Management research
Guide for institutions and professionals

# Management research

Guide for institutions and professionals

Roger Bennett

Prepared with the financial support
of the UNDP Inter-regional Programme

Management Development Series No. 20
International Labour Office   Geneva

Copyright © International Labour Organisation 1983

Publications of the International Labour Office enjoy copyright under Protocol 2 of the Universal Copyright Convention. Nevertheless, short excerpts from them may be reproduced without authorisation, on condition that the source is indicated. For rights of reproduction or translation, application should be made to the Publications Branch (Rights and Permissions), International Labour Office, CH-1211 Geneva 22, Switzerland. The International Labour Office welcomes such applications.

ISBN 92-2-103303-1

*First published 1983*
*Third impression 1987*

The designations employed in ILO publications, which are in conformity with United Nations practice, and the presentation of material therein do not imply the expression of any opinion whatsoever on the part of the International Labour Office concerning the legal status of any country, area or territory or of its authorities, or concerning the delimitation of its frontiers.
The responsibility for opinions expressed in signed articles, studies and other contributions rests solely with their authors, and publication does not constitute an endorsement by the International Labour Office of the opinions expressed in them.
Reference to names of firms and commercial products and processes does not imply their endorsement by the International Labour Office, and any failure to mention a particular firm, commercial product or process is not a sign of disapproval.

ILO publications can be obtained through major booksellers or ILO local offices in many countries, or direct from ILO Publications, International Labour Office, CH-1211 Geneva 22, Switzerland. A catalogue or list of new publications will be sent free of charge from the above address.

Printed in Switzerland                                                                                                  VAU

# CONTENTS

Introduction .................................... 1

Chapter 1  Why bother with research ................. 5

    1.1  Attitudes to management research ........... 6

    1.2  Needs and purposes research can meet ....... 8

    1.3  Some examples of relevant research ......... 12

    1.4  The need for a balanced policy ............. 14

    1.5  Relationship of research with programme development and consultancy ................ 15

    1.6  Relationship of research to education, training and development .................... 17

    1.7  Implications of developing a research role .. 19

Chapter 2  The nature of management research .......... 23

    2.1  The meaning of research .................... 23

    2.2  The research process ....................... 25

    2.3  Research and the managerial process ........ 27

| | | |
|---|---|---|
| 2.4 | Management research and the social sciences . | 30 |
| 2.5 | Approaches to research ...................... | 32 |
| 2.6 | A different perspective ..................... | 37 |
| 2.7 | Deciding on the appropriate form of research | 40 |

Chapter 3  Establishing what should be researched ..... 49

| | | |
|---|---|---|
| 3.1 | The main requirement ........................ | 49 |
| 3.2 | The research programme ...................... | 50 |
| 3.3 | Determining research needs .................. | 52 |
| 3.4 | Getting the research programme going ........ | 67 |
| 3.5 | Planning research ........................... | 71 |

Chapter 4  Methods of management research ............. 81

| | | |
|---|---|---|
| 4.1 | Levels of research .......................... | 81 |
| 4.2 | Levels of rigour ............................ | 83 |
| 4.3 | Criteria for choice ......................... | 85 |
| 4.4 | Basic approaches ............................ | 86 |
| 4.5 | Principal research methods .................. | 90 |
| 4.6 | Some techniques of research ................. | 110 |
| 4.7 | Further reading ............................. | 114 |

Chapter 5  How research can be organised .............. 115

| | | |
|---|---|---|
| 5.1 | The basic dilemma ........................... | 115 |
| 5.2 | The need for organisational task fit ........ | 116 |

| | | |
|---|---|---|
| 5.3 | Where are you now? | 116 |
| 5.4 | The structural component: organisational alternatives | 121 |
| 5.5 | The managerial component | 128 |
| 5.6 | The servicing component | 133 |
| 5.7 | The financial component | 136 |

**Chapter 6  Using the results of research** .............. 143

| | | |
|---|---|---|
| 6.1 | A framework of research utilisation | 143 |
| 6.2 | Barriers to using research | 145 |
| 6.3 | Factors conducive to research | 149 |
| 6.4 | Areas in which research can be used | 152 |
| 6.5 | Disseminating research findings | 160 |

**Chapter 7  Developing the researchers** ................. 167

| | | |
|---|---|---|
| 7.1 | The competent researcher | 168 |
| 7.2 | Identifying the "competent" researcher and research training needs | 172 |
| 7.3 | Approaches to developing researchers | 174 |
| 7.4 | Writing the research report | 185 |
| 7.5 | Careers in research | 191 |

**Chapter 8  Conclusion: guidelines for action** .......... 195

| | | |
|---|---|---|
| 8.1 | Some conclusions concerning policy | 195 |

| | | |
|---|---|---|
| 8.2 | How to improve dissemination and application | 198 |
| 8.3 | How to use this book to improve research in in your institution | 202 |

Appendix 1  <u>Annotated bibliography</u> ................... 207

    1. Introduction ................................. 207

    2. Structure and use ............................ 208

    3. Brief review of key areas .................... 209

    4. Alphabetical bibliography .................... 215

    5. Further references ........................... 242

# INTRODUCTION

If we look around us, there are few things in life that have not been subject to the influence of "scientific endeavour": to a process studying an aspect of life (e.g. biology, physics, medicine) with the aim of developing a systematic body of knowledge. From this body of knowledge, we can work on ways to improve life and living. The range of influence of scientific endeavour is enormous. We can see it: in the provision of drugs and medicines to help fight disease; in the development of faster growing and higher yielding crops; in our ability to produce more and efficient products and machinery/equipment; in our capacity to build models (e.g. on computers, in simulation laboratories) of how to put a man or vehicle into space; in our increased capacity to use modern electronic aids, such as micro-computers; in our understanding of the way people behave and work in different countries and different cultures, and so on. Problems still abound, no less than those to do with the distribution of food and wealth. Scientifically, these can be handled. The political will to do something about these problems is often missing. Unless people want to do something about problems, scientific endeavour will lie fruitless.

Research is part of scientific endeavour. It is that part which explores the unknown (e.g. unknown facts, unknown applications of theory) and contributes to building knowledge and theory from which practical action can be developed. As will be shown later, there are many different types of research and a number of different methods that can be used for carrying out research.

Management research can, and does, make a contribution to the development of relevant approaches to the management of organisations and enterprises. It helps identify, critically examine, generalise and disseminate useful practical experience: indeed, management research builds on practice, draws from it, and the ultimate criterion of its effectiveness is in the practical application of research results. However, the potential of management research is far from being fully utilised. Many management institutions treat it as a stepchild. They feel that they can easily survive without research, just by reading what others have written. Or, they are short of resources and, since their research programme may generate little income, they would cut it before any other activity. In many institutions, there is a shortage of experienced researchers and a lot of confusion on what should be researched and how, what to do with results, how to use research findings in training programmes, whether research is of any use to consulting work, and so on.

In a dialogue with a number of management development institutions in both developing and industrialised countries, the ILO Management Development Branch has identified these and other problems of management research. Institution heads and their research directors discussed with us their growing concern about research, as well as the problems involved in orienting research, managing it, and selecting, preparing and motivating staff for research. A number of management development institutions with whom the ILO co-operates were then consulted on the idea of preparing a special guide to management research. Their answer was enthusiastically positive and the UNDP agreed to support the work through an inter-regional project entitled "Co-operation among management development institutions". Indeed, one of the objectives was to make good experience with research available to other institutions and thus strengthen their co-operation.

The work programme was organised as follows. In the first stage, the ILO Management Development Branch defined the scope of the project, developed an outline of the guide and identified a suitable author. One person was designated: Roger Bennett, Director of Research at the Thames Valley Regional Management Centre, and Editor of the Journal of European Industrial Training. The idea of a team of authors was rejected in this case in order to develop a homogenous and logically structured text that could serve as a guide rather than a book of readings. It was easy to pursuade Roger to undertake the task although he was fully aware of the difficulties involved. He approached the project as a real challenge.

In the second stage, the guide was written and the manuscript circulated to 30 institutions in both industrialised and developing countries. This helped test the assumptions on whose basis the guide was prepared and collect comments reflecting experience from various parts of the world.

The following institutions and their directors, research directors or staff members were particularly helpful and their comments and ideas were reflected in the final version of the guide: Instituto de Estudios Superiores de Administración (IESA), Caracas, Venezuela (Henry Gómez); Centre d'Enseignement Supérieur des Affaires (CESA), Jouy-en-Josas, France (Romain Laufers and Roland Reiter); National Management Development Centre (OVK), Budapest, Hungary (László Horváth and Tamás Zoltán); Institute of Finance Management, Dar es Salaam, Tanzania (Kami Rwegasira); Cyprus Productivity Centre, Nicosia, Cyprus (Haris Constantinou); Thames Valley Regional Management Centre, Slough, United Kingdom (Morris Brodie); Ecole Supérieure de Commerce de Lyon, Lyon, France (Philippe Albert); George Washington University, Washington, DC, United States (Gordon Lippitt); Management Development Centre, Khartoum, Sudan (Sowar el Dahab Ahmed Eisa and Mahmoud Abdel Halim al Rahman); and Indian Institute of Management, Ahmedabad (Ramadhar Singh).

In addition, the author received useful materials and references from a number of colleagues in the United Kingdom, including John Child of the Aston University Management Centre, Ian Mangham and Cyril Tompkins of the Bath University School of Management, John Burgoyne of the Lancaster University Centre for the Study of Management Learning, David Chambers, Anthony Hopwood, Derek Pugh and John McGee of the London Business School, Richard Stapleton and Alan Thomas of the Manchester Business School and David Buchanan of the Scottish Business School in Glasgow.

We wish to extend our very sincere thanks to them, as well as to all those who could not be named but whose experience helped to design and prepare this guide.

In the third and final stage, the author worked on the definitive text, interacting with a number of colleagues in the management development profession and endeavouring to make maximum use of the valuable guidance and new materials provided by co-operating institutions. It is for the reader to judge whether this collective effort has produced a useful result.

ILO Management Development Branch,
Geneva, November 1982.

# WHY BOTHER WITH RESEARCH?                                1

As was made clear in the introduction, there is a vital need for research into management. Primarily this need arises because the management technologies and approaches developed in one country or one sector of a country do not always readily apply elsewhere. In the advanced industrialised societies, there is a need to find out more on how to fruitfully use micro-electronics, its impact on management and society, and on how work and leisure patterns will be changed. In the developing countries, the need may have more to do with building up local data bases (e.g. on types and number of industries, employment distribution, economic modelling for planning a rural/semi-industrialised economy, appropriate ways of managing less educated workforces, etc.) and with managing state enterprises, small businesses, social programmes and the like. For example, in Venezuela, an opportunity for developing research came through the need to study population. One aspect was concerned with social and economic policy trade-offs brought about by rapid population growth, whilst the second focused on managing a family planning programme. This attracted support from international foundations and led to the development of a sound reputation for the Instituto de Estudios Superiores de Administración (IESA) at Caracas.[1]

Importing approaches from one country to another may not work. For example, copying the Japanese approach may

---

[1] See D.C. Korten (ed.): <u>Population and social management: A challenge for management schools</u> (Caracas, IESA, 1979).

fail because cultural attitudes and values are very different. In order to work effectively, such approaches will have to be fitted to the culture. In developing countries, management research must serve mass-based needs and demands, using local resources to provide information and knowledge for local consumption and utilisation. It must address local management issues and problems, and get at the basics (e.g. food, housing, health, education, etc.) as far as these are the proper concern of managers and policy makers. It must help local decision makers and managers to come up with better solutions to these problems. Carrying out research for wider international consumption and publication is a secondary requirement. Yet in "advanced" societies the reverse is often true. This means that approaches adopted elsewhere become well known to staff in management development institutes in the developing countries. The temptation is to look at them as universal principles that can be applied in local situations, and can undermine the enthusiasm to carry out local research. This, combined with a lack of tradition and trained staff for research, can lead to attitudes which go against the development of a strong, practical research capacity. Thus, research into management is concerned with identifying and generalising - where possible - best management practice and achieving a fit between practice and the needs of local enterprises.

But attitudes to research can vary enormously, even within a single country. Recent research in the United Kingdom compared attitudes to research of managers and management developers. In developed countries too, differences in attitudes exist.

## 1.1 Attitudes to management research

In this research, respondents were asked to give a view on 14 different statements that had been derived from previous interviews and discussion with a number of managers and academics (in terms of how strongly they agreed or disagreed with each statement). The views were reasonably similar although large differences did occur for certain statements. For example, whilst most managers are rather uncertain about whether to neither agree nor disagree that <u>managers are afraid of research</u>, the management developers seem to agree they are.

Both groups appeared to agree that <u>the only research that gets done is what the researchers want to do</u>, although management developers seemed to agree more strongly with this statement than did managers. Neither group was of the view that <u>most management research is a waste of time and money</u>. Managers were in stronger disagreement with this statement than were management developers. Both groups were of the view that <u>organisations aren't all that keen to have research done</u>. They also agreed that <u>most managers don't know how to use research findings</u> although the management developers held this view a little more strongly than did the managers. On the question of <u>credibility of researchers</u>, the managers appeared to be somewhat uncertain, whereas management developers agreed they lacked credibility. The final difference was over the question of whether <u>research provides an objective impartial view of the managers' situation</u>. Management developers agreed with this more strongly than did the managers. Both groups seemed to disagree that a <u>manager isn't much good if he needs research to help him in his job</u>. In a parallel survey similar findings were achieved. Managers, however, felt rather more strongly that currently, research is largely initiated by researchers who are not sufficiently familiar with the managerial world and lack credibility. Disillusion with current research practice was widespread, most managers believing that it is not cost effective or relevant to the problems they face. At the same time, managers and management developers agreed that managers did not know how to use research findings and that appropriate research would be helpful.[1]

The more negative attitudes are clearly destructive. The person holding them tends to see all forms of research through the same pair of very dark glasses. There can be no doubt that some research has been on the fringes of what managers and academics as a whole would regard as useful. Yet there is a large body of other research which has been of relevance and use to managers and management developers. There is nothing more helpful than useful

---

[1] A report of the combined findings is given in R. Bennett and J. Gill: "The role of research in a regional management centre", in <u>Management Education and Development</u>, Dec. 1978.

relevant research, i.e. research that meets well defined needs.

## 1.2 Needs and purposes research can meet

Whilst each institute must develop its own approach to and policy for research, aiming for a distinctiveness that will give the research some character and appeal, there are a number of needs which in general highlight the case for a research activity.

### The requirements of the work of the institute

These will vary, depending upon the nature of the work. Some institutions will be involved with short courses or in-company management development programmes, where there will be a requirement to establish training needs, to devise effective ways of meeting those training needs, and to evaluate the success with which they have been met. Research approaches can not only help in this respect but also build up a body of knowledge and experience about such practices. Where diploma and degree activities are concerned, it is clearly necessary that the institute is able to show a healthy research activity from which contributions to both staff and course members are seen to flow. Research helps generate a more demanding and lively intellectual capacity, and contributes to making the teaching material much more relevant, personal and direct. Whilst teaching is invariably based on using other people's research findings, it can be made much more relevant and lively if the trainers can refer to their own research findings.

### Research can also help facilitate staff development

Whether staff carry out research for a higher degree or not, it adds to the knowledge, experience and wisdom of the staff member and must therefore be considered as an important staff development activity. Whilst by no means the only way of developing staff, it is certainly one which adds freshness and critical awareness to what the member of staff is doing.

### Developing and extending the professional competence and experience of staff

The pursuit of research aims, publishing research

findings, and applying these findings to learning and managerial situations can have a major influence on the professional effectiveness of staff and improve the chances of keeping up to date in the subject.

## Demonstrating and enhancing the role and reputation of the institute

A capacity to undertake meaningful research relevant to the levels of work aspired to and the subject areas taught by staff, enables the institute to improve its reputation and maintain a visibility for its work that might otherwise be difficult to achieve.

## Increasing its publications record

Clearly, increased publications of the right quality will help enhance the reputation and status of staff and the institute. This is another means whereby the visibility can be increased.

## Giving encouragement to consultancy

Often, staff with a history of demonstrated academic ability through research and publications attract consultancy inquiries to the institute. The links between research and consultancy must be thought through; they do not exist in isolation.

The contribution of research to management training can be set out more specifically. For example, the Pakistan Institute of Management in Karachi sees research being able to assist in the following areas:[1]

- identifying and analysing management and other problems of business and industry;

- identifying the training needs of those managers and executives involved in helping to solve these problems;

---

[1] S. Alvi: "An overview of research for management training", in Pakistan Management Review, Second quarter 1980, pp. 83-90. The article aims to give some useful advice on how research can be conducted with respect to meeting these needs.

- improving management teaching and training practices and techniques;

- preparing Pakistani management training materials and cases;

- carrying out immediate and long-term evaluation and follow-up of the effects of training.

The range of purposes attributed to research by staff in United States management centres varies as shown in illustration 1.

| Illustration 1: Ranking of purposes attributed to research | |
|---|---|
| PURPOSE | RANK |
| develop/generate knowledge/theory and aid understanding of the unknown | 1 |
| keep staff abreast of field and contribute to teaching | 2 |
| help solve problems/doing things better | 3 |
| establish application in general | 4 |
| build prestige/increase visibility of self and institution | 5 |
| generate means of analysis and thinking/learning | 6 |
| evaluate training and learning | 7 |
| develop future consumers of research | 7 |

It will be noticed that the majority of these purposes are concerned with academic requirements of knowledge seeking and teaching, although the emphasis varied between the institutions (for example, those who had "made it" were often more concerned with application than those who were still trying to). Illustration 2 shows how research objectives tend to be perceived by managers and academics in the United Kingdom.

Illustration 2: Ranking research objectives

| OBJECTIVES | RANK ORDER | |
|---|---|---|
| | Managers | Academics |
| making a contribution to the development of more effective management practices | 1 | 1 |
| developing more effective ways of teaching/training managers | 2 | =2 |
| developing skills and competence of management teachers | 3 | =6 |
| creating a better understanding for managers of situations in which they have to manage | 4 | =2 |
| producing more knowledge about management practices | 4 | 9 |
| assessing the usefulness of existing services/courses | 6 | 8 |
| helping managers to solve problems | 7 | =2 |
| providing more relevant material for management teachers | 8 | =6 |
| identifying the needs for new types of management services/ courses | 9 | 5 |
| developing new theories about the process of management | 10 | 10 |

Clearly these findings will not apply to other institutions in other situations and countries. In a later section of this guide we shall describe an approach which can be used to establish specific research needs and objectives. These listings do, however, give a broad indication of the range of needs and objectives which can be pursued through research.

## 1.3 Some examples of relevant research

There are some well-known examples of research that has influenced management thinking, training and practice. These contrast sharply with much of the research that is reported in the highly academic and purportedly "reputable" journals. Whilst much of the purely academic research never progresses beyond those journals, relevant research does. It often (but not always) starts out as research aimed at producing new knowledge and theory, and gets published in the academic journals. It then becomes developed, refined, "picked-up" and used, and often published in a more popular and generally available form. Some will start out as clearly being problem-oriented, and contribute to theory as well.

A major example of relevant research is the "Hawthorne experiments". These were initiated in response to a real managerial problem - poor performance. The first studies looked at the effects on performance of working conditions (heat, light, ventilation, rest periods, etc.). Comparisons between experimental groups (i.e. those studied) and control groups (those not studied, but whose performance was monitored) showed performance increased in both. Factors other than work conditions were influencing performance. This led to studies of the effects on performance of social (group) control and of attitudes. The findings indicated that social factors had a big influence on performance. These findings - grossly summarised here for purposes of this example - led to the development of the so-called "human relations school" of management, which has influenced management training and practice for decades.

Another "landmark" piece of research was that carried out by the Tavistock Institute of Human Relations in countries such as India and the United Kingdom and in industries ranging from coalmining through weaving/spinning to airlines. This research focused on relations at work, but this time with respect to technology. It demonstrated that work must not be thought of as purely a social activity nor as a technical activity, but in terms of both. The concepts related to "socio-technical" systems and related design considerations owe a great deal to these studies.

In the field of <u>organisational design and structuring</u>, the pioneering research of Rensis Likert has produced world-wide impact. This research established relations between the nature of the organisation and overall performance. Concepts such as "linking-pin" and overlapping group structures are much used in the literature and in managerial discussion.

One of the most widely known sets of notions are those developed by Douglas McGregor. Managers in many organisations have been heard to describe them in terms of "Theory X or Theory Y" assumptions. A good deal of research has been carried out, identifying styles of management with levels of output and organisational characteristics. We now know much more about the conditions and circumstances in which certain styles are more or less effective than others.

Some major studies have looked at what managers actually do in their work. For example, in the United Kingdom, Rosemary Stewart has produced some interesting frameworks for analysing managerial work. More important, however, is the use of these frameworks in training and developing managers.

A good example from the developing countries is concerned with <u>managing development programmes</u> intended to relieve those who live in absolute poverty. A recent publication draws together experiences from Asia, Latin America and Africa.[1] The cases given show how the conventional bureaucratic structures and procedures of development agencies contribute to programme failure. Research in this area is highly relevant to the management needs of developing countries.

These few brief examples illustrate the impact that research can have on organisational managerial practice.

---

[1] D.C. Korten and F.B. Alfonso (eds.): <u>Bureaucracy and the poor: Closing the gap</u> (Singapore, McGraw-Hill, 1981).

Not every piece of research will have international impact and acclaim. It can, however, develop along lines which will have relevance to management training and practice, and avoid the extremes of an approach which is too theoretical. But should all staff be encouraged to do research?

## 1.4 The need for a balanced policy

In considering the role of research in a management institution, we should take a sensible middle of the road attitude. Not all members of staff should be expected to undertake research, or are capable of doing so. Their skills have to be used in the direction in which they can be best employed. Good teachers should be allowed to teach, and not forced to do research if they have neither the inclination nor the potential to do so. Similarly, not all areas of management needs and problems are either susceptible to or need researching. An institute must, therefore, develop a research policy. The idea of having a research policy is crucial. Such policies are needed for a number of reasons, some of the important ones being:

- to enable the institute to fulfil its main role;

- to provide a service to industry and other organisations where it is currently not provided;

- to facilitate the greater use of existing knowledge.

To develop research in a completely ad hoc manner wastes effort; to duplicate what is already happening, wastes resources; to do nothing would be to deny the important place of research in management education, training and development. For any policy to be effective, some key ingredients are necessary. These are:

- to establish the objectives to be pursued (how else do you know if your policy is effective?);

- to have some underlying theme of themes or areas of work for research which are important to both the institute and clients;

- to have a means of measuring progress;

- to have the general support of those directly and indirectly involved with the policy.

This all means that there must be a thorough discussion of the need for research amongst staff in the institute, the development of a clearly stated research policy, and working towards a set of attitudes or a culture which recognises the importance of research but also accepts that it is not an all important and all embracing characteristic of an institution.

## 1.5 Relationship of research with programme development and consultancy

It can be argued that there is little need to bother with research since most of what it can possibly offer institutes and their clients can be catered for through normal developmental and consultancy activities. This argument rests on the definitions and scope given to each of these activities. Some people do not accept a distinction between research, new programme development and consulting. It is important to make one, however, because it helps to identify the contribution each can make to management development and training.

The primary function of most members of an institute is to "teach" - using the word "teach" in its widest sense to embrace the many different training and learning activities involved. However, just as all manufacturing and service organisations have certain requirements for maintaining, improving and changing their products, so too does the management institute. Just as there are overlaps and linkages in a manufacturing organisation between research, development and production, so too there will be between research, development and consultancy in a management institution. The main distinctions between them can be illustrated, and point to differing skills, knowledge, attitudes and experience needed by staff to carry them out.

<u>Programme development</u> is the process whereby continual improvement is sought in the range and adequacy of the institute's services, the courses provided and the material used. In general, research and consultancy form important primary inputs to the development process. Programme development can take place at two basic levels:

(i) developing existing activities – a constant effort to improve the effectiveness, efficiency and quality of present activities and to encourage adaptation;

(ii) developing new activities – matching current activities against the requirement to contribute to the development of effective management and providing new activities where gaps are shown to exist or where a current activity is no longer adequate and necessary.

Research provides a primary output to the development of new services (with, of course, some spin-off for existing services). Whilst consultancy has a greater role to play in feeding back ideas to the development of existing services, it can also uncover new areas in need of research. Each member of staff should, to some extent, possess the skills necessary to undertake development work. Essentially these skills involve observing what is happening, evaluating what is happening against the objectives from which the activity sprang and relating inputs from research and consultancy to the outcomes of that evaluation.

Consulting involves offering advice to managers in areas of concern and providing solutions to specific problems. The body of information upon which the academic can call is already known and, often, the problems are recurring. Where new areas of difficulty arise the consultancy approach may develop into a research approach, applying more rigorous procedures. This is not to say that consultancy approaches do not use research techniques – they do. The fundamental difference, however, lies in the setting and testing of hypotheses and the relationship with the client.

Not every member of staff can be expected to possess the skills required to undertake consultancy work, although it can be argued that the teaching activity to an extent rests on some of them. The skills are concerned with communicating ideas to management, understanding the views of management, analysing and defining the problem/situation, coping with political differences, and organising time and commitments effectively. Underlying most of these are a range of social and interpersonal skills which not everyone possesses. None the less, the institute should encourage the development of general consultancy skills - for example, by placing an inexperienced member of staff to work on an assignment with a competent consultant.

Research is concerned with discovering new information and relationships and expanding and verifying existing knowledge and can be considered as a careful inquiry or examination. Whilst both research and consultancy are "careful inquiries", consultancy does not itself purport to bring about or be concerned with new information and relationships. In addition, as with consultancy but probably more so, not every member of staff can be expected to possess the necessary skills. These include many consultancy skills as well as certain conceptual and analytical skills a consultant may not require. Thus, whilst a researcher is likely to make a good consultant, a consultant is less likely to make a good researcher.

Therefore research, development and consultancy are separate but linked processes; development can take place without a research or consultancy activity; but effective development rests on research and consultancy for which few members of staff may possess the necessary skills.

Some differences between research and consulting are illustrated in figure 1.[1] It should be noted that this represents only the extreme cases of the differences between them. Often they share common properties and methods as in the case of planned change using an action research approach.

## 1.6 Relationship of research to education, training and development

Research and teaching are closely related. Both concern knowledge: research generates it and teaching helps people acquire and use it. There should exist, therefore, a pool of knowledge and experience within an institute upon which its members can draw. Those who teach and train managers should also help generate that pool of knowledge. Students and course members who help generate their own knowledge and then compare it with the results of other

---

[1] With acknowledgement to Morris Brodie for his contribution to the development of this table.

**Figure 1 Factors differentiating research and consulting**

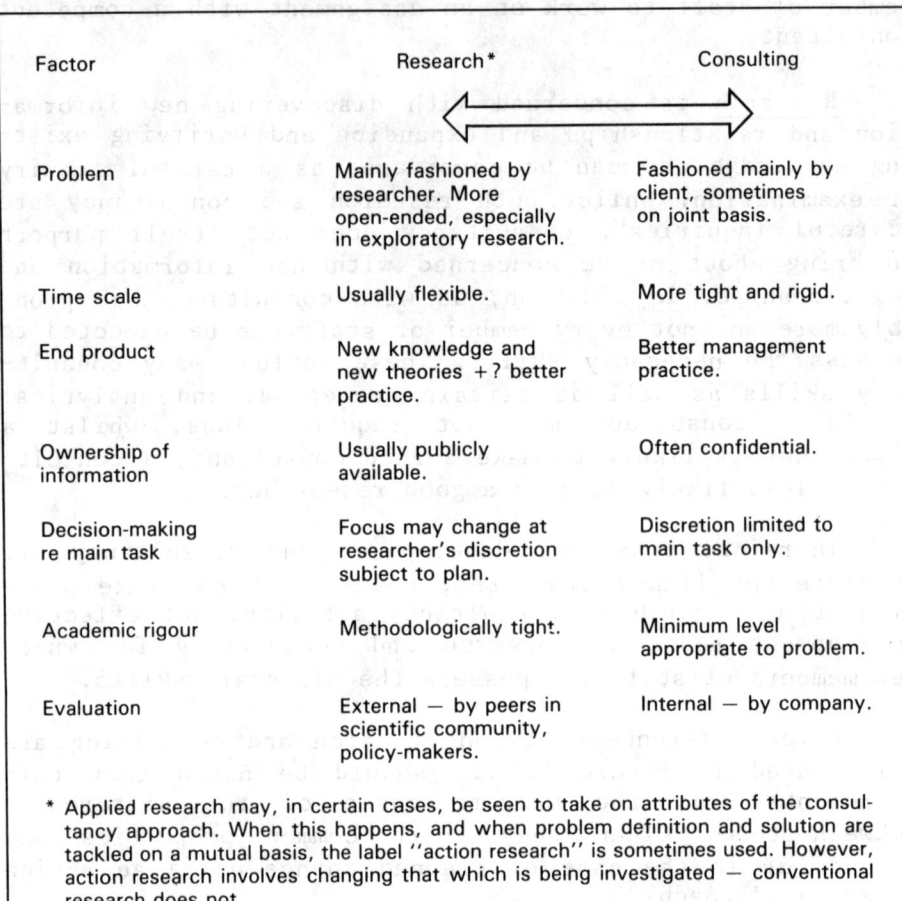

| Factor | Research* | Consulting |
|---|---|---|
| Problem | Mainly fashioned by researcher. More open-ended, especially in exploratory research. | Fashioned mainly by client, sometimes on joint basis. |
| Time scale | Usually flexible. | More tight and rigid. |
| End product | New knowledge and new theories +? better practice. | Better management practice. |
| Ownership of information | Usually publicly available. | Often confidential. |
| Decision-making re main task | Focus may change at researcher's discretion subject to plan. | Discretion limited to main task only. |
| Academic rigour | Methodologically tight. | Minimum level appropriate to problem. |
| Evaluation | External — by peers in scientific community, policy-makers. | Internal — by company. |

\* Applied research may, in certain cases, be seen to take on attributes of the consultancy approach. When this happens, and when problem definition and solution are tackled on a mutual basis, the label "action research" is sometimes used. However, action research involves changing that which is being investigated — conventional research does not.

research more readily accept it. Ownership of information is a powerful learning weapon.

In addition, both are concerned with problems: teachers and trainers are concerned with how to help managers solve problems and manage effectively: research can help provide information about the situations in which the managers operate. Both research and management teaching are concerned with "understanding": research helps us understand the world around us, whilst teaching helps us understand the knowledge, concepts and ideas that managers can use to improve their work. As we have seen, research and teaching are linked with development: research as a primary input, especially in assessing the possibilities for development; teaching as a means of capturing essential developments and building them into practice.[1] Finally, both are concerned with theory: research with helping to build and test theoretical formulations; teaching with pushing theory into application and practice. These links are illustrated diagrammatically in figure 2.

Some major European and American institutions have established a clear relationship between research and educational activities. For example, the role of research at INSEAD has been described in the following terms: "In an institution which is dedicated primarily to its educational goals and therefore to the delivery of high quality teaching, the essential function of research is to contribute to the intellectual growth and development of its faculty. Production of knowledge is only a secondary outcome. This is reflected in the role of the research co-ordinator, who at the same time and in close association with the dean, is in charge of career development. Unlike the case in most United States schools, research does not come out of doctoral programmes but starts from the educational role. This creates difficulties and problems but also, we think, more relevant research, more individual development, and less professional dissonance and career dichotomy."[2]

## 1.7 Implications of developing a research role

The discussion so far has been in favour of bothering to develop a research role and capacity. Many people would argue that each management institute should have some level of research capacity. But there are implications to this. These may be summarised as follows.

---

[1] At the Norwegian School of Management, Pat Joynt has developed a research-based approach to management education. See P. Joynt and M.L. Rytter: "Experiments with experience: A new strategy for management education", in Journal of European Industrial Training, 1981, No. 7, pp. 23-26.

[2] C. Faucheux: "Current research at INSEAD", in Strategies for management research and development in Europe (Manchester, Manchester Business School, 1972).

**Figure 2  Management education and research**

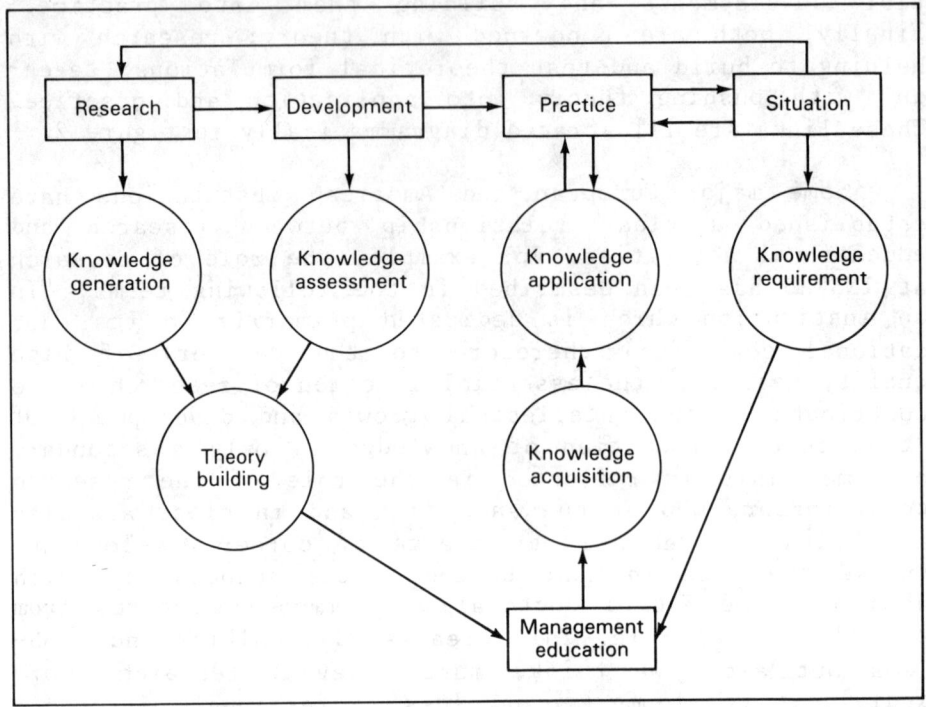

Attitudes

Some members of staff may consider research as a soft option to teaching, a break from the real work of the institute, an unnecessary means of obtaining a higher degree, or an intrusion on academic life. A research activity should not be forced upon staff where such attitudes exist but rather its utility demonstrated through the application and development of research findings. Where positive attitudes prevail, these can be built upon and chanelled into appropriate research with encouragement and opportunity.

Time

Research absorbs time. Where staff are concerned with the registration and supervision of research students' workloads will need adjusting. The amount of supervision time required will vary according to whether such students are part-time or full-time. The management and control of research assistants working on externally funded projects will require time. Obviously, those staff directly involved in carrying out research themselves will have a commitment to time. This is especially true if experience necessary to supervise research students is to be acquired.

Money

Research costs money. A prime cost is that of the time of staff doing research, whether faculty members or contract researchers. Members of staff carrying out research require quiet work rooms, equipment, good library facilities, travel allowance, registration fees, reproduction of material and the like, and perhaps even a research assistant. Research students may need improved research literature resources in the library – for a group of research assistants, the physical resources (space, equipment, etc.) required to carry out the research will have cost implications.

Beyond these specific implications lies a more general one – namely, the effects that a substantial and growing research capacity can have on the institute as a whole: on its culture, structure and management. Often research changes the attitudes and expectations of staff; it can break down barriers between academic disciplines, course or activity groupings (or at least show that they exist); it can sometimes require marginal re-organisation of the institute in order to accommodate research; and often the management problems will increase – managing research workers and those involved with research poses different problems than does the management of teachers, trainers and developers.

It is necessary, therefore, to consider and evaluate the advantages and disadvantages of developing a research capacity. This can be done in the following manner:

(1) call a meeting of senior staff (preferably all staff if the institute's faculty is not too large) and discuss the pros and cons of establishing or enhancing a research capacity;

(2) draw up a check list/questionnaire of all the pros and cons and ask each member of the institute to assign an importance or weighting to them out of ten,

where ten is the greatest importance being attached to any particular factor;

(3) analyse the results, write up a short working note and distribute to staff;

(4) call a second meeting of staff to discuss the outcomes of this mini-evaluation activity.

It would not be surprising if the conclusion reached is not that we shouldn't bother with research but rather why have we not bothered with it before!

In addition to clarifying the need for research, this exercise will also identify members of staff who are keen to do research. They can be encouraged to form the nucleus of a research group. This is the most important starting point. However often and long the senior staff of an institute may talk about the need for research, it will only be translated into practice when at least one member of staff actually gets things going. If you are at this point, read on. This guide is designed to help you take things on from there.

# THE NATURE OF MANAGEMENT RESEARCH     2

## 2.1 The meaning of research

To talk about the meaning and nature of management research may seem irrelevant and unnecessary. We have glimpsed it in the introduction and in chapter 1 and, since so many people do it, some at least must know what it is about. Yet views differ. Some people consider research a cosy, personal activity to indulge in from time to time from the safety of an armchair, with access to a pile of books. Such "research", or <u>private study or desk research or literature search</u>, is of immense value in helping us to keep up to date and improve our personal stock of knowledge. It can provide ideas for improving training or establish the basis for the start of a major piece of investigative or empirical research. Whilst some would call this form of research nothing more than "armchair theorising", it has a very important part to play in management research by establishing what is already known and therefore not in need of research, unless in a totally different context (for example, researching the effects of applying to the learning situation previously researched motivation models or of using Western styles of management in different cultures).

For others, the term "research" is <u>rigorous scientific activity</u> aimed at developing new bodies of knowledge. It conjures up pictures of the physicist in his laboratory, carefully making sure that nothing changes except what he wants to change, and noting the results. This, too, is an important conception of research. Whilst in the social sciences it is difficult to control and change the things we want to in our research, we can set up experiments and simulations which allow us to get close to this scientific approach. We can use models and computer programmes to predict the way the economy might move (with well-known margins of error!); we can examine factory loading and space requirements before putting up the building (preventing us finding it is too big or too small); and we can design training courses which use particular methods and compare them with courses for similar managers but using different methods.

Neither extreme is wrong - they simply illustrate that research is not neatly separable from the world in which it takes place and can therefore take on different shapes forged by the "reality" in which it exists. They do, however, have one thing in common: both are concerned with the <u>systematic development and acquisition of knowledge</u>. The first starts with an existing base, the second with the aim of generating or extending the base. What is done with that knowledge which often distinguishes social scientific research - and particularly management research - from some other research. We are concerned also with its application. Whilst in, say, the scientific engineering field, application is separated from research, this is less true in management. Some forms of research embrace both action and problem-solving in the managerial world. This tends to blur the distinction made in chapter 1 between research, development and consultancy. But though the edges are indistinct, the core differences still exist.

We can derive from such considerations a <u>definition of research</u> that fits both the generally held view and the more specific, management-related view. Research can be seen as a systematic process of discovering, acquiring and using knowledge. Put more formally, research is <u>a systematic, careful inquiry or examination to discover new information or relationships and to expand/verify existing knowledge for some specified purpose</u>.

The "specified purpose" is usually a problem, and the problem may belong to the researcher or the manager; it may be academic (i.e. a problem of theory) or applied (i.e. a problem of practice). Since there is nothing more practical than a good theory, academics and managers should have a combined interest in research.

But what is management research? Clearly, it is a systematic, careful inquiry into anything to do with management. Since all enterprises are managed, the scope for such inquiry is very broad. There are, as we shall see, processes which are fundamental to management that may be the subject of research. But there are many things which are not "management" that impinge upon the process of management. They may well be the subject of their own research specialisms but will still contribute to management. Accounting research, for example, may be very specific to accountancy but will still have an impact on management. The collection of basic data on industries may not be classed as management research but can still provide useful information and a means of getting research started. External agencies may be willing to fund what appears to be non-management research that can provide routes into research more closely related to the managerial process. There is, therefore, a blurred distinction between what is and is not management research.

## 2.2 The research process

The research process usually starts with a problem or question. The problem/question may be the researcher's - he may wish to know which learning theory best explains different levels of performance in different situations. The problem may be initiated by a manager who wants to decide on the best technique for developing greater participation. In either case, the requirement is for some information that will shed light on the problem and help make a decision to solve it. It may be that solutions are not the end result of the research: an outcome might be the development of a new theory or body of knowledge. Whatever the end result, the starting point is represented by an urge to find out, to explore, to evaluate - in short, to do research.

There are other steps betwwen these end points. Having defined, or at least acknowledged, the problem or area of interest, the researcher may carry out a preliminary study. This will enable him to set out the parameters of the problem and to gain some idea of the essential information to be sought. Such exploratory studies, free from too much bias or preconceived ideas, help point the research in the right direction. For example, the problem may concern inadequate commission earnings of salesmen immediately after finishing training. The temptation here is to blame the training. An exploratory study (usually much less costly that the full treatment) might uncover poor supervision during the first weeks of the job, or lack of understanding of the commission scheme, as possible alternative explanations. If this preliminary work is thorough, the next stages can be less embracing than might otherwise be the case. From this work the researcher may well set up an <u>hypothesis</u>, or a series of hypotheses, to test against reality. In simplest terms an hypothesis is an imagined answer to a real question. In our example, the question would be "What causes low levels of commission earnings in immediate post-training periods?" The answer, as we have seen, might be based on guesswork, theoretical inspiration, or an appreciation of the factors involved, or indeed a combination of all three. In our case, the hypothesis might be that, in immediate post-training periods, salesmen will earn low levels of commission if inadequate supervision persists.

Having framed this hypothesis, the researcher then <u>seeks information or data</u> to test its validity. He might decide to check records for low earnings, and see what situations led to them; or he could monitor earnings and performance levels in two sales forces, one of which had a high ratio of supervision and the other a low ratio. The data collected would then be <u>analysed</u> and subjected, possibly, to several statistical tests to determine whether the proposed "answer" holds true or not and with what degree of confidence or faith it can be accepted. The results of this analysis and deliberation would be <u>interpreted and communicated</u> - via reports, seminars, planning groups or whatever - to the "client". This phase can be a difficult one but need not be as inconclusive as so often is the case. The process is shown in figure 3.

It should be stressed that the research process may not necessarily be geared to the testing of hypotheses. Often a researcher will be more interested in the exploratory stage, with a view to developing a number of alternative hypotheses for later testing by himself or others. If this proves successful, a useful contribution will have been made to management knowledge.

**Figure 3  Major steps in research processes**

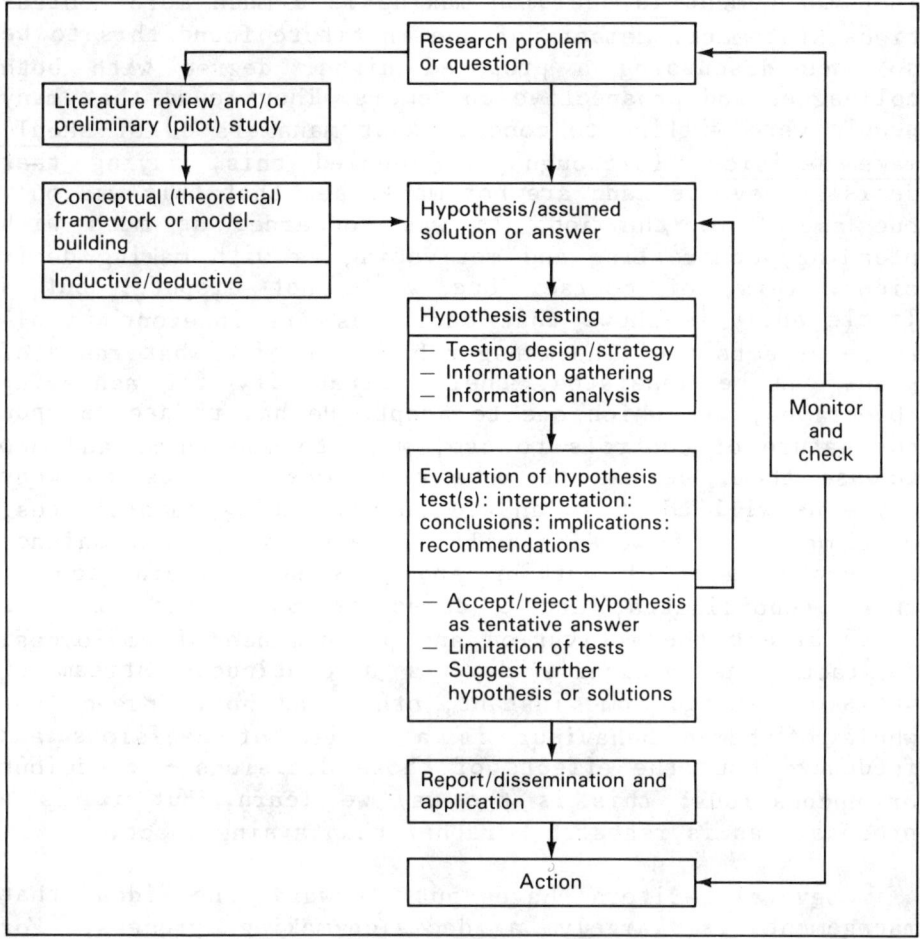

## 2.3  Research and the managerial process

Chapter 1 examined the relevance of research to management education and we concluded that research and "teaching" are, or should be, mutually supportive. But what about management practice? Do the same conclusions apply?

They do. The research process and the management process are similar. Furthermore, managers are often their own researchers. The good manager is, at least unconsciously, a good researcher. Both management and research are decision-taking processes.

That managers make decisions can hardly be denied. That management is decision making is a much more contentious statement. Members of one institute found this to be so when discussing a proposed higher degree with both colleagues and prospective customers. They found that many people were willing to concede that managers do or should make decisions (although some denied this, saying that decisions evolve, and are not made) but that this was only one aspect of the job. It was concerned as much with planning, controlling and motivating as with making decisions. This, of course, one would not dispute, but a little analysis shows that decisions are inherent in all these aspects too! The manager has to decide what range of plans can be generated, their suitability for achieving objectives, and which one to adopt. He has to decide upon the nature of controls to use, when to use them, and how to use them. He has to make decisions also as to what style he will adopt as an aid to motivating subordinates, what methods of working will achieve an optimum balance between economy of working and personal satisfaction of these subordinates, and a dozen or more other factors which affect the motivation and performance of employees. In fact, the manager's day is a continuous stream of decision making: some instant, others ad hoc. Indeed, the whole of human behaviour is a series of decisions and feedback about the effects of those decisions - conscious or unconscious: this is the way we learn. But it is a process - as is research - rather than a single act.

Several writers have put forward the idea that management is largely a decision-making process. For example, Simon makes the point that decision making is so nearly co-extensive with management that we can treat it as if it were fully so.[1] Similarly, Emory and Niland open their book on making management decisions with the following statement: "Decision making pervades the activities of every business manager - indeed, of every rational person. And decision making is all pervasive in business activities, for not to make a decision is itself a decision".[2]

---

[1] See H.A. Simon: The new science of management decision-making (New York, Harper and Row, 1960).

[2] See C. Emery and P. Niland: Making management decisions (New York, Houghton Mifflin, 1968), p. 3.

Management and decision making are both processes concerned with objectives. Problems arise and have to be solved. To do this, information must be obtained, alternative solutions sought and evaluated, and the chosen solution implemented and monitored. Management _is_ a decision-making process, as a little self-analysis will demonstrate to even the most sceptical amongst us. These stages of the managerial decision-making process are virtually the same as those the researcher goes through. Some major differences are:

Time: the manager is often short of this and may be unable to be as rigorous as needed in collecting and analysing information. Researchers usually have more time and are judged, in part, on the quality of information collected and analysis as well as on the end results.

Experience: managers are usually very experienced in the problem area and in dealing with the changing complexities of their situation. The researcher can bring to bear upon that situation considerable research-based experience which can be of value in obtaining and evaluating information.

Urgency: managerial problems often require quick solutions, whereas research has a longer time horizon. The temptation for the researcher to do a "quick, cheap job" must be resisted.

Impact: managers are responsible for the careers of employees and the families they support and for sums of money of often immense proportions. The fate of people, the profit earned by investors, the result of the next election ... all can hang on a manager's decision. At best, the researcher's efforts will provide a base for an exciting new tomorrow (in some small way, usually) and at worst, the research report will rest, unread, on a bookshelf: it can be ignored without any real implications for the "real world"! It may, and probably does, have an impact on his career prospects and reputation.

Despite these differences, research has an affinity with the managerial process and an important role in helping managers through the application of its techniques and methods to identifying problems, collecting relevant and timely information, and sorting out solutions. We should, however, bear the following points in mind when assessing the role of research in management.

---

Illustration 3: <u>Key points in assessing role of research in management</u>

Research and researcher are not infallible

Managers must be involved in the research if it is to be of use to them

Researchers must not be hedged in by endless constraints

Much valuable information and experience exists within the organisation itself

"Packages" or "ready-made" solutions to managerial problems should be throughly evaluated through research

Researchers should not be seen as replacing the manager as decision-maker

Researchers should be expected to provide supplementary information to enable the manager to take the necessary decision

Research methods and techniques can help managers in their own information-seeking activities

Research can be of indirect help by providing case material, knowledge, issues, etc. about decision making for the development of managers

---

2.4 <u>Management research and the social sciences</u>

The management process is largely concerned with people: people make decisions, they implement them or resist their implementation, they monitor the results and are affected by those results. Indeed, many writers define management as a process of achieving results through people. It is not surprising, then, that the study of management is claimed to come within the perspectives of the social sciences; namely, disciplines such as psychology, sociology, social anthropology, economics, history and geography. It is also not surprising that much management research is of a social scientific nature. Many of our most difficult theoretical and practical problems have to do with people in organisations: how to train them; which learning theories work best; appropriate managerial and leadership styles; what motivates people at work; which theories of motivation best explain work behaviour; how we should design jobs and organisations to optimise human satisfaction and organisational effectiveness - these and many more issues continually occupy the thoughts and time of many management researchers. The concepts, theories and ideas of "behavioural science", that subset of social science concerned with individual and small group behaviour, has dominated the research scene.

Yet management, and the training of managers, embraces other considerations. Management is about finance and economics: it is about operations planning, modelling, and quantitative analysis; it is about information, cybernetics, systems theory and computers; it is about politics, power and culture. These areas are also subject to research, but receive far less attention than research in behavioural science. Too much management research is behavioural science orientated. We need more of the other kinds. Often, too, behavioural science theories are based on research carried out in non-management areas, such as in psychology where many concepts derive from studies of animal behaviour. Whilst these concepts get picked and used in management education, we need more directly relevant research about management itself. This is growing, but greater efforts are still required.

Often, useful relevant research is carried out in institutes which do not appear to be concerned with management, where the term "management" does not appear in their titles. There exist, for example, institutes of administration, of business, of administrative studies, or of finance. There are staff colleges and training establishments. Each may be carrying out good management research, or well placed to do so. They should be encouraged in their efforts.

It is not easy to carry out management research. The field is complex; the main subjects of research (people) have relatively free will; circumstances change beyond our control. As a result, research may be ineffective, or of little use to anyone other than the most theoretical academic. To be useful, research in management should help solve problems, either of theory or of practice. Ineffective research does neither, yet we need both, for management is all about deciding things and doing things. As we shall now see, different approaches to research emphasise different aspects of the theory-practice relationship.

## 2.5 Approaches to research

There are, as indicated earlier, a number of different approaches to research. Whilst it is easy to argue (as some do) that research is research, whatever form or shape it takes, there does exist a sharp contrast between those approaches aimed at <u>purely academic or theoretical problems</u>, and those concerned more with the "day-to-day" difficulties of <u>management in practice</u>. There is, too, the often associated difference in the degree of "scientific method" adhered to in carrying out the research. In the physical sciences, it is much easier to have rigid control over an experiment: to formulate a hypothesis, design a rigorous research project, control all variables, and look for the answer.

---

Illustration 4:   <u>The theory-practice divide</u>

A good deal of management research has been initiated for <u>reasons of theory</u>. Many of the early studies of technology and organisation structure, undertaken in countries as far apart as India and the United Kingdom, were carried out because the researchers wanted to explain the relationship between the two. Such research contributed to the development of organisation theory. Indirectly, it has stimulated considerations about the practice of organisation design. At the level of the individual person, much research has focused upon various issues of motivation from a theoretical point of view. Some recent research in Israel as well as the United States has been explicitly concerned with the theoretical aspects of expectancy motivation, but also giving due consideration to the application of the findings to current problems of practice.

> Often, research is started for reasons of practice. Managers frequently request help in changing their organisation structures or designing jobs and work systems to improve motivation and performance. Research carried out on job design in Norway, Sweden, the United Kingdom and the United States have not only solved problems of practice but shed light on the weaknesses and strengths of the relevant theories and concepts. An important programme of research undertaken by the Asian Institute of Management concerns rural development management. It has produced findings of importance to practical management issues as well as developing case studies, notes, concept papers and other materials suitable for classroom use, and the development of faculty who are now familiar with the problems of the rural development manager and how to train him.
>
> These examples show that good, effective management research mixes theory and practice, even though it may be initiated for reasons of one or the other.

In the social sciences generally, and management in particular, this is rarely achievable. So what form or forms of research are relevant? Let us examine a number of identifiable approaches which might loosely be argued to exist on a continuum going from "theory-orientated" to "action-orientated", on the assumption that there are many kinds of research, not just one. This analysis is based on the typology put forward by Clarke.[1] He uses three dimensions for establishing the typology:

(1) Is the research concerned with clarifying and resolving theoretical issues, or with solving a practical problem in one enterprise?

(2) How is the research disseminated and diffused? Through learned journals? Reports to sponsors in the organisation?

---

[1] P.A. Clarke: Action research and organisational change (New York, Harper and Row, 1972).

33

(3) How is the researcher involved with his audience? Is it a single case, where only one audience exists (e.g. members of the scientific community or the research sponsors)? Or a multiple case where the researcher is both solving a practical problem and contributing something to our knowledge base?

Combining these dimensions produced five types of research, which are described here together with a sixth and more recent approach which has interest and relevance for management and social science research. This is not a scientific classification, and the boundaries are blurred. It does help us though, to think about the type of research we want to do.

## Pure basic research

Pure research arises from the need to develop a basic discipline. It is concerned with resolving, illuminating, or exemplifying a theoretical issue. It aims to enhance knowledge and understanding of the world around us. The findings are published in learned journals for the benefit of scientific colleagues and are of a high level of generality. They may take years before they add to our general stock of knowledge or become part of the armoury of practising professionals (e.g. personnel, OD, training specialists) in organisations or even before they become part of the thinking of people concerned with other types of research.

## Basic objective research

This research tackles a general problem of the application of knowledge which can arise in many contexts but does not aim to solve a particular practical problem. The findings are often published in both learned and professional journals with the aim of transmitting the outcomes of the research to scientists and to the practising professionals. Thus, the level of generality is still high and the people receiving the feedback about the research are professionally trained and/or academic. It is usually publicly funded and sometimes written up in a manner which the management teacher/trainer finds easy to pick up and use.

Evaluation research

This kind of research aims to assess some aspect of the performance of an enterprise (e.g. the effects of a change from authoritarian management to management by objectives; the change in behaviour of managers after receiving a three-week programme in human relations; the cost and social benefits of a United Nations road development programme to the economic activities of, say, a town of India). It usually analyses the effectiveness of such change programmes. It rarely actually tries to change things. The problems it tackles are essentially practical (as opposed to theoretical) and the results usually conveyed only to the sponsoring organisation through specific reports (although they may sometimes be published in professional journals to illustrate, for example, the use of a new research technique). Evaluation research is often sought by enterprises looking for a sophisticated method of collecting information and the appearance of "scientific neutrality" or impartiality. Arguments exist about the role and utility of evaluation research but there can be little doubt that it is an area in which management academics and practising managers can stand together looking at the same problem with mutual interest.

Applied research

This form of research is aimed at solving a specific, practical problem within an enterprise or sponsoring organisation. It does so through the application of appropriate knowledge. An example would be the use of our existing knowledge of human motivation to make changes to job/work organisation design in order to improve job satisfaction; or to apply our knowledge of human learning to improving training designs for management programmes. The results may or may not be written up: the recipient of the findings is the sponsor. Sometimes the research is published in case study form in professional journals.

This restricted dissemination usually means that applied work does not contribute to our existing stock of knowledge. It can, in fact, become rather insular, running the risk even of applying knowledge which is known to be inadequate. To carry out applied work effectively, the researcher has to be able to read the learned and professional journals with an eye to spotting theoretical developments and their relevance to applications of the sort in which he is interested.

Action research

This is a form of research where action (e.g. the solution of a problem, usually regarding some aspect of organisational change and development) is both an outcome of the research and a part of the research process. It aims to tackle problems which have relevance to theory and to report the findings to sponsors, scientists and practising professionals via reports and professional journals.

Action research thus has three task masters - the sponsor, the behavioural science practitioner, and the scientific community. This imposes many strains upon the researcher and his research. The main purpose of action research is to improve the stock of knowledge for the sponsoring (i.e. client) organisation. This can, and does, cause problems in disseminating the findings to a wider audience. However, where sensible, open and trusting collaborative research is carried out, publication of results is usually possible (albeit in disguised or anonymous form), providing opportunities for adding to our knowledge in general about management organisations. Its critics argue that, since the researcher is changing what is being researched during the process of the research, the project cannot be replicated. If it cannot be replicated, its findings cannot be tested in other situations. This prevents general knowledge being developed. Thus, it cannot contribute to theory. These points are difficult to refute, unless the notion of action research is changed. However, as a means of improving the utilisation of the research carried out, it has a lot to commend it to management researcher. It is important to bear in mind that the researcher is actually involved in the change process, at least by providing information collected through surveys, etc., to a group of organisation members, possibly before, during and after the change. He thus loses what some would argue is the key to good research - a critical, detached objectivity.

New "paradigm" research

This is a fairly recent addition to the range of approaches adopted for management research. Just as action research gave rise to considerable enthusiasm from the late 1960s on, so new paradigm research seems set to become a front runner in the 1980s. As its name implies, it is based on a new model or framework for research. It claims that research can never be neutral and that even the most static and conventional research exposes needs for change in what is researched. New paradigm research centrally involves inquiry into persons and relations between persons, and is based on a close relationship between researcher and researched. The research is a mutual activity of a "co-ownership" form, involving shared power with respect to the process and outcomes of the research. Those being researched can, for example, decide how the research will be done, in what form and with what questions being asked. The researcher is a member of the "community" and brings to it special skills and expertise. He does not dictate what shall happen. In contrast to the "old paradigm" with its emphasis on "hard", objective, tight and quantitative research, the new paradigm approach seeks to develop "a new rigour of softness". It links knowledge with participation, with action, with qualitative data, with the person as "a whole", and with values. In short, it states that "the outcome of research is knowledge. Knowledge is power. The wrong kind of research gives the wrong kind of power. The right kind of research gives the right kind of power. Research can never be neutral." This is an exciting approach, particularly when put over by one of its enthusiastic adherents. In terms of utility, it clearly has a place in helping research get started in situations where more conventional approaches are difficult (e.g. prisons, mental hospitals), where the real feelings of a person need to be examined (e.g. a manager facing a group decision going against him), and where personal and small group experiential learning is a key focus (e.g. T. groups), among others. It is clearly action orientated, and might be said to be seeking the ultimate in truth and knowledge in social science. Its rate of adoption will very much depend on availability of the necessary skills among staff in management institutions and its acceptability to practising managers.

## 2.6 A different perspective

As noted earlier, these forms of research represent different degrees of departure from or adherence to what we might call the "theory-action" divide. Theory-orientated research (as represented by "pure basic" research) is concerned with generating new knowledge, and developing new concepts and models - pushing back the frontiers of knowledge. Action-orientated research is concerned more with providing information to help serve current needs, solve existing problems or generate decision alternatives in a managerial action context.

Obviously, both forms of research are necessary. Without the development of new concepts, new theories, and new principles, little technological progress would ever be made, even though it may take decades for a new idea to find a pragmatic outlet. The same is true of management research. We need the many excellent basic research programmes currently being carried out in order to provide new ideas, techniques and processes for future managers. But we also need to systematically translate these sometimes highly theoretical and academic findings into relevant and practical managerial applications. It is this translation into practice which many managers do not see taking place, and therefore they rightly criticise the academic management community.

These three aspects of management research (knowledge, action and translation of knowledge to action) may best be summarised and further developed by reference to figure 4. The vertical axis represents the two extreme forms of research while the horizontal axis demonstrates their main emphasis. Thus, point A shows that knowledge-orientated research aims mainly to explain the world we live in and to further our understanding of it, yet it can also aim to progress towards predicting and controlling events, at a theoretical level at least (point B). The process A-B may be called an "inventive" one since it is concerned with producing new theories, ideas, etc. and testing their validity. Such research can also be aimed at developing understanding of everyday problems and controlling/predicting their outcomes (process C-D). This might be termed a "reactive" process since essentially we are concerned with reactions to problems arising in ongoing managerial situations. Often, help cannot be given to the manager in process C-D because either few or no new methods or ideas have been developed in the inventive process A-B, or, if they have, little attempt has been made to translate them into useful, working principles i.e. the "adaptive" process B-C.

**Figure 4  Types of research and their use**

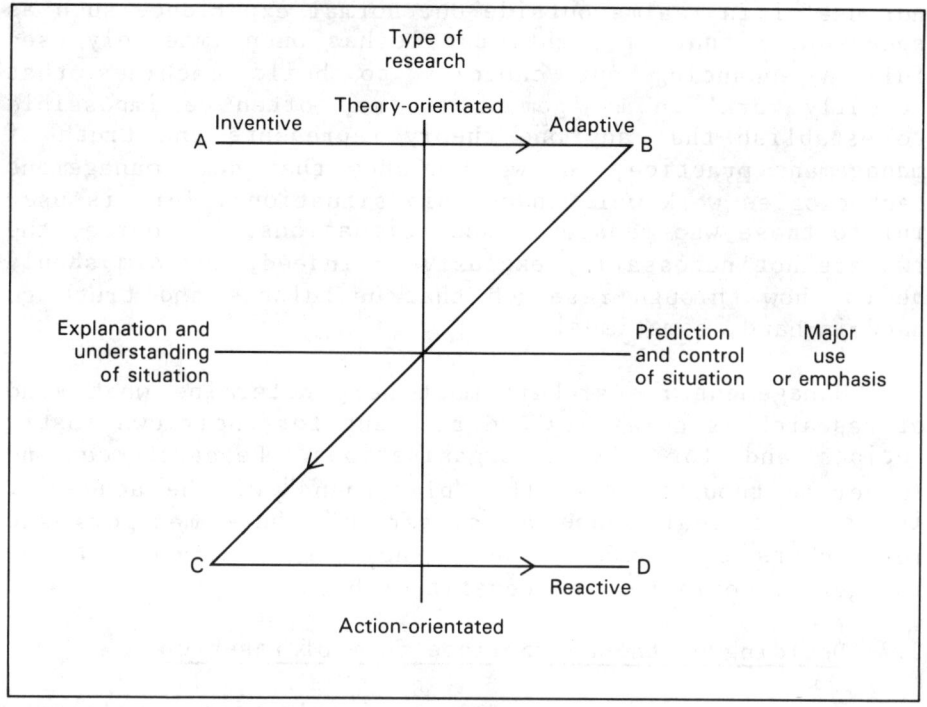

Perhaps an example will help to illustrate the relationship between these processes. One of the most frequently heard questions, historically and currently, is "How do I get my people to improve their performance and give their best?" It is a question asked by all sorts of managers in a variety of situations, and has been the subject of endless research programmes. Essentially, it is a very practical question and one would hope that managers (and others) would react by undertaking action-orientated (i.e. reactive) research. This is now becoming the case, as many of the reports in the national daily papers testify: witness the much-talked-of Volvo and Saab "experiments", not to mention many others which do not hit the headlines with such frequency and intensity.

To summarise, research is concerned both with "truth" and "usefulness". Some research - the theory-oriented - seeks often what is "true", to find out exactly what the "facts" are and, through a process of trying to refute the theory which explains these facts, present the real state of knowledge. However, it is not necessarily "useful" to know that something is true. Indeed, the reverse may be so. Newtonian physics has turned out to be neither true nor useful in realms outside our normal experience such as speeds near that of light. But it has been immensely useful in enhancing our capacity to build machines that actually work! In management, it may often be impossible to establish that any one theory represents the truth of management practice, but we can show that some management technologies work well in certain situations. This is useful to those who manage in such situations. Of course, the two are not necessarily exclusive - indeed, our aim should be to show through research that usefulness and truth go hand-in-hand, sometimes!

Management researchers must help determine what kind of research is necessary and relevant for their own institutions and for client organisations. Research can no longer be thought of as the "playground" of the academic: it is in a real sense a "classroom" where managers and researchers can combine their knowledge and view of the managerial world for the benefit of both.

## 2.7 Deciding on the appropriate form of research

How, then, does a management institution decide upon the nature and style of research it should adopt? What are the factors which determine the extent to which it shall engage upon knowledge-seeking or knowledge-applying research? Clearly, there are a number of considerations to be taken into account. We will consider some of the key ones here.

### What kind of institution do we have?

This is a critical question. Knowing where you are now helps shape where you want to be and the difficulties to be overcome in getting there. Is yours a mainly teaching institution? If it is, at what level? What form of research is appropriate to its teaching role? Is it more concerned with professional training as opposed to academic training? If it is, perhaps a more action-oriented type of research is appropriate? What research is currently taking place? Is there any research culture and tradition? If not, introducing research will be very difficult unless it is directly related to the main activities upon which staff are engaged.

What kind of institution do we want?

Research activity is undoubtedly one of the best ways of helping to reshape the image and approach of a management institution. In the United Kingdom a number of management institutions took deliberate research policy decisions some 10-15 years ago and are now enjoying the benefits. They saw their previous work to be going stale and recognised that the institution would not be able to reach out for different forms and levels of work without a research capacity.

Whether the change is from a highly academic approach to more action-centred learning activities or vice versa, is irrelevant. What is relevant is the type of research that will aid the process. To become more academically respectable requires research that can be published in learned journals - here you are really concerned with "inventive" research. Making the change to more in-company, action learning endeavours implies the need to publish in professional and popular journals and to be engaged in "adaptive" or "reactive" research. The key issue is: how big a change (if any) is required to get from where we are now to where we want to be? For some institutions the change will be too great for research alone to bring it about. Here we enter into the realms of "politics".

What sort of staff do we have and do we need?

Not all staff can be expected to undertake research. If they have been used to teaching and running management programmes as their primary activity, with perhaps heavy teaching and administration work loads, they are not likely to have the time or inclination to do research. If they were hired because of their practical experience, they may have little interest in research unless it is clearly action-oriented in the "reactive" style. Staff who have good academic qualifications and are keen on speculative-type teaching may be more interested in knowledge-oriented research of the "inventive" sort. The really professional management trainer might find "adaptive" research appealing. Developing the right kind and style of research may require you to modify your staffing and recruitment policy. Do you build in research as a selection criteria? What sort of research experience/potential do you look for? Can you reward a staff member for carrying out good research and achieving publication? Is there a promotion/career route for the research-oriented as well as training/administration-oriented member of staff? Knowing the kind of staff you have and need will be of importance in determining the form of research to adopt. The following checklist (illustration 5) may be helpful in assessing your staff. It is based on stereotypes of management academics as seen by both academics and managers. Where do your staff fit?

Illustration 5:   Academic stereotypes

The isolate        seeks to convince other academics of the value of his research through academic publications; if message "trickles" through to managers, all to the good, but not worried if it doesn't; interested only in pursuing personal research interests (if topical, these add to his visibility).

The pragmatist     seeks to convince clients of value of his research through popular publications (frowned upon by much of the academic community) as well as convincing peers via academic press; hopes message will get through; may carry out "confirming" type research where possible - testing validity of theory in practice.

The translator     understands research process and has done some; a good teacher; translates academic jargon and sophisticated research into practical terms, maybe writing it up; produces readable books and articles; may assume also the role of "educator".

The persuader      uses research in teaching MBA-type students and tries to demonstrate/persuade of utility of research in hope that students will take it back to client community, and be active.

| | |
|---|---|
| The educator | attempts to get groups of managers, trainers and others together to listen to and discuss research findings of self or colleague; attends professional rather than (or as well as) academic conferences to exchange views. May also be a "liaiser". |
| The liaiser | goes out talking with client community to establish their interests, problems and needs; drops off a few reprints of articles in popular form; suggests names of colleague(s) who might talk further, or suggests he has a further chat; maybe directs manager to useful other sources of information or help. |
| The missionary | seeks to "sell" his ideas and research to specific organisations in relation to specific problems; uses research output in consultancy work; keen to take on specific problembased projects; attempts to link users with research via any practical mechanism. |

In a rough and ready way, these "stereotypes" fit the "theory-action" continuum of research approaches. The "isolate" is much more likely to be concerned with inventive, knowledge-seeking research, whereas the "missionary" will very much be into action-oriented research of one form or another. The other roles represent shades between these two, but with a bias towards adaptive research.

<u>What forms of activity are you/will you be engaged upon?</u>

Research for its own sake is a luxury few management institutions can afford. The research approach you adopt needs to be related to your work activities. Are these: mainly taught courses, leading to an academic award? (if they are, "adaptive" type research might have relevance); mainly short courses, run either in-company or in the institution? (here a mix of adaptive-reactive research might be possible); mainly of a one-off, tailor-made form, working in and with companies on, for example, action learning, project-based or self-development type activities? (if it is, then reactive research is most likely to be of relevance, particularly action research. Adopting new paradigm research should be reserved for experimental situations, involving skilled staff). An institution with a mix of management education, training and development activities, comprising diploma and master degree/PhD work, short courses, project-based learning programmes, seminars, action-learning, etc., will face difficulties in developing a coherent approach to research unless its organisation structure provides conducive focal points. This might take the form of staff groupings based on task or "product" activities. A more clearly identified research approach can be related to particular groups and staff interests.

What kinds of clients do you/will you have?

It has to be said that not all enterprises and their managers are interested in research - either in taking part in it or in using the results. For the most part, managers are able to deal with their own problems in their own ways. Some will, on recognising a problem that might require a research-based solution, get in touch with a management institution. Others will not. Some will be sympathetic to approaches to let you carry out research within their enterprises; and again, others will not. Some will see a need for assessing the impact of the training work you are doing for them and an evaluation type of research will be called for. Others will see a need to involve an action research approach with the organisational change programme they are discussing with you. Opportunities to carry out knowledge seeking research may be very rare, except as a spin-off from a more action-oriented project. Knowing the kind of enterprise managers you are dealing with will give an added perspective to your view of the form of research that is relevant to your own institution. Like academics, managers come in different stereotypes. Which of the following represent the managers you deal with?

---

Illustration 6:   Manager stereotypes

The agnostic      doesn't read journals or books; dislikes academics or tolerates them;

|  |  |
|---|---|
|  | avoids conferences or seminars; knows problems only too well but refuses to believe research or academic work has anything to offer; never goes on courses. |
| The convert | reads popular journals; attends seminars and conferences on "in" topics; listens to academics; knows the jargon; pretends to understand his problems; does nothing about using research to help solve them. |
| The influencer | educated in management field; reads the popular journals and books; seeks to influence colleagues to be more accepting toward academic concepts and research findings; introduces such ideas at meetings and other appropriate opportunities. |
| The activator | educated or not, believes in role management research can play; invites researcher to study problem or allows access when requested, if appropriate. |
| The innovator | educated in management or other field; reads popular journals and books; attends seminars and conferences; seeks out credible academics; understands his problems; attempts to use joint research approaches where relevant; willing to try something new; accepts change as part of organisational life. |
| The donator | inspired by willingness to part with money for genuine attempts to improve managerial practice; may be generally philanthropic; not necessarily educated in an academic sense; keen not to see worthwhile approaches and activities go under for the lack of financial support; may well be an existing client who believes in your work. |

Who has the money?

In many cases the availability of funds for research is the deciding factor in determining the kind of research you undertake - at least initially. As we saw previously, the IESA in Venezuela "broke into" management research through population studies. Staff interests and those of powerful funding bodies came together well. Having established a reputation, it became easier to negotiate funds for other projects. Visibility in the "money market" is important. Sometimes, a quick survey of a topic or issue for a client with the money and power to do something with the results is a good way of establishing both visibility and reputation. It may deflect you initially from your main goals, but it can be helpful in creating a research capacity.

If you are fortunate to have a number of "innovators" amongst your clients, you should be able to develop any form of research as long as it is relevant to the corporate managerial body at large. A sound research relationship can be developed with the "activator" on topics that have specific relevance to him - this will normally lead to mixes of adaptive/reactive research (e.g. evaluative, applied and action research). The "influencer" will be interested in hearing of the results of any research you are carrying out but may not be prepared to get involved. One avenue for identifying and cultivating managers with a keen interest in research is through the courses and programmes you run. Do you have good "persuaders" on your staff?

Which approach to research is for you?

Obviously there are many factors to take into account in answering this question. We have briefly discussed some of them in the sections above. In coming to a view, you may find the checklist presented in figure 5 to be of help. Whilst this can in no way be considered an exhaustive or accurate listing (particular circumstances will change the emphasis shown), it does provide an indication of the kind of research that might be relevant to your institution, given that certain factors prevail. In using this figure, first work down the list of factors, and read off against each one the type of research approach that will possibly be relevant to you. Then add up the number

**Figure 5  What type of research? A summary checklist**

| Points for checking | Possibly relevant research approach | | |
|---|---|---|---|
| | Inventive | Adaptive | Reactive |
| **Nature of institution:** | | | |
| Research | * | * | * |
| Teaching — no research | | * | |
| — some research | * | * | |
| Training/development — no research | | * | |
| — some research | | * | * |
| Consultancy and advisory services | | | |
| — no research | | | * |
| — some research | | * | * |
| **Staffing:** | | | |
| Qualifications — academic | * | | |
| — professional | | * | |
| — experience | | | * |
| No research training/experience | | * | |
| Some research training/experience | * | * | * |
| Teaching-oriented | * | * | |
| Learning/practice-oriented | | * | * |
| **Activities:** | | | |
| Higher degrees | * | * | |
| Qualification courses generally | | * | |
| Short courses in institutions | | * | |
| In-company courses | | * | * |
| Project-based | | * | * |
| Action-learning | | * | * |
| Self-development | | * | * |
| **Clients:** | | | |
| Closely linked on e.g. action learning programmes | | * | * |
| Providers of students for courses | * | * | |
| Ad-hoc relationship/contact | | * | |

of "stars" you have circled under each of the headings "inventive", "adaptive" and "reactive". The one with the highest number is the one to look at first. But remember there are constraints that may deflect you away from this "logically" derived profile: money, power, staff interests - all will have a bearing on what you decide. And don't miss out on opportunities when they arise - if a donor appears, make him welcome and get started. Whichever approach you adopt, there is the specific requirement to determine what should be researched. We will tackle this issue in the next chapter.

# ESTABLISHING WHAT SHOULD BE RESEARCHED 3

## 3.1 The main requirement

As we have seen in the previous chapter, there are a number of different approaches to research. What sort of research is mainly needed in management? The answer depends on several things. One is the state of knowledge and theory available and its adequacy in explaining and predicting managerial phenomena. We have numerous concepts describing particular aspects of management; what we lack in many fields is sufficient hard information of their utility in practice. Secondly, management is in itself an applied or practical "discipline". We might expect that management research should also have an applied orientation. Whilst this is so in some respects, a lot of management research tends to be of an "academic" nature, if not theory-orientated. Thirdly, the interests and orientations of staff members must have an influence on the nature of research carried out. Those who have followed a primarily academic route will mainly be interested in academic research, but not exclusively. Others in management education and training will have come from a career in management itself. They will often have a more practical orientation - many will not be interested in research at all. It would seem, therefore, that the kind of research mainly needed should have an action or practice orientation to it. This should not be to the exclusion of knowledge-seeking or theory-orientated research. If we blindly use research only as a tool for solving today's problems we shall not be generating the capacity - the concepts and frameworks - for dealing with tomorrow's difficulties. There is a fundamental interaction between theory and practice: research helps develop that interaction. Without it, our role as management educators, developers, trainers and consultants will quickly become sterile, wither and die, because research can be useful not only to managers and organisations but to the work we do as management developers (e.g. in enriching our teaching).

To have decided that research has an important part to play in the affairs of a management institution and that a particular approach, or range of approaches, should be adopted, are crucial steps in the development of a research capacity. Such steps will have established a commitment, a policy, a philosophy regarding researching. They will not have led to any sharply defined research interests, needs or problems. What is needed is a research programme.

## 3.2 The research programme

The nature of the research programme will, therefore, depend upon

(1) the research policy adopted;

(2) the type(s) of research approaches most favoured;

(3) a set of research projects.

Guidance has already been offered on (1) and (2). How can research projects be established? This can be achieved in one of two ways.

### Ad hoc programmes

The projects can develop in an ad hoc manner. That is, as a particular interest, need, problem or area of research presents itself, someone takes the initiative in setting up a project and actually doing some research. Research initiated in this way can be appealing: it responds directly to the need and it can capture the interest and enthusiasm of the faculty member. Both are important. On the negative side, such an approach leads to fragmented (and sometimes wasted) research effort, a dissipation of research effort, and the failure to build up a developing and continuing body of research, knowledge and practice.

Thematic programmes
---

An alternative way is to develop a thematic approach. By this is meant a programme of research that links projects together within a coherent framework. The framework may be based on either a single theme (e.g. a major subject area, or a set of common problems) or a set of related themes (e.g. a group of subject areas that comprise the main inputs to the training work, or a set of issues that cut across a number of different industries/managerial levels). The major disadvantage here is that it can be costly in time, effort and money to get the programme launched. Individual projects and initiatives flourish more quickly - they also perish more quickly if they are not embodied in more thematic research. Balancing this are the momentum and magnetic qualities of thematic programmes. If a member of staff leaves, there are usually enough left to keep the research going. Additionally, student projects can often be attracted to thematic research, as can staff on sabbaticals. This helps research to grow and flourish. There are many examples of thematic research: the studies of organisational behaviour and structure at the University of Aston, United Kingdom; the Ohio State University's leadership research; the quality of working life research in several European management institutes - these, and others, have grown from small beginnings along a theme of continuing relevance to either knowledge/theory, or action/practice, or both.

The research in such institutes is based on what we might call an "enduring research theme". They have taken a key management, organisational or social (as in the case of IESA in Venezuela on population) issue and developed a lively and continuing research theme. Many institutes work together on similar themes, creating a "research stream". It can be helpful in getting your own research started to become linked to and identified with such a research stream. One way of tapping this stream is to have one of your staff do a research degree at one of the main institutes. That staff member may then be able to develop further some aspect of the research in your own institution. Another way is to have a visiting member of faculty from the main institute spend time with your staff in setting up research. This has been tried in many places and can work well if you have enough competent staff with basic research skills who can learn from the visiting professor, and provided the research is based on local needs. Simply importing the visiting professor's own research may do little to develop research relevant to the needs of management and management teaching in your area and institute.

## 3.3 Determining research needs

A variety of methods can be used. Some will result in ad hoc projects being initiated over a period of time, others in thematic research. All will help develop research which will be useful to the management institute, its staff and its clients (both individuals and enterprises).

### Personal interests

Many institutes find that research gets started because a particular member of staff is vitally interested in some special area or issue. Something plays on the mind and won't let go until a research project is in progress. It may be an academic interest, in the sense that a part of the discipline is inadequate; it may be an interest in method, often associated with learning; or it may be an interest in what managers actually do, in terms of, say, the way they spend their time. The important thing here is not so much the research area itself but more the enthusiasm for doing research. This must be captured, nurtured and channelled. A way of doing this is for a senior member of a faculty to be given responsibility for research - as a co-ordinator, a supporter, a leader - and for this person to hold discussions with individual faculty members. Talking over professional interests can lead to the identification of research possibilities. If two or three staff show genuine keenness, they can be helped, counselled and supported. A small core of research will then build up, bearing in time the fruits of publications, student projects linked with the research, enriched training and consultancy and, it may be hoped, the enthusiasm of other staff. The programme of research which this leads to may or may not be ad hoc - this depends on the extent to which the personal staff interests connect up with each other. It is just possible, for example, that the interests of the lawyer, the accountant and marketing specialist can find mutual expression in researching the problems of setting up new businesses. The senior staff member with responsibility for research can help to bring them together.

## Specialism interests

Most staff in management institutions have a specialism or set of related specialisms which form the basis of their skills and knowledge and the contributions they make to management education, training and development. Research needs can often be identified through an assessment of the state of knowledge and practice within the specialist area. If several specialists within a given area are employed by the institution, small group seminars can reveal areas of common interest and concern. Seminars involving specialists in related fields (e.g. production management, operational research and quantitative methods; personnel management, financial management and social accounting) can be particularly fruitful in producing ideas for research which are multi-disciplinary and inter-disciplinary in character. If such research needs can be identified and fostered, the effects of group momentum can be harnessed. The potential for developing thematic research programmes is quite high. On the other hand, single specialism research may lead to useful ad hoc projects. There is, of course, often a strong link between personal interests and specialism interests that may take staff along divergent research paths. This is no bad thing, except that considerable fragmentation of research effort can arise from it.

## Programme interests

This refers to the programme of work and activities of the institute, such as training courses, in-company development projects, organisational development activities, consultancy work and the like. Each will pose a series of research needs including identifying future programme activities and priorities, developing new approaches, evaluating existing activities, and producing programme material. A potentially rich source of research needs is the training needs analysis upon which many programme activities are dependent. This may reveal training and development requirements about which little is known. A systematic research-based study might be called for in order to throw light on the training need; or an experimental approach to meeting the need might be developed.

Gaps in knowledge and training competences might be revealed, suggesting research-based staff development as a possible solution. Surveys of clients to assess attitudes to particular training approaches can highlight potentially beneficial ways of meeting the identified training need. A careful analysis of a number of training needs analysis reports offers a relatively quick and cost-effective way of mapping out interesting and useful avenues of research. The identification of <u>problems and difficulties with training methods</u> experienced by staff can add to the range of programme-orientated research needs. An example of this would be the development of leadership styles with groups of managers of differing cultural backgrounds. The method most successful with one group may not work with another. Why? What factors are involved? Which methods are most suitable for which groups? Can some groups not be trained in leadership styles? These are good research questions. Another source of research potential is <u>the resource material</u> used in the programme of activities. Acquiring new knowledge and information, developing case study material and problem "incidents", in relation to the training needs and methods, can form the basis of research projects. Research can be used as a means of generating, testing and developing such material. Whilst an inherent danger with these sources of research needs is a totally "produce-orientated" research programme, there is the considerable benefit of being able to link specialism and client needs.

Institutional interests

Every management institute will have its own interests and needs for research. These may be powerful enough, particularly in the infant stage of developing its research capacity, to give considerable shape to the research programme. Staff development needs are especially potent. The use of research-based higher degrees is a common means of developing staff and upgrading levels of qualifications. This may be related to the personal interests of staff or to the requirements of their specialism. Programme development is also a strong spur to research, especially in areas where the institute does not possess any or much strength. The use of research for developing potential consultancy strengths represents another strong institutional interest. Staff members with good research track records and reputations often find themselves being called upon by the client for help and advice. Public image, reputation and visibility of the institute are factors of considerable influence in identifying research needs and releasing sufficient organisational commitment and resources to make something happen. A danger here is, perhaps, that this method will lead to a rather insular, in-bred and introspective type of research being developed. It will meet the needs of the institution and to a large measure those of its staff, but will it relate at all to the requirements of the clients, of the region or of the economy of the country? Again, the senior staff member has an important contribution to make in helping to bring about a balanced programme of research.

## Client interests

A management institution's clients have a vast array of possible research needs. Regular contact with clients arising from normal working relationships may not be sufficient to identify research needs. Specific visits, based on a well-prepared set of questions, may be required. Systematic studies using questionnaires and interviews can prove valuable. Seminars at which staff and managers come together to probe particular problem areas are often fruitful in identifying areas where research can play a vital role. Throughout such activities, it will be important to keep in mind the possible distinction between the needs and problems of the organisation and those of individual managers. Quite different research strategies can arise from them. For example, a study of where, when and how managers do their most creative thinking could be carried out without having to negotiate access to companies. A sample could be built up from managers on courses and membership lists of professional bodies. It may not be representative of the entire managerial population but might well yield very interesting data. On the other hand, a study of how companies use creative managers would require a totally different approach - one that would be highly dependent on gaining access.

## National interests

Research needs in management are often influenced by national interests and requirements. The particular emphasis placed within national governmental policy on areas such as education, social welfare, employment, industrial development and training will have a bearing on organisational and managerial priorities. Variations will exist between sectors, and with respect to time scale. Government agencies publish reports and discussion documents indicating priorities and time scales. They may even go so far as to spell out recommendations for research. This network can be turned into establishing contact with relevant committees, working parties and individuals which provides a good information source. Joint collaboration in, for example, the running of conferences on specific aspects of relevant government policy can open ideas and avenues for mutual development. The process can be painfully slow and is not one on which to rest the entire research programme. It can, however, lead to research which is highly relevant to the managerial needs of a particular sector of the economy.

Systematic approaches

A number of institutions are deriving considerable benefit from adopting a systematic approach to the identification of research needs. There are, no doubt, many variants, but the following have been found to work quite well.

(1) It is possible to use <u>regular seminars</u> for identifying and updating research needs and requirements. This can involve either staff on their own, or with managers and others. Staff seminars can be initiated by checking out staff interests in research. The first seminar can be based on a discussion of these interests. The outcome should be an agreed list of areas in which staff feel research could usefully take place. Certain members would be invited to prepare short discussion papers which would contain:

- a statement of what the area was all about;

- a review of the key research recently carried out in the areas on a national/international basis;

- an assessment of where the research is going, the gaps, etc.;

- a statement of fruitful areas for development and their relationship with staff/institution/ client interests.

The papers would then be presented at a second seminar (or several seminars if the number of papers is high) and conclusions reached about the need for research in specific areas. These conclusions can be fed into joint staff/manager discussion groups, to establish the relationship of designated areas of research to the practice of management. Priorities would then have to be determined and a research programme set out. All that is then required to get it moving!

(2) A broader based and more probing approach is the use of the <u>"expert" panel</u>. At its <u>simplest level</u>, this approach is much like the use of seminars on a regular basis for a specified period and is sometimes known as the "nominal group" technique. The so-called "experts" are people drawn from industry, consultancy, the academic world and so on who have special interests or competencies. A number of sessions are arranged at which panel members are required to do certain things. This might take the following form:

> Session 1: panel members are each asked to put forward and discuss, say, three areas which they feel will be important to managers/companies in the near future. These are recorded by staff and a short report produced.
>
> Session 2: members discuss report and agree the most and least important areas, problems or issues - most/least important to themselves?, the country? or whoever. A second short report is produced.
>
> Session 3: members discuss second report and are asked to highlight which of the important areas are susceptible to a research approach, what kind of information is needed and in what form ......

A final report is prepared, containing a proposed research programme. Further sessions can be held to update the report and help monitor progress.

A <u>more sophisticated and non-interactive approach</u> can be used. This involves a similar type of procedure but without the seminars. It uses the tools (or some of them) of management research to help identify management research needs, and is based on forecasting techniques. Although demanding in terms of time and staff skills, it does bring into sharper focus the problems of management and push them into magnitudes of priorities. The key steps are:

1. invite senior managers, management teachers/trainers and others as relevant to become members of the panel;

2. develop a research instrument, i.e. a survey questionnaire outlining the key areas of the managerial/organisational process and ask members to describe the main problem they would expect to occur in each area;

3. collect the questionnaires, analyse them and list the problem areas described;

4. design a second questionnaire based on these problem areas, requesting panel members to rate or rank the relative importance of each problem;

5. analyse, categorise and compare the findings to see which problems are rated with an acceptable degree of agreement between panel members;

6. develop research programme recommendations and provide feedback to panel members;

7. update and revise from time to time, generally or within specific sectors.

A good example of this approach is the management research agenda study carried out by the Centre for Management Development in Lagos, in co-operation with the ILO, on behalf of the Nigerian Council for Management Development. Their work is summarised in illustration 7. Another example, from Canada, shows an agenda derived from a national conference of senior management educators. This is shown in illustration 8. Finally, the development of the research programme at the Instituto de Estudios Superiores de Administracion (IESA) is given as a further example in illustration 9.

Illustration 7: **The Nigerian management research agenda**

This illustration shows how some of the tools and techniques available to management researchers can be used to identify management research needs. The approach shown was developed by the Nigerian Council for Management Development through its operational arm, the Centre for Management Development. The Centre has a mandate which includes "the sponsoring, promotion and conduct of research into all aspects of management and allied subjects in relation to the Nigerian situation". But where to start?

The chosen starting point was the Nigerian management research agenda study, conducted in co-operation with the ILO. The need for the study was evident, namely to establish a link between what is researched and the real and important problems confronting managers in Nigerian organisations. But which problems should be tackled? It was this basic question that helped shape the study.

The study was based on the "Delphi panel" approach, and took place in early 1980. Top managers, management teachers and scholars were invited to become members of a non-interacting panel. Their purpose was to identify the major problems that could be expected to confront Nigerian managers during the next three to five years. A total of 62 people took part in a two-phase survey.

Phase 1 consisted of circulating a questionnaire designed around key elements of an organisation as an open system. Panellists were asked to describe the major problems they thought would occur at each of five activity points: input, transformation, output, feedback and environmental interface. Forty-four panellists completed the form. Over 600 problems were identified but reduced to 439 for methodological reasons. This was achieved by using separate persons to code and categorise the statements. Only those achieving consistent coding were retained. These were used in phase 2.

Phase 2 was also based on a questionnaire. This time, panellists were asked to judge the relative importance of each problem statement on a scale of 1 (little importance) to 10 (extremely important). A greater number of panellists (61) completed this more straightforward questionnaire. By calculating means and standard deviations, an "acceptable level of agreement" was determined, taking 1/3 of a standard deviation around the mean as the cut-off point. This allowed 23 statements to be retained, which were then ranked on the basis of their mean scores. Groups of more and less important problems were thus identified.

The critically important problems identified were:

1. It will be necessary to train workers to appreciate the limits of modern equipment. Otherwise, millions of Naira will be lost yearly as abusive treatment results in equipment breakdowns.

2. There is a need to educate both managers and union leaders in the intricacies of developing and operating a modern industrial relations system.

3. Organisations will have to develop relevant, realistic and fair methods for objectively evaluating the performance of employees at all levels.

4. Organisations which do not have effective and comprehensive training programmes will find it difficult to adapt and grow.

5. Infrastructure deficiencies (roads, communication, electricity, water, etc.) will severely hamper some operations and totally cripple others.

6. Numerous decision activities (e.g. planning, control, investment, product mix, etc.) will be hampered by a growing shortage of relevant, reliable and timely statistical data on both the micro and macro levels.

7. Pressures for more efficient allocation and utilisation of organisational resources will require the use of far more effective techniques

in such areas as job design, cost analysis, and productivity measurement.

The problems thus elicited formed the basis of the management research agenda. Proposals to implement the agenda have been developed, and include its extension to sectors other than modern industry.

---

Illustration 8: The Canadian research agenda[1]

The priority research agenda arose from a national conference of the Canadian Federation of Deans of Management and Administrative Studies held in 1980. It was recognised that their research must now address business education itself, and not just the traditional business specialisms. The following agenda was derived:

1. Research to broaden the management education curriculum. It is generally agreed that "non-cognitive" skills, such as negotiating, interpersonal communications and ethical decision making, will be increasingly required of all managers. How can such skills be taught or developed?

2. Research to streamline the management education curriculum. It will not be possible to include in the pre-career training of managers everything that the manager of tomorrow will need to know. What subjects should be deleted or reduced to

---

[1] See R.R. Rehder: "American business education - Is it too late to change?", in Sloan Management Review, Winter 1982, pp. 63-71. See also Managing in the 1980s: Choosing themes for management research, Report of the National Conference of the Canadian Federation of Deans of Management and Administrative Studies (CFDMAS) and the Administrative Sciences Association of Canada (ASAC), held in Toronto, Canada, 29-30 September 1980 and 2 February 1981, pp. 23-24.

make room for more essential or appropriate subjects?

3. <u>Research to implement lifelong continuing professional education for managers</u>. Changing circumstances, new challenges, and fresh knowledge now compel managers to continue their learning throughout their careers. How can this continuing professional education be provided most effectively?

4. <u>Research on training for "results-oriented" management education</u>. Business schools are increasingly impelled to evaluate their efforts by results in terms of measurable increases in student capacities rather than merely in terms of inputs (class hours, professorial credentials). How can a "management by results" system be developed and installed?

5. <u>Research on producing the distinctive skills and knowledge required by managers of different kinds of organisations</u>. Managers of governmental, non-profit, voluntary and other kinds of agencies and organisations are drawn increasingly from the graduates of business schools. How can such managers be better prepared?

6. <u>Research on installing the international understanding and capabilities needed by prospective managers</u>. Canadian businesses, industries and other organisations will operate more and more in an interdependent global environment. How can managers be prepared for such new challenges?

7. <u>Research on recruiting and training managers from non-traditional segments of the population</u>. More women and members of minority groups must be drawn into effective management positions, both to achieve social equality and to produce the larger cadres of managers our society needs. How can such people be identified, recruited, trained and appropriately used?

8. <u>Research on educating for entrepreneurship</u>. The traditions of risk-taking, venture management,

invention and other innovative aspects of management need reaffirmation and revitalisation. How can individuals be identified and prepared for such crucial roles?

9. <u>Research on preparing managers to cope with the emerging relationships of Canadian organisations with new external constituencies</u> (e.g. government, consumers, labour organisations, etc.). External pressures, constraints and relationships will impinge increasingly on the manager's role. How should managers be prepared to deal with these pressures?

10. <u>Research on educating managers to understand changing values, philosophies and life-styles</u>. A transformation will continue concerning the values of managers and of other groups or segments of the population. How can managers for the future be educated to understand their own values and contribute to the social and cultural formation of shared ideals and purposes?

---

Illustration 9: <u>Research at IESA</u>

During IESA's present stage of development, RESEARCH represents a BASIC INSTRUMENT for:

1. generating knowledge of the social, political, economic and cultural environment in which public and private Venezuelan organisations operate;

2. developing and adapting managerial and administrative technologies in order to promote desired changes in the afore-mentioned environment;

3. participating in the analysis and discussion of issues of national interest in order to generate a better understanding of the country's problems;

4. contributing to the development of the basic disciplines (sociology, psychology, economics,

etc.) which underline the analysis of administrative and managerial problems and which, in Venezuela, do not generally address intervention in reality as a means for promoting change.

Research pursued in accordance with the aforementioned guidelines is vital for the development of teaching and consulting activities that go BEYOND A SIMPLE TRANSFER OF MANAGERIAL AND ADMINISTRATIVE TECHNOLOGIES DRAWN FROM THE EXPERIENCE OF OTHER ENVIRONMENTS.

RESEARCH DEVELOPMENT IN IESA is ORIENTED, among other things, ALONG THE FOLLOWING LINES:

1. EXECUTION OF RESEARCH PROJECTS WHICH RESPOND TO THE ACADEMIC INTERESTS OF THE INSTITUTE. This means being more PRO-ACTIVE without scorning external research demands in order to deal with some specific needs of public and private organisations.

2. The research promoted by IESA should cover, in principle, BROAD SUBJECTS THAT HAVE A HIGH MULTIPLIER EFFECT as regards the repercussions that questions raised and knowledge generated will have on various areas and problems.

3. THESE RESEARCH SUBJECTS SHOULD BE PARTICULARLY MOTIVATING (GENERATING GREAT ENTHUSIASM) at least for IESA professors and, if possible, they should have potential impact for the teaching activities of the institute. This means guaranteeing the continuity of the research projects both at individual and institutional level.

4. Giving greater IMPORTANCE to activities related to RESEARCH INTO THE PROFESSORS' career development (promotions, etc.).

5. Exploring the possibility of executing RESEARCH PROJECTS JOINTLY WITH OTHER ACADEMIC INSTITUTIONS.

In accordance with the above-mentioned lines of action, the concrete objectives for 1982 (based on work already in progress or needing completion) are as follows:

1. To initiate research on the relationship between STRATEGY AND STRUCTURE IN VENEZUELAN ENTERPRISES. (At present, the exploratory phase of this research project is being concluded.)

2. To initiate a project on PROFESSIONAL CAREER PATTERNS IN VENEZUELA.

3. To revise the needs and possibilities of research in STATE AND SMALL- AND MEDIUM-SIZED ENTERPRISES, with the aim of creating openings for research in these fields.

4. To PREPARE MONOGRAPHS relating to the following subjects: structure and strategy of the private enterprise, design and administration of social programmes, equality of educational opportunities, finances.

5. TO PREPARE PUBLICATION OF THE FOLLOWING BOOKS: (based on ongoing and completed research)

- The management of social programmes in Venezuela

- Study of Venezuela (collection of 21 essays on various subjects about institutional sectors of the country and political, social and economic structure of the country)

- Competition between private enterprises: industrial concentration and its effects in Venezuela

- Policy implementation in Venezuela

- Women in education in Venezuela.

6. To initiate the publication and distribution of IESA's work papers series.

(3) A similar approach is one based on the use of surveys. This can allow a broader set of interests to be represented through a larger number of participants. Two methods are commonly adopted: interviews and questionnaires. Whilst interviews are more time consuming than

questionnaires, they allow more probing, exploratory and detailed information to be gained. They also set up a more personal relationship between the staff member carrying out the survey and the participants. Many more participants can normally be covered by a questionnaire survey. The two can, of course, be used together. A typical survey-based approach would be:

1. small group of staff members meet to discuss the nature of the survey and agree upon its objectives;

2. staff members of the group individually visit a small number of managers, consultants and management teachers/trainers to conduct unstructured interviews; the aim of the interviews is to gain some information about the way management research is viewed, problems it can/ should tackle, degree of involvement in research, and so on;

3. staff members meet again to share information and to agree on the basic structure of a questionnaire. One staff member is asked to design the questionnaire;

4. when draft questionnaire is ready, staff members meet to discuss and modify it;

5. modified questionnaire is then pilot-tested by asking a small number of managers consultants and teachers/trainers to fill it in. They are then inverviewed briefly to gain reactions to the questionnaire, to detect ambiguities, difficulties, etc.

6. questionnaire is modified and produced in final format;

7. during the time spent on the above, two activities can take place

    - determining the method of analysis of data,

    - drawing up a sample of people to whom the questionnaire will be given/sent. This might include members of professional bodies, managers in local companies, consultants, teachers/trainers in own and other institutions;

8. questionnaires are circulated. As they return, analysis gets under way;

9. major findings are discussed by staff members and conclusions/recommendations agreed;

10. a survey report is produced and circulated within the institute for debate. A summary can (many would say <u>should</u>) be sent to those who took part in the survey;

11. reactions to the report are discussed and an agreed research programme set out.

This is an interesting and useful research activity in its own right. Apart from yielding reasonably systematic information about research needs, it will give a sense of research achievement to those involved and demonstrate what can be achieved.

The political process

Each of the approaches just described is useful in analysing and mapping out research needs and programmes. They are systematic, if not rational, approaches. All such approaches, however, can only be useful in the "right" political context. Shared research interests may not be matched by shared power to get things going, or access to money to fund the research. Defining policies and needs may therefore be much more of a political process than a straightforward managerial analysis type of process. The major determinant of research interests at one point in time may later change - a key staff member leaves, a "donator" may be under pressure to redirect resources. Identifying such major determinants may be difficult, but further references to figure 5 may throw up the key ones.

3.4 Getting the research programme going

Getting research started is possible if the requirements so far discussed are taken into account. In summary, these requirements were:

- deciding that research is a necessary and important activity in the institution;

- determining the type or range of approaches to

- research most relevant to the mix of institutional, individual and client expectations and perceptions;

- working out a policy for research, including objectives and a means of monitoring their attainment;

- identifying appropriate and relevant research needs, with respect to broad sets of interests and problems that will shape those needs.

These are important factors, yet without a commitment and interest from staff in getting research going, nothing will happen. Whilst this can be achieved in a number of ways, it is often more effective if several are used at the same time.

## Staff research

It is unusual (and probably unhealthy) for a management institute not to have a member of staff working towards a higher degree. The degree may be obtained by research or course work. Most taught masters' degrees contain an element of research, for example through a project activity. Where a member of staff has been involved in such an activity, and where it has been relevant to the work of the institute, a good basis exists for developing research. Such staff members should be involved in the research programme. They should be encouraged to take part in identifying research needs, extending their own research interests - thus maintaining that urge to do research which is so necessary if anything is to happen.

## Student research

Some institutes use projects as part of the learning process. The problem or topic to be investigated is chosen by the course member or the sponsoring company, is part of a strategy for building up research or investigative work in particular areas. Linking project work to a research theme is a common way of getting research going. This is especially true of projects carried out on post-graduate/post-experience programmes. Projects which build upon each other - where the recommendations of one report help initiate further project work - can result in useful, systematic research being started.

Contract research

This involves selling research as a service to clients. A necessary prerequisite is at least one member of staff with sufficient research skills to make such a service possible. There are snags. The client may well wish for confidentiality to be guaranteed, and this will prevent publication. In turn, the build up of a visible research activity may be frustrated. Against this can be set the funds such a service will generate. These can be used to "buy in" research capacity.

Buying-in experience

This requires finance to be available and must be based on participation of your own staff and local industry. Such funds can be generated through contract research, allocated through internal budgetary mechanisms, or acquired from research grant-awarding bodies. The latter will, however, require some track record or reputation to be demonstrated - rather a lot to ask of an institute starting out on the research road. Buying-in poses problems of career paths, job security and continuity of research. These are not easily overcome without substantial funding. The best use of such people is in an advisory capacity.

Selection of staff

A number of these issues lead to the necessity of staff members being interested in and capable of doing research. If they are not already around and cannot be developed, then selection can be used as a means of priming the institute with research-orientated members. If research is made a specific and explicit selection criterion for certain posts, and promotion/rewards are related to it, the chances of getting the necessary staff will be increased. Paying lip service to it will have dangers. A staff member appointed to carry out research as part of his/her job, and prevented from doing so, will quickly become disillusioned.

Quick surveys

Research-minded staff can often quickly establish a programme of research through the use of questionnaire and/or interview type surveys. The management research agenda described in illustration 10 did this. Starting off with ambitious in-depth studies, lasting several years and involving detailed follow-up of participants (as in some longitudinal research) may be exciting initially but can soon lead to demoralisation when results are slow to emerge. Surveys can be carried out quite competently by a reasonably experienced staff member, are relatively cheap and easy to start, and offer quick results which can find their way into published articles. After a few years and several surveys, a reputation and visibility should start to emerge. But don't carry out surveys just to get research going: they must be part of the programme and strategy of research, and gather data about a topic, problem or area that is important to the institute, its staff and its clients. If a "management research agenda" type study is carried out, further survey areas will be revealed. A useful starting point might in any case be to carry out a survey of management education, training and development requirements of companies in the local area, in a particular industrial sector or across the country as a whole.

Collaborative efforts

To establish research in a sector or country is difficult for any one institution, particularly if that institution is not experienced in this activity. A more fruitful way is to seek to establish collaborative working links with other institutes or bodies which have a shared interest and some experience in research. There must be a contribution from both sides to make it work. One party or set of parties might provide the experienced programme leader, the others less experienced programme faculty, or rooms, or secretariat services, or whatever is required to make the collaboration beneficial to all parties.

---

Basically, establishing the programme comes down to having one or more members of staff dedicated enough to get it started. They will need help, support and a meaningful research agenda. Help, support and the agenda will, however, not result in research without those staff.

---

## 3.5 Planning research

Planning the research activity embraces the identification of research needs, the setting of research objectives, and the establishment of the research programme itself. But this is planning to do research: what about planning for actually carrying out the research? Are there any key steps in the process of carrying out research and what are they? Whilst some differences occur, depending upon the nature of research involved (for example, planning research involving a group of people requires more emphasis to be placed on certain co-ordinating activities than does individual research), the main steps are fairly common. They occur at two different levels: the managerial level and the operational level.

### Managerial planning

This is an extension of the process of establishing the overall research programme (i.e. "policy planning") and involves the translation of the policy plans into plans about how to achieve them. The main constraining factors must be identified before it is possible to plan effectively. There are five key elements involved in managerial planning. These are:

(1) Identify and secure the necessary <u>financial resources</u>. Without these, little or no research will get done. Major items will be staffing costs (e.g. research assistants), travel, secretarial/clerical support, printing, materials, postage and telephone. The money to pay for these will have to be found from somewhere, either the internal budget or external sources (such as grant-awarding bodies, sponsoring companies). This is an important topic and we shall return to it in chapter 5 of this guide.

(2) Secure a commitment of <u>staff time</u>. Whilst this, too, has financial implications, they are part of the internal accounting problems. Many institutions budget for a number of hours for pursuing research. These must be allocated to the various projects and the staff carrying them out. Regular reviews are needed to ensure that the time is being spent wisely and fruitfully. Clearly, the major allocations should go to high priority projects, leaving some available for research management/administration/co-ordination. Workloads and time estimates will

therefore be required for each research project. These can be arrived at only through experience, and even then it is not possible to be highly accurate in setting times against particular research activities. But this is in the nature of research.

(3) Select and appoint <u>the researcher</u>, where appropriate. For certain projects, it will be necessary to have assistance in the shape of a full-time research worker. Making such an appointment will require careful thought. What sort of person is required? What skills, knowledge and experience are needed? At what salary level can/should the person be appointed? How much responsibility will the person be expected to carry? (A research assistant who is just another "pair of hands" is quite different from a researcher who will be expected to initiate action, negotiate with companies, interview senior managers, etc.). Such questions can only be answered if you have thought out what the person will be required to do and set this out in the form of a job description. This description can be used as the basis for drawing up the job advertisement and, of course, determining the selection and appointment criteria. Candidates should be interviewed by the person in charge of the project and a senior member of staff. The nature of the work and the conditions of appointment should be made clear. On appointment, a period of familiarisation will be necessary before the research can start. If this can include some degree of involvement in developing research plans and giving final shape to the project, a greater commitment will be developed.

(4) Ensure that <u>appropriate and adequate research supervision</u> is available. This is needed at two levels: someone (or a group?) to supervise the overall research programme (this will normally be the senior staff member with a research co-ordinating role), and individual supervisors of research projects. At the <u>research programme level</u>, the main supervisory requirements will be to keep an eye on overall progress, making sure that projects are started and completed on time, that staff/staff time are available for the research, that budgets are not exceeded, that new funding is sought, and so on. At the <u>individual project level</u>, supervision will mainly consist of ensuring that the project moves forward, that specific phases are carried out properly, that advice and sources of help are made available to the researcher, that working papers and

progress reports are prepared, that the researcher has a sympathetic person to listen to his/her problems. Research can be a lonely activity. It is important, therefore, that the researcher is not isolated from the rest of the staff. Equally, it is important that quiet workrooms are available in order that researchers can escape from everyday activities of the institute. Some researchers - usually those who are inexperienced - will require close supervision: others will want to be left alone to get on with the job but have access to sources of help when difficulties arise. This demands a sensitive balance between putting on pressure to achieve results and giving plenty of freedom and scope for individual action.

(5) Establishing and monitoring <u>research output</u>. There is a danger that research can become an end in itself, a way of life almost. Whilst there is a lot to be said for "living and breathing" research, it can lead to non-achievement in terms of the specific outputs you are seeking. "Outputs" include such things as research reports, publications, diagnostic tools, guides, new products/programmes, solved problems, or whatever relates to the project/programme objectives. To some staff, these things will readily be seen as important, necessary and useful: to others, they will simply get in the way of the main activity, researching. Establishing a <u>research output plan</u> may be desirable if only to develop commitment to the end products and provide a set of benchmarks for measuring "success". Such monitoring does not take place solely at the end of the project. Progress reports, pub- lished articles, etc., can be achieved whilst research is in progress. This helps also in keeping motivation going and giving researchers a sense of achievement.

Illustration 10 includes a short description of procedures established by the Cyprus Productivity Centre. Similar guidelines are used by many management institutions in both industrialised and developing countries.

---

Illustration 10: <u>Procedure for planning and control of research projects at the Cyprus Productivity Centre (CPC)</u>

A major problem faced in the planning and control

of research is making sure that projects get completed, and on time. The CPC have instituted a procedure for tackling this problem. Essentially, there are three aspects to the procedure:

1. Following the finalisation of their programme of activities, and specifically, the "research programme", each research project leader, in consultation with other officers who will work on the same project, prepares and submits to the director a "research proposal" in the format shown below.

2. Research projects start following respective discussion of this "research proposal", i.e. prepared as soon as possible after the finalisation of the reseach programme, at the beginning of each six-month planning period.

3. During the execution of each research project, two progress meetings of the project leader (and other group members if appropriate) with the director takes place. These progress meetings are initiated by the respective project leader, the first after the preparation of the respective questionnaire and prior to any field work is completed and prior to the date analysis stage.

## Research Proposal

Objective(s): This section contains a brief but convincing statement why it is important for the CPC to undertake the research project, followed by a clear and precise statement of the project objective(s), in such a way as to reveal to the reader the exact boundaries of the investigation.

Methodology: In this section, a short but clear account is given in respect of (a) definition of the project "universe", (b) choice of appropriate sampling techniques and sample size, (c) data collection techniques, and (d) data processing techniques. The above can constitute subsections of this section.

Estimated time and cost: In this section, the estimated hours to be expended by each officer concerned on

> the specific research investigation are given, as well as the services expected to be required from institutions or persons outside the CPC (i.e. for field work, etc.). Further, the expected cost of the investigation (excluding the cost associated with the officer-hours, but including travel cost for field work as well as services from institutions or persons outside the CPC), itemised by source of cost, are quoted and a schedule of execution given.

## Individual operational planning

So far, the concern has been mainly with planning the context of research. What about the content, the actual operational process of carrying out research? Are there any aspects here that need to be planned, or is research just simply something that happens? There is, indeed, a real need to plan research in that it helps introduce some semblance of clarity into a process which is (often) notoriously blurred. The following steps should help.

(1) Clarify the <u>research objectives</u>. It quite often happens that those who carry out the research are not necessarily the same people as set the initial research objectives. It also frequently is the case that, even where the staff involved did set the objectives, the passage of time will have rendered them less clear. In either case, it is important to review and clarify the objectives. Do we still understand what we are trying to achieve? Can they, on reflection, be met in practice? Are they too broad or too narrow? Are they still important? Asking such questions <u>before</u> the research starts may well prevent frustration, anger and dejection at a later stage. Talking over these questions with colleagues, course members or clients will provide a good test.

(2) Do some <u>background reading</u>. Many researchers find it difficult to resist the urge to rush out and start measuring things, designing questionnaires or interviewing people. If such temptation is not overcome, serious problems might occur later on. Important insights available from other research, guidance on the best use of particular methods, pitfalls that should be avoided, concepts that have special appeal or relevance - all of these, and more, can be missed if time is not spent on reading some

of the key, relevant literature. A thorough literature search is not always needed at this stage. Researchers must, however, be aware of the major research in and around their own area of interest, if only to avoid repeating what has already been done.

(3) Initiate a proper <u>literature search</u>. Depending upon the nature of the research, this will be the first major activity of the project. Not all projects will require a systematic literature search. For example, much evaluation research is carried out not to advance knowledge but to determine the effects of, say, a new training programme. In such a case, background reading on relevant approaches and similar research is all that will normally be required, just to check on methods and effects of similar training. A project aimed at testing a new hypothesis of, say, the influence of economic conditions on managerial decision making, will need to be grounded in the findings and context of other research. Although most of the time spent searching the literature will occur near the beginning of the project, time should be regularly devoted to it until the very end. This will enable significant, current other research to be drawn upon. Planning the literature search is important. There will be a need to work back through past issues of relevant journals. Look out for major review articles: they can save a lot of time and effort. If recent, only a small amount of updating will be required. Make notes of the material you read, keeping an accurate record of the reference. A card index system is essential. Carry a few cards around in your pocket: they can prove very useful when you are browsing through a bookshop, talking with a colleague or thinking alone, and when no other writing material is to hand on which to capture a precious thought or record a reference.

(4) Review the <u>research methods</u> to be used. The background reading (and literature search, if one is carried out) will provide the basis for reviewing and finally deciding upon the methods to be used. As we shall see in chapter 4, many methods exist, and some can be effectively used in combination with each other. Where a project comprises several stages of research, plan all stages before any of them starts. They may have an influence on one another. For example, in researching the causes of high turnover or absence among factory workers,

one might require two stages. The first might be an exploratory study, using group interviews, to find out the range of likely causes. The second might be a questionnaire survey of all employees, based on the interview findings. It might be preferable (subject to background reading/literature searches) to start with a full-scale questionnaire, and use interviews to follow up the findings and probe in more depth. Which way you do it depends to a great extent on what you are looking for: in this case, most likely causes, or detailed knowledge and understanding of known causes.

(5) Work out <u>time and timing required</u>. An estimate of the time required to carry out the project may already exist. If it does, check it. It will more than likely not be enough. If it is not, make a list of all the key activities in the project and put times to them. Then consider when the time will be required - this is "timing". Both are important. A questionnaire survey, for example, may be estimated to take six weeks. One week may be required to design and test the questionnaire but spread out over several weeks or even months. Sending out questionnaires may take just a few days, whilst analysing them may require several weeks - but two or three months after they were sent out. Thus, the six weeks of work might be spread out over an elapsed time of four to six months. Planning what happens, when and how much time is needed becomes important. A useful technique for doing this is one borrowed from operational research - network analysis or critical path analysis. Even simple bar charts can be helpful. An example of a bar chart applied to a research project is shown in illustration 11 and figure 6.

Illustration 11: <u>Bar chart planning aid for evaluation project re impact of a four-module sales managers training programme</u>

This illustration is based on a semi-hypothetical case. A company was embarking upon a training programme for its sales managers. In order to evaluate its impact, a research consultant was employed to carry out evaluation research of a "before and after" type. A three-stage project was agreed upon comprising unstructured interviews before the programme started (stage 1), structured interviews before and after each of the four modules (stage 2), and a post-programme questionnaire survey (stage 3). In planning the project, the consultant used a simple bar chart derived from a breakdown of project activities and an estimate of the time each activity would take.

The bar chart in figure 6 shows that certain activities were planned to overlap. Others required elapsed time between them (such as sending out questionnaires and starting to analyse early returns). This identified dead periods into which other activities can be planned, from, say, another project. The bar chart also shows that the consultant has not allowed enough elapsed time between certain activities. For example, in G, a gap of time would be required between the company receiving the report and the consultant conducting the seminars. This is careless planning. A more itemised set of activities and the use of network analysis would have enabled the consultant to spot these problem areas. It would also have allowed for a more realistic elapsed time estimate - from start of project to finish - to be made: 80 days is too tight.

(6) Give consideration to the reporting requirements involved. Writing up a research project can be a painful experience. Just how painful depends on how much thought and preparation is put into it. If adequate planning is given to this important activity, the pain will most probably turn into genuine pleasure. How the write-up is done depends a lot on personal preference and time-scale. Some people much prefer to write up everything at the end of the project. This may be possible on a short time-scale. For a project lasting several years, it may be difficult to recall the early stages of the work. If a continuing write-up is not favoured, then working documents and progress reports should be prepared as the research proceeds. Where a continuing write-up is embarked upon, be prepared at a later date to modify, or even scrap, earlier material. Ideas, quality and style will develop and change. Reporting may also take the form of journal articles, books and the like. These will require a

**Figure 6 Example of bar chart planning aid**

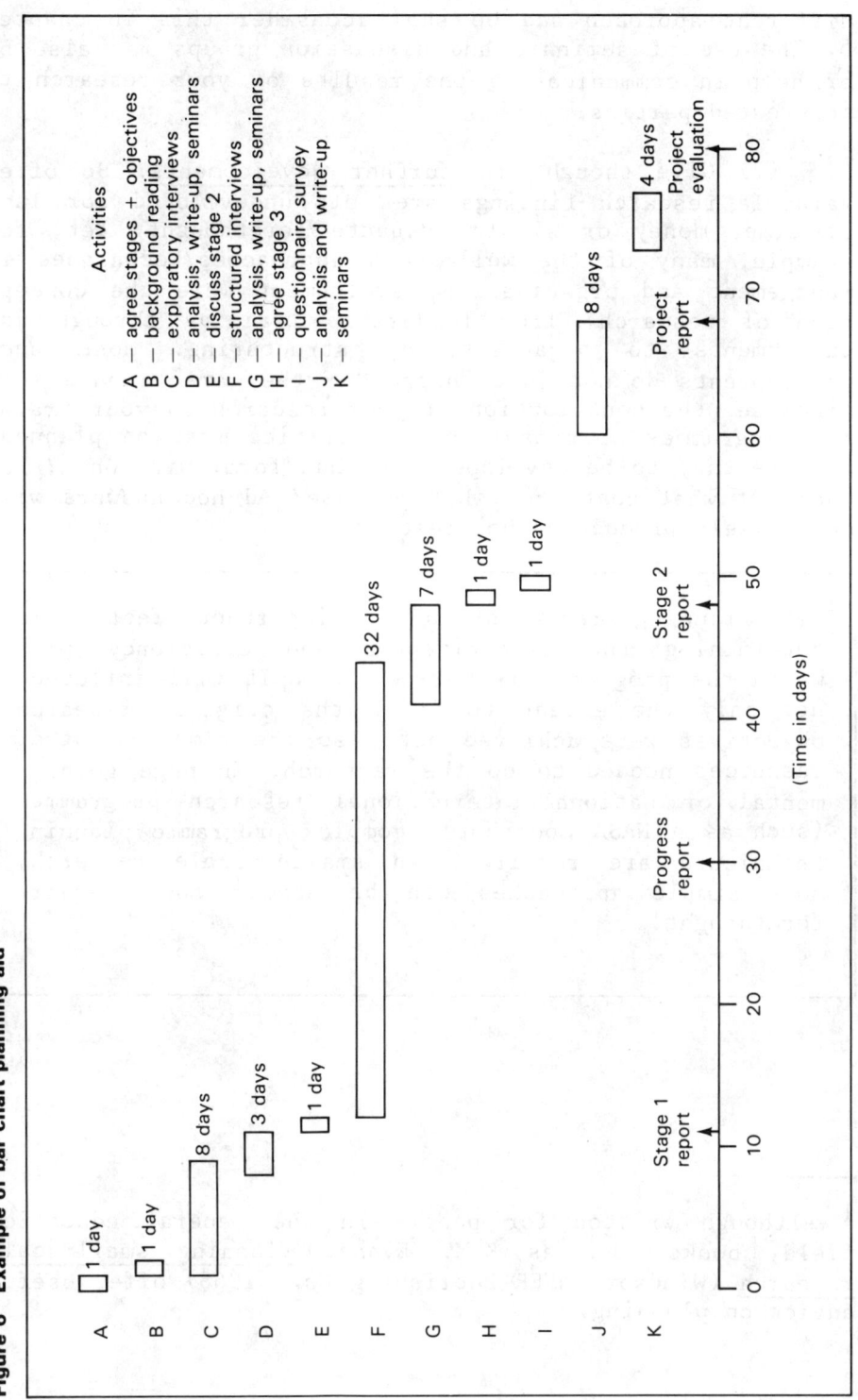

different approach and we shall consider this in chapter 5. The use of seminars and discussion groups may also be of help in communicating the results of your research to interested parties.

(7) Give thought to <u>further developments</u>. So often valuable research findings are left undeveloped for lack of time, money or simply adequate forethought. Yet, for example, many of the well-known approaches/techniques in management and organisation development were the conception of research, from leadership training through job enrichments to organisational structuring. Most such developments do not just "happen" - they are planned for. Likewise, the contribution of your research to your training programmes or consultancy activities must be planned. How are they to be developed? In what form? With whom? For whom? At what cost? For what purpose? Ad hoc answers will most likely produce ad hoc results.

---

Planning research is an important factor in determining the effectiveness and efficiency with which the programme is carried out. It will influence not only the extent to which the original research objectives were achieved but also the time and other resources needed to do the research. In huge governmental or national/international research programmes (such as a NASA moonshot), complex programme planning techniques are required. In smaller-scale research, more simple approaches can be used.[1] Both require forethought!

---

[1] Although written for people in the general education field, books such as K.M. Evans: <u>Planning small-scale research</u> (Windsor, NFER Publishing Co., 1968) offer useful advice on planning.

# METHODS OF MANAGEMENT RESEARCH 4

Research aims to help solve problems and puzzles; investigates the relationships that exist in the world around us; builds bodies of knowledge that some might refer to as a "science". Whilst few people yet regard the body of management knowledge as constituting a science (notwithstanding subject areas such as "management science" and "behavioual science"), the investigation of managerial issues, problems and interests can take on a scientific aura, depending on the methods of research used. In this chapter we discuss briefly the main methods of management research. Many excellent texts exist which describe them in great detail. In appendix 1, the reader will find suggestions on where to find more detailed guidance on particular methods. Our purpose here is to introduce them. First, however, a brief look at the different levels at which research can take place, and at the levels of rigour involved. This will help place in perspective the nature of management research and the role of key methods in carrying out research. At all times, though, it should be remembered that the main aim of management research is to help improve the practice of management. If this is used as a key criteria in selecting methods, our search and choice will not be fruitless.

## 4.1 Levels of research

Research takes place at different levels of scientific sophistication. Different disciplines or areas of study have established different states of knowledge. They also have different hoped-for outcomes and uses. Disciplines such as physics emphasise accurately predicting what will happen and how to control events. In contrast, much research into wildlife focuses on describing and understanding events. The latter is clearly necessary to attain the former. Particular methods are more relevant to one level than to another. Thus, observation and recording are important in studying wildlife; experimental design and sophisticated data analysis and modelling in getting a man on the moon. Sciences follow a similar pattern of development and progression. In management we still have our observational studies (e.g. of what managers do), but we also attempt prediction (for example, reactions of group members to different managerial styles). There are four levels of research which are not mutually exclusive – they overlap, and neither do they form a rigid hierarchy. For example, it can be argued that classification comes before description, in that we group things and then look for the common properties in each grouping. Usually, however, we start with a description of objects and events, and establish that some are similar to and different from others.

Description

Describing what exists is the most basic level of research. For example, research to improve our knowledge of management processes in different countries is descriptive. Thus, analysis of job descriptions and observational/diary studies are used. Another example are studies which attempt to describe managerial traits, looking for those that characterise the successful or eminent manager (the "great man" theory approach). Such studies yield information which allows us to draw up a profile of a particular manager – i.e. his managerial style. We may then be able to classify managers according to similarities in profile or style. Whilst an important starting-point (it helps to "map out" the research terrain), describing "what is" may not necessarily improve our knowledge of management.

Classification

Observational research often throws up similarities and differences in what has been studied. It may show, in the case of managerial styles, that democratic styles occur in certain situations in particular countries (but not in others) whilst more authoritarian approaches seem persistent in yet different circumstances. This allows us to classify, or categorise, the things we are studying, on the basis of known, natural characteristics.

## Explanation

Having reached the stage of being able to fit things into classifications and of being able to document similarities and differences, the researcher naturally asks why? Why do these differences occur? What causes the similarities and differences? Why do certain approaches to management prevail, or even predominate, in some countries, but not in others? How do such styles arise in the first place? The researcher seeks to understand what is happening and to represent this in theoretical developments, models and propositions. Thus, descriptive and classificatory work establishes a basis for building theory. We are able to describe much about the world around us, and the different forms of life that have existed (using, for instance, a classificatory system known as "cladograms", which relate certain life forms to each other) but we are still asking the questions "why" and "how"!

## Prediction

All sciences try to reach the level where they are able to "predict". Using established theories and formulae, researchers want to be able to say "if X, then Y". Most researchers in the physical and advanced sciences can now do this. In the field of management, truly predictive theories are rare. Whilst the testing of hypotheses may take on this predictive form, we are still trying to understand and explain what managers do. Our methods of research are now geared to this, relying more on field studies and field experiments than on the experimental designs of the laboratory scientist. Whilst researchers in disciplines such as psychology conduct laboratory experiments, most management research takes place in managers' workplaces.

## 4.2 Levels of rigour

When choosing among research methods, one must also consider the amount of rigour required. The term rigour is used to refer to the extent to which the method employed strictly adheres to the fundamental requirements of research design. Three levels of rigour have been identified.[1]

## First level

The first level of rigour embraces those methods which offer a qualitative and narrative approach to the analysis of variables. Such methods offer minimum scope for classification and enumeration of the variables being studied. The methods include authoritative opinion, the single case study, and narrative history. Such methods can be used for indicating important variables and hypotheses which might then be tested by using more rigorous methods. They should not be ruled out purely on the grounds of their low level of rigour. Their utility lies in a capacity to handle issues which more rigorous approaches may not be able to deal with. This is especially so in exploratory studies.

## Second level

At the second level of rigour, measurement, particularly in a quantitative form, becomes important. These methods include survey research, longitudinal or time-series analysis and uncontrolled experimentation. Here the emphasis is changed from illustrating and describing situations and potentially important variables to one of measuring and manipulating certain variables and their relationships to one another. Usually such methods enable us to argue that something is related to something else. They seldom allow us to establish a causal relationship, i.e. that (a) causes (b) or if (a) then (b).

## Third level

The third level of research approaches the scientific method used in the physical sciences. Here the research is concerned with manipulating variables in order to test for causal relationships, to seek out those variables which have a critical or important impact on what is being

---

[1] See R.J. House: "Scientific investigation in management", in <u>Management International Review</u>, 1970, No. 5, pp. 139-150.

studied and the key relationships involved. Thus, if the research aims to establish why something occurred, then research methods at this level of rigour are necessary. This involves experimentation, either in a laboratory or in a controlled field setting.

Research should be at the highest level of rigour appropriate to the objects and needs of research itself. Pursuing rigour for its own sake is not necessarily an advantage. Information derived from first and second rigour methods is important to the development of theory. It is far more effective to carry out controlled experimentation, for example, on variables known to be important than on variables which turn out to be trivial. The issue is not one of deciding on the best method, for there is no such thing. Some methods are more appropriate than others to the purposes of the research. We cannot explain or predict if the bases of classification and description have not been established. It is likely that, for much research in the management field, first and second level methods will be of use to the researcher. Experimentation will, in most cases, be restricted to constructing and verifying theories.

## 4.3 Criteria for choice

In addition to the two criteria that we have already examined, there are three other points that should be borne in mind when choosing an appropriate research method.

### Answering the research questions

The method must allow the research question to be answered. It is clearly important to know and thoroughly understand what questions you are seeking to answer. A clear statement of the research questions will enable both the level of research and level of rigour to be more adequately determined. It will also enable a check to be made on the understanding of the nature of the research problem involved.

### Current state of knowledge

If little is known about the variables involved in the research problem then more qualitative, exploratory research methods will be needed. If, on the other hand, a review of the literature shows that a good deal is already known, it is then possible to isolate the key variables involved. This would then determine the extent to which a hypothesis or hypotheses could be established and made available for testing. This, in turn, would lead to a choice of method which allowed hypotheses testing to be carried out. However, even where the variables are known in advance, their very nature may prevent the use of experimental research methods.

The nature of the variables involved

The choice of method is governed by the extent to which the variables can be manipulated and measured in a controlled way. In the physical sciences, it is often possible to make the subject of the research do what you want it to do. In the social sciences, this is not always true. For example, if we are interested in testing a hypothesis about the relationship between managerial style and productivity of employees, we need to control the style adopted and the situation in which it is used. This is rarely possible. The right situations may not arise and even where they do, the people involved may not allow us to control what they are doing for our research.

4.4  Basic approaches

The "scientific" or conventional approach

Before we consider the principal methods of management research, we must refer to the major steps of the research process outlined in chapter 2 (see figure 3). This depicts the key steps of the research process: the "scientific method". This consists of four logical steps, namely, (1) setting up a hypothesis, (2) developing a method, (3) gathering the data and (4) drawing conclusions. These assume that a problem exists and that something will be done about that problem once conclusions have been drawn from the data gathered. Scientific method and common sense are quite similar. Both develop from the determination or formulation of ways of thinking about the world based on information received and conclusions drawn. The differences hinge on the notions of being systematic and controlled. Common sense usually derives from experience and other people's views, rarely systematically garnered. Scientific method ensures that systematic approaches and procedures are used. Likewise, experiences may not be controlled in the sense that most people do not deliberately seek to experience certain things simply in order to draw conclusions from them. In scientific method, the researcher deliberately sets out to control what is looked at, what is measured and how it is measured.

Scientific method is one of four methods of knowing. The first is the method of tenacity. Here, we know something to be true simply because many people fervently say or believe it to be true. The more it is repeated, the more valid the truth becomes. Here there are dangers. Many people, centuries ago, held tenaciously to the view that the world was flat. The second method of knowing is the method of authority. If well-respected and authoritative sources says that something is so, then it must be so. The Bible is one such source. Tradition and public sanction can add to the authority of a statement of belief. Thus, if, for example, a government bases its approach to managing the economy on a well-respected tradition of economics, spokesmen may give the impression that such an approach is "correct". Whilst such an approach is dangerous for research, we have to accept that it is an important part of life. If a subordinate asks a manager how to solve a problem, the latter may well answer from a position of experience and authority. This may be taken for granted. If it were not so, the time taken to solve problems and make decisions would be inordinate. A third way of knowing is the method of intuition, or as it is sometimes known, the "a priori" method. This is based on the notion that people will reach the truth because their natural inclination will be to do so. It is based on the notion that intuitive propositions should agree with reason and not necessarily with experience. It might thus be termed a "rationalistic" approach. But whose reason does it agree with? Different people will come to different conclusions using different processes of reason.

The scientific method has a key characteristic possessed by none of these other three methods, namely, self-correction. Scientific method has built-in checks which are so conceived and used that they control and verify the researcher's work and conclusions. This helps produce objective, verifiable knowledge. Put another way, theory derived from the scientific method is something more than the researcher himself. The other three methods are much more subjective, and therefore result in theories based more on the experience, reason and intuition of individuals.

Methods used in management research are more objective, systematic and controlled; they approach the ideals of scientific methods. If scientific method is considered to be the anchor of the third level of rigour, then we have a bench-mark against which to compare and contrast the other methods. This does not mean that these other approaches are any less acceptable, useful or "correct" than scientific method.

## The reasoning process

In research we seek facts from which to draw conclusions. Drawing conclusions depends on the researcher's ability to reason logically. Scientific method is a logical reasoning process based on two important methods of reasoning: inductive and deductive. The <u>inductive method</u> consists of studying many individual situations in order to develop generalised conclusions. This procedure is followed in most research projects, when new facts are being studied, new truths revealed and new general propositions or theories put forward. An example is the Aston studies on organisational structure, where hundreds of organisations were studied and general dimensions of structure put forward. Four conditions[1] are necessary for effective induction, namely:

- observations must be correctly performed and accurately recorded;

- observations must cover cases that are representative of the population from which they are drawn;

- observations must cover a sufficient number of cases;

- conclusions must be confined only to the statements that are substantiated by the findings and are not over-general or too inclusive.

---

[1] For further explanation of these and other aspects of reasoning, see V.T. Clover and H. Balsley: <u>Business research methods</u> (Ohio, Grid Publishing, 1979).

With the <u>deductive method</u>, reasoning starts from a general principle or rule generally regarded as fact, and assesses a specific fact or case that seems to fit the rule or principle. This involves reasoning from the general to the particular. For example, the conventional principles of management (planning, controlling, co-ordinating, etc.) are regarded as general statements about how managers operate and perform. A researcher, in assessing the effectiveness of several companies, might use measures to be able to gain information on each company on each "principle". A company not using one of these principles, might then be reasoned to be ineffective, or likely to be so in the future. Two conditions are essential in this type of reasoning:

- the general principle or rule must be correct, i.e. true;

- it must also be applied only to those cases that properly come under its scope.

Such reasoning processes help us determine cause and effect. We must, however, in seeking such relationships, be sure that the cause and effect conditions exist; that no other unknown conditions cause the effect; whether more than two conditions are interacting to bring about the effect; that we have distinguished correctly between basic and secondary causes. If we follow these relatively simple rules, the conclusions drawn from our reasoning or inferences about our data will stand up to rigorous scrutiny.

<u>Model building</u>

An important part of the research process is the building of models to represent cause, effect and other relationships. Whilst the term "model" is used in many ways,[1] it basically refers to a dynamic framework or schema that helps portray the key concepts, propositions, etc., of our theory. Models may be highly conceptual or theoretical (theory itself being a model), developed at the start of a piece of research, and then tested through the process of data gathering, analysis and reasoning.

---

[1] See C.W. Emory: <u>Business research methods</u> (Homewood, Illinois, Irwin, 1980), pp. 38-39.

They may also be the end products of research, with only a weak conceptual framework having been in existence at the start. Model building is now a sophisticated process, using computers and advanced statistical procedures, e.g. in developing economic models for predicting future movements in the economy and in looking at population growth, etc. Models have their place, as Helmstadter[1] argues, but research is more than building models. The gathering of basic facts, for example, can be a most useful exercise in itself.

## 4.5 Principal research methods

Many different methods can be employed in exploring a problem situation, helping solve a problem, or establishing acceptability or otherwise of a hypothesis. Some of these methods can complement each other.

Let us now briefly review the main methods, remembering that they have varying degrees of "scientific respectability" and that methods of "low respectability" are sometimes very useful.

### Historical research

Whilst in one sense all research is historical, i.e. it is impossible to analyse data at exactly the same time as it is collected, and interpretation is based on the past, a particular method of research is the historical approach. It may take one of two forms: it may be concerned with an historical problem in management or it may be an historical approach to a current management problem. Where historical problems are concerned, particular problems are faced by the investigator. A key problem is separating fact from opinion or myth. When the problem under investigation is more recent, then data and facts may be available but not collected in the form needed to describe and understand the problem. The problem can be looked at in one of two ways: the researcher can collect data and describe the field at a point in time (this is known as a cross-sectional study) or the researcher can describe the development of the managerial problem over a

---

[1] G.C. Helmstadter: Research concepts in human behavior (New York, Appleton Century Crofts, 1970), pp. 37-38.

period of time (in this case it is referred to as a longitudinal historical study). For example, historical researchers interested in political leadership could examine the approach used by Hitler or Churchill in the Second World War, and describe the circumstances within which both were operating. These are cross-sectional studies. On the other hand, researchers might look at the development of political leadership from before the First World War to after the Second World War and seek to identify changes in style. This would be a longitudinal historical study.

Historical research also helps solve current problems by examining what has happened in the past. In management education and training, we often use the case study approach in a similar way. Students and trainees look at the historical development of a company, the problems it has faced, and its current situation, in order to suggest future directions and strategies the company might adopt. Similarly, the literature reviews carried out prior to a research study are an historical approach. Often, a literature review leads to the development of hypotheses which can then be tested through other research methods. Thus historical research methods can generate hypotheses. They can also be used to test hypotheses through what has been called the "ex-post-facto" design of research. Such a design follows the main steps of scientific method. However, many variables about which information is collected will be historical. Whilst the relationship between a current problem and historical variables might be established, it may be impossible to say one has caused the other.

There are traditionally three basic steps in the historical method: (a) the collection of data, (b) the criticism of data, and (c) the presentation of data. Whilst these steps occur in all research, they are limited by the fact that the events being studied have taken place before the time of the study. Thus, in using the information collected, researchers have to exercise their own opinion, interpretation and judgement of the data, their validity and meaning. Although the researcher's data can be checked with other information recorded at the same time, problems exist. Other information will no doubt have been recorded for other purposes and conclusions drawn will be limited. Another drawback of the historical research method is that, in order to show the extent and nature of sources of information used, any research report will be lengthy indeed. It will also usually be highly descriptive and may lack the more quantitative approaches to measurement.[1]

---

Illustration 12: <u>Historical analysis of inflation's impact on profits</u>

Research can take place at one point in time (cross-sectional) or over a period of time (longitudinal). Most longitudinal studies go forward in time: historical research clearly does not, yet is a form of longitudinal research.

This example from Israel illustrates a form of historical research. To gauge the impact of inflation on profits, a time period is essential. Professor Flink and his colleagues at Bar-Ilan University, chose the period 1968-74 to see what effects different levels of inflation had on reported profits (net of tax), incidence of corporate income tax, and dividend cover.

The data were obtained from published reports of the 19 industrial firms listed on the Tel-Aviv Stock Exchange during the 1968-74 period. Three specific years for analysis were chosen: 1968 was the first full year after the Six-Day War and inflation was only 2 per cent; 1971 was the first subsequent year of two-figure inflation (13.3 per cent); and 1974 was the (then) latest year for which statements were available - and inflation had reached 56.2 per cent.

Various technical procedures were used for adjusting net income, using data from the companies' published annual financial statements. The methods of adjustment used were: cost of goods sold; depreciation; and monetary holding gains. Other technical

---

[1] A well-known publication based on historical research into the growth of major American companies is A.D. Chandler: <u>Strategy and structure: Chapters in the history of the American enterprise</u> (Cambridge, Massachusetts, MIT Press, 1962).

> adjustments were needed: e.g. restating items in the income statement in terms of the purchasing power of the Israeli pound at the end of the year. The authors' article provides details of all the procedures used.
>
> The analysed data was presented in tabular form, comparing each company and providing the median. The data suggested, among other things, that adjusted gains tend to be less that nominal earnings, even when monetary gains are included, and that a substantial portion of adjusted profits in an inflationary period derives from the gains of monetary holdings.
>
> Similar studies can be carried out in areas such as sales turnover and profitability; wage payment levels and employee turnover; extent of management training and achievement of performance targets, and so on. Whilst such studies are historical, they can be used to throw light on current problems. In such cases, the term "ex-post-facto" research is often used.
>
> ---
>
> Taken from S.J. Flink, A. Birati, and M. Ungar: "The impact of inflation on the profits of listed firms in Israel", in Accounting and Business Research, Autumn 1978, pp. 253-257.

## The case study

The term "case study" usually refers to a fairly intensive examination of a single unit, such as a person, a small group of people or indeed a single company. Case studies involve measuring and studying what is there and how it got there. In this sense it is historical. It can enable us to explore, unravel and understand problems, issues and relationships. It cannot, however, allow us to generalise, that is, to argue that from one case study the results, findings or theory developed apply to other similar case studies. The case looked at may be unique and therefore not representative of other instances. It is, of course, possible to select several case studies to represent certain features of management that we are interested in studying. This can lead us to an experimental design from which theory and generalisations may flow. Two types of study can be carried out. <u>Exploratory studies</u> seek to discover significant variables and relations, and to lay the foundations for perhaps more scientific work aimed at testing hypotheses. For example, it might be wondered what variables most influence effective management: a case study, probing through discussions with and observations of the people involved, might throw some light on this question. It might then be possible to predict how the variables would be related to each other in other circumstances and to test this particular prediction. This would take the second form of study, namely, <u>hypothesis testing</u> rather than hypothesis generating. Here the researcher would seek data, perhaps from many different situations aimed at proving or disproving the validity of the hypothesis.

Such studies do not attempt rigorous control - this is both a strength and a weakness. The strength is that we obtain a greater realism in the research; the weakness is that things may get out of hand (sudden incidents erupting), destroying the validity of the research. They can be costly and time consuming, and may, of course, not produce shattering conclusions. For many management research requirements, however, the results can be rewarding.

Where several case studies are combined within the research design, the label "field study" may be used.

The case study approach, like the historical method, has two functions. Whilst the intensive investigation of a single manager or group of people or organisation may be carried out solely to increase our knowledge of management, often it is done to make practical improvements. Contributions to general knowledge are incidental. The case study approach may therefore have research, consultancy, and management training objectives. The case study method has four steps. The <u>first</u> is determining the present situation. The research worker may have only a vague impression of the research problem. He needs descriptive information which will determine as clearly and accurately as possible the present status and circumstances of the case being investigated.

The second step is to gather background information about the past and the key variables. The researcher often compiles a list of possible causes of the current situation. The third step is to test hypotheses. The background information collected will have been analysed for possible hypotheses. Now, in this step, specific evidence about each of these hypotheses can be gathered. This step aims to eliminate possibilities which conflict with the evidence collected and to gain confidence for the important hypotheses. The culmination of this step might be the development of an experimental design to test out more rigorously the hypotheses developed, or it might be to take action to remedy the problem.

Taking remedial action is the fourth step of traditional case study method. The aim is to check that the hypotheses tested actually work out in practice. Some action, correction or improvement is made and a recheck carried out on the situation to see what effect the change has brought about. It will be apparent that the case study method enables rich information to be gathered from which potentially useful hypotheses can be generated. It will also be gathered that it can be a time-consuming approach. It is also inefficient in researching situations which are already well structured, i.e. where the important variables have been identified. Where this is the case, other methods should be employed. The case study method is extremely useful in exploratory studies where our main interest is in developing a rich variety of suggestions. They lack utility when attempting to reach rigorous conclusions or determining precise relationships between variables.

---

Illustration 13: Case studies on the use of evaluation

This example is drawn from the world of education in the United States. It concerns the use of the case study method as a means of exploring the utility of evaluations - evaluation of evaluation, in other words. The researchers felt that "naturalistic research methods" (i.e. involving case studies, field investigations, participant observation) best met the main considerations guiding their research. These were:

- need to attend to consequences over the long term;

- sensitivity to the context in which programme actions are taken;

- exploration of the many consequences of evaluation;

- systematic attention to the evaluation as a process.

As the authors state, "naturalistic methods are particularly, perhaps uniquely, appropriate for the careful study of individual social settings and social process" (p. 32).

Each of the case studies focused upon a particular educational evaluation programme, especially the persons who shaped the process, how the evaluation fitted the total operation of the school programme, and how it influenced decisions made about the programme.

The study involved a retrospective, in-depth interview approach, and a review of documentary evidence to provide supplementary data. The basic procedure adopted was:

- select sites for study, based on personal and professional knowledge of evaluation programmes, via contacts in public educational agencies;

- make initial contact with a potential site/host (at senior level) to explain study, seek cooperation and answer host's questions and stress anonymity;

- collect documents, etc., describing the programme;

- conduct first round of private interviews with the site programme director, principal, etc. Interviews were open, non-directive, to gain as much data as possible about the programme;

- develop list of questions aimed at tracing evaluation impact and utilisation;

- carry out interviews with expanded "pool" of participants;

- develop and write up accounts, look for corroboration; draft and re-draft case study and circulate to participants for review in further interview;

- circulate open-ended questionnaire about case study to participants and finally re-write.

Such an approach has many applications in social science - and in management education and training. Change programmes (often involving action research) have to be (or should be) evaluated; factors leading to the adoption of a particular management style need to be explored; relationships involved in a successful management development programme can be unravelled - these and other areas can be explored using case study, or naturalistic research methods.

---

Taken from M.C. Alkin, R. Daillak and P. White: <u>Using evaluations - Does evaluation make a difference?</u> (Beverly Hills, California, Sage Publications, 1979), Chap. 2.

---

Case study research is also used in management teaching. A major use is to write up the data as a <u>teaching case study</u>. Such case studies are quite different from research case studies, and require special skills and attention in their writing-up and use as a learning vehicle. Research case studies provide rich data from which to develop lively, practical and interesting learning material.[1] Other uses include comparative analyses of management technology in different companies; "for instances" in classroom teaching, and many more. Research case studies provide rich, detailed information that can enliven the learning process.

---

[1] On writing and using case studies, see J.I. Reynolds: <u>Case method in management development: Guide for effective use</u> (Geneva, International Labour Office, 1980).

## The survey

This is the most widely adopted method in the social sciences and probably in management research also. Surveys are usually cheaper, quicker and broader in coverage than most scientific experiments. But on the other hand, they often lack the control and in-depth study of the experiment. They also lack the richness and depth of meaning of a case study approach. Relying mainly on the techniques of sampling, interviewing and/or the questionnaire, the survey can provide useful information on many issues faced by managers. For example, managers may wonder how employees feel about the training provided; what subjects foremen think should be given priority on supervisory management courses; whether members of the organisation think participation is a good thing; or perhaps what young managers think about their career prospects. It may be that basic facts about the make-up of local industry, the distribution of employees, the movement and growth in population, the main sources of wealth/income generation, the centres of key purchasing power, the nature of marketing issues, and so on, are not available locally or nationally.

These issues can be explored using survey research methods, involving research instruments (for example, questionnaires, checklists) which, if constructed and tested adequately, can produce useful information. In short, surveys are based on a very simple procedure: if we wish to know what people think about certain things, we must ask them.

Surveys produce much information. Thought must therefore be given before data are collected and as to how they will be analysed. Otherwise severe problems can arise causing frustration and even the abandonment of the project. Many excellent techniques of analysis exist - from slogging it out by hand to computer processing - and are described in a number of sources.[1]

Surveys, if used wisely, produce useful information quickly. But people may not want to respond to questions;

---

[1] See, for example, the publications by Oppenheim (1960), Kerlinger (1973) and Weisberg and Bowen (1977), annotated in appendix 1.

may give false answers or misunderstand its purposes. These can be avoided, or reduced, only if one is careful.

The survey can be used for <u>two quite different purposes</u>. The <u>first</u> is to describe current practices and events. Such are termed polls. The purpose of a <u>polling survey</u> is mainly to distribute responses or answers to an item. They can be used to determine the extent to which certain practices are common or certain trends becoming apparent. They can be used to compare practices among organisations. They are therefore valuable for establishing a body of data on which to base comparison. <u>A second use</u> of the survey is for analysis. <u>Analytical surveys</u> go beyond simply describing the current state of practice. A polling survey of one organisation may show us that all managers exercise an authoritarian style of management, but it enables us to say little else of importance. For example, why do all managers exercise such a style and how does that style influence the performance of the organisation? Analytical surveys may help us answer such questions. Questions on the factors related to, for example, performance and style in an organisation can be built into the questionnaire and we can start relating data on one to data on another. Statistical analyses can be made of the information collected. Whilst analytical surveys may enable us to establish relationships between variables, they do not demonstrate how they are related. Furthermore, they do not tell us causes. More light can be thrown on such issues through the use of controlled case studies or experimental research designs.

Surveys are widely used to collect information and observations over time. Such longitudinal analysis enables us to identify not only which variables are related to each other, but also how those relationships change with time. If, in addition, we can control the circumstances in which the observations are made, we can test hypotheses. Such control is seldom achieved in management research; this is a main drawback of longitudinal studies.

A longitudinal study may be turned into an uncontrolled experiment by collecting information from a number of people at one point in time, making some change to the circumstances and then collecting more information later. The problem here is again that we can seldom control what happens as a result of our introduced change.

Illustration 14: <u>Survey of operations research (OR) utilisation in Greece</u>

Survey research methods have often been used to collect factual and attitudinal data. For example, the Technical University of Greece in Athens was interested in finding out how operations research (OR) was used by firms in Greece. It was hoped that the findings would interest OR people in other countries similar to Greece. Our interest is more in the method.

A questionnaire was sent to OR practitioners in 20 big private and public organisations (about half in each sector). The questionnaire covered areas such as organisational and functional status of OR, work done by OR people, impact on the firm, implementation problems, and so on. Participants were contacted twice on a personal basis: once to introduce and clarify the survey, and again to discuss matters not covered in the questionnaire.

A question was included on other organisations (e.g. names and addresses) which participants knew used OR. This would have expanded the survey population, but proved fruitless. Most of the users were already covered by the initial survey mailing list. The survey included industries such as textiles, cement, domestic appliances, construction, transportation, oil, heavy manufacturing, services and finance, as well as some key public services. Employees ranged from a few hundred to several tens of thousands.

This is clearly not a "representative" sample survey. Participants were not drawn at random and do not cover all aspects of industry in Greece. In a sense, it is a "consensus" survey, since the key users of OR were identified and a check made (via the question referred to above) on other known users. The results therefore tell us something about the state of OR utilisation in Greece. It was concluded to be rather poor - a fact attributed to the character and level of socio-economic development of the country.

Such surveys can be conducted on all manner of topics, e.g. the use of behavioural science techniques, the rate of adoption of management by objectives, the nature and variety of financial accounting techniques employed, among many others. The information gained can provide important training/consultancy indicators for management institutes, and valuable comparisons for industry. Reports containing such data can be sold commercially.

---

Taken from C.P. Pappis: "A survey of OR utilisation in Greece", in European Journal of Operational Research, No. 6, 1981, pp. 248-251.

Illustration 15: <u>Comparative international survey of organisations</u>

From time to time, examples of outstanding research are published. A recent illustration is a survey of international differences in work-related values. In essence it is a simply designed piece of research, but yielding massive amounts of data and complex analysis. It involves a large international computer manufacturer who developed an international attitude survey programme between 1967 and 1973, which produced a data bank from answers to 117,000 questionnaires covering 66 countries. The problems, both human and technical, were enormous.

A supplementary survey, carried out at IMEDE in Lausanne between 1971 and 1973 on a different international population using a questionnaire in English only, reproduced comparable results. Statistical analyses involved frequency distributions, correlations and factor analyses of data across individuals; analysis of variance by country, occupation, sex and age; and ecological correlations and factor analyses. It is a good example of how a survey conducted for purposes of managerial action (e.g. feedback and action discussion groups) has also been used to develop significant theoretical insights.

> Taken from G. Hofstede: <u>Culture's consequences</u> (Beverly Hills, California, Sage Publications, 1980). At nearly 500 pages, a long but interesting read: too long to be adequately summarised here.

## The experiment

The classical method of the physical sciences is the experiment. Most physical science researchers aim to set up a situation in which all the variables can be controlled or varied at will. They usually try to hold all variables constant except one. By varying this one and monitoring changes in the "output", the relationship between variables can be carefully studied and documented. In essence, the researcher seeks to vary one of several independent (or input) variables, whilst measuring the effects on the dependent (or output) variable(s), keeping intervening variables constant. For example, we can vary the petrol mixture fed to an internal combustion engine and note the difference in speed or power achieved, and at the same time, keeping, say, pressure or load constant and controlling temperature in the laboratory. When dealing with human behaviour, it is not possible to strictly adhere to this approach, although sometimes we can get reasonably close.

Such an approach clearly meets the requirements of scientific method. It does not, however, meet all the requirements of management and social research. Experimentation is a particularly desirable method where research questions take the form of hypotheses which state that "if (a) then (b) follows", rather than those hypotheses which seek to describe a phenomenon or where the primary purpose of the research is to develop or verify theory. It is not especially useful in exploring a field, describing phenomena, and suggesting or generating hypotheses for testing.

Although true experiments are rare in management research, some approaches come close. For example, it is possible to vary the instructional techniques used for training managers and to measure the achievements. Here, however, control over intervening variables such as ability, intelligence, orientation and the like, is difficult but the use of matched groups (i.e. different groups of managers who have roughly the same IQ, etc.) undergoing different "treatments" takes us nearer to the scientific method. But this approach is not foolproof. We cannot control, for example, the activities of managers outside of work - their love lives, drinking habits, arguments with spouses, etc. - which may well affect performance. We can, none the less, recognise them and account for them. In getting close to the true experimental design, the researcher has to attempt to gain complete control over the situation by determining exactly who will take part in the experiment and which participants will or will not receive whatever experimental treatment given.

An example of true experimentation which can be used to study human behaviour, and particularly that of management, is the <u>pre- and post-test control design</u>. Here two groups are used, each group containing managers who have been randomly assigned to the group. Data are then collected about the individuals (for example, a questionnaire may be administered to establish their attitudes to work, managerial style, biographical details in terms of background, age, etc.). Some change is then made in one group, but not in the other. The change might be, for example, to send one group of managers to a training course. Once the change has been made, further observations or data collection are made. The data collected before and after the change in both groups is compared. The researcher clearly is looking for a difference in data in the group which experienced the training compared with the group which did not.

Experiments are broadly of <u>two types</u> - <u>the laboratory experiment</u>, where the problem to be studied is divorced from other facets of the real world surrounding it, but not connected to it; and <u>the field experiment</u>, where attempts are made to study the problem in its real setting and to minimise the influences of seemingly unconnected facets or variables. Whilst most experiments in management research are likely to be field experiments, the existence of training schools, simulators, and so on, make laboratory experiments quite attractive - even though the results may have little significance in the real setting.

Laboratory experiments

A laboratory can be considered as any setting in which the researcher is able to closely control the conditions under which observations are made. A laboratory may therefore be a training room, a specially designed or set up part of an organisation, or any other setting which gives the researcher more control over the circumstances. The aim is to control as many as possible of the influential independent variables not pertinent to the immediate research problem. Thus, theoretically relevant variables are isolated and measures taken of the response of dependent variables when either independent or intervening variables are manipulated.

Laboratory experiments are useful when it is not possible to test a hypothesis in a real-life setting. It is important, however, that the variables to be tested can be simulated or replicated in a laboratory. Often it is necessary to attempt to repeat laboratory experiments in real-life settings to demonstrate the relevance of the findings to the real-life situation.

The field experiment

With the growth and development of statistics, special laboratories for experimentation are no longer necessary for adequately controlled research. Through the use of replication (i.e. repeating the experiment on several groups), randomisation (i.e. assigning participants and/or treatment/changes to groups by a random process), and certain statistical control (i.e. mathematically adjusting results to account for the effects of uncontrollable variables), field experiments can be carried out with little interference from the normal activity and with several variables being manipulated at once. The use of experimental and control groups is the most common approach to controlling a field experiment. As with the true experimental design, in a controlled field experiment, the experimental group consists of a group of people subjected to the treatment. The control group must be sufficiently similar to the experimental group to allow comparisons to be drawn between the two.

For example, imagine the data preparation room in a large computer installation and suppose that the managing director of the company believes an authoritarian approach to the management of data preparation personnel will lead to improved performance. A field experiment might test this hypothesis. Data preparation personnel could be randomly divided into two groups; one the experimental group, the other the control group. The experimental variable would be the style of management adopted for each group. In the experimental group, it might be changed from authoritarian to democratic and perhaps back again to authoritarian, whilst in the control group it would be held constant at authoritarian. Performance of both groups would be measured, before and after the change had been made in the experimental variable in the experimental group. However, as the famous Hawthorne experiments illustrated, it is possible in such an experiment that some other variable is influencing performance. In one of the Hawthorne studies, performance measures were taken of experimental and control groups: performance continued to improve in both groups, even when the conditions of the experimental group reverted to those of the control group. The variable causing change in performance in both groups was the attention given to each group. An experimental design, involving the use of unobtrusive measures and approaches, can be developed to control such a variable.

Problems in experimental research

Experimentation aims to produce valid evidence for findings and theories. Problems do exist. Most research in management is concerned with human behaviour and there are many specific rival hypotheses which can threaten the validity of research studies.[1] It is possible to explain the research results or the observed events in several different ways and these need to be considered (they have been labelled internal validity).

(1) <u>History</u>. Due to the interaction of people with their environment, and the fact that it is impossible to carry out an experiment at a single point in time, there

---

[1] For a full explanation of these threats, see D. Campbell and J. Stanley: <u>Experimental and quasi-experimental designs for research</u> (Chicago, Illinois, Rand McNally, 1966).

is always the danger that some external event will occur and influence the managers being observed.

(2) <u>Maturation</u>. People change with time often independently of any specific event. It is necessary, therefore, to control or account for processes within the organism which can make the participants different at the end of the experiment from what they were at the beginning, regardless of any environmental manipulation.

(3) <u>Testing</u>. The act of measuring in the behavioural sciences alters what we are measuring. Thus, for example, asking people to respond to an attitude statement may get them thinking about their own attitudes. It must be shown that the experiment did not cause this to happen to a large extent.

(4) <u>Instrumentation</u>. We often change and develop our research instruments during the research process. For example, researchers may have learned to do their job better; on the other hand, at the end of an experiment, they may have become fatigued and may not be paying as much attention to their observation. Where pre- and post-test questionnaires are used, it may be necessary to use slightly different forms. We need to know, therefore, whether the experimental differences observed are the result of the experimental variable or of the research instrumentation itself.

(5) <u>Statistical regression</u>. Measurements of behavioural characteristics often include errors due to chance. For example, managers who initially score high on attitude towards democratic management may have achieved that result partly because they were in luck on the day they completed the questionnaire. Since chance seldom strikes in the same way on two successive occasions, we would expect that those who originally scored high or low on our attitude scale would regress towards the mean over time. This would influence the outcome of any experimental treatment given to groups of managers selected on the basis of such scores.

(6) <u>Selection</u>. Normally, we aim to select participants for an experiment randomly from the population about which we hope to make general statements. Experiments

where participants are not selected randomly may suffer from some form of bias being introduced. Such bias may be unconscious and subjective. This will influence the results of the experimentation.

(7) <u>Experimental mortality</u>. Not all participants in an experiment will stay the course. Some drop out because they lose interest in the experiment, change jobs, or become ill. Where this occurs to a large extent, the results may have been unduly influenced.

(8) <u>Selection maturation</u>. Some of those who volunteer or accept an invitation to take part in an experiment may have some quality which reflects maturity possessed by few others in the population. For example, in hospital studies, patients who volunteered to take part in studies are often those who would have recovered anyway, due to their maturity, with or without the specific treatment offered.

(9) <u>Reactivity</u>. The reactions of people who are aware that an experiment is taking place are often different from what they would be in a non-experimental situation. The Hawthorne study is a good example of this.

There are also <u>external dangers</u> to the validity of experimental research findings. We need to question the extent to which the results found in one group can be generalised to the population as a whole. Unlike the dangers posed by internal validity, it is rarely possible to identify and account for the limitations to generalisation. Such restrictions on generalisation need to be critically assessed.

Finally, consideration should be given to the ethics of research and experimentation. Because there are so many internal and external threats to the validity of experimental research findings, it is tempting to carry out research in an unobtrusive manner by getting participants to change their behaviour or undergo a treatment without their knowledge. Some researchers find that this is ethically unacceptable; others argue that, as long as the participants are not damaged or put under stress, any means of getting valid data is acceptable. There are no hard and fast guidelines on this: researchers must form their own views on what is ethical.

Illustration 16: <u>Experiments with performance</u>

"True" experiments in the social sciences are difficult to find - true in the sense that they adhere to the scientific method. The most notable experiments concern the causes of high and low levels of performance or productivity. Such studies involve experimental conditions in which work layouts have been changed, leadership styles varied, or simply equipment and related factors altered (as in F.W. Taylor's early experiments). Probably the most famous are those associated with Elton Mayo and his colleagues, the "Hawthorne Experiments".[1]

The early experiments took place between 1924 and 1927 at the Hawthorne Works of the General Electric Company in Chicago. They were based on traditional assumptions of early industrial psychology, and studied the relationship between illumination and efficiency. General Electric manufactured light bulbs and was interested in the possibility of relating lighting to performance, thereby increasing their own sales.

Two groups of workers were involved. In the "control" group, illumination remained unchanged during the experiment, whilst in the "experimental" group, light was increased in intensity. This simple experimental design allowed the researchers to vary the (for them) independent variable of illumination and study its effect on the dependent variable - level of output. If output increased in the experimental group but not in the control group, it would have been shown that better lighting increases performance. Unfortunately, output increased in <u>both</u> groups, thus denying the researchers their hypothesis. Some other variable was at work, and further experiments were needed.

One involved a specially selected group, operating in a variety of changed conditions, the last of which was a reversion to original conditions of heating, lighting, rest pauses, and so on. Output continued to climb throughout. Further studies, involving attitude surveys, suggested attitude towards work was an important factor, along with the so-called "Hawthorne effect". The latter refers to the fact that people subjected to special conditions (i.e. being the centre of attention), will feel special and their attitudes will thus change. This is important in much management research - the research itself may change what is being researched.

The use of elements of the scientific experiment (e.g. control groups, matched groups, random assignment of members to groups, careful control and manipulation of variables) is still an important aspect of management research.

------

[1] Numerous accounts exist. A most readable version is J.A.C. Brown: The social psychology of industry (Harmondsworth, United Kingdom, Penguin, 1954), Chap. 3.

## Combining methods

Whilst for many purposes a single method may be appropriate, the possibility and advantages of combining different methods should be considered. Often, it is impossible to carry out research with a single method. For example, we can study the politics of management using several different methods. An experimental design might involve two companies, each company with several different plants managed by general managers. We could select the companies on the basis of, say, similar technology, size, location, and so on, in order to control certain variables. The experimental variable might be attitude towards the general manager. Survey research could find first what the attitudes were in each different plant. In true experimental fashion, a change could be introduced (this might constitute providing additional information in one of the plants but not in the others, or sending three of the managers on a training programme but not the other, or similar changes). A longitudinal study using questionnaires and observation could then be made to monitor the effects of the changes over time. Historical research methods might be introduced to establish the antecedents from which the political behaviour of the managers appear to derive. The combination of research methods helps us garner a wealth of information and maintain control over the study. However, since each method has its own limitations, their combination may limit the validity of the research findings.

---

Illustration 17: Combining methods

The Hawthorne studies referred to in illustration 16 also represent an example of using different research methods - in this case experimental design and attitude surveys principally. However they did not constitute the original research design.

A recent example is a study of trainer effectiveness carried out in the United Kingdom for the Manpower Services Commission.[1] The work began with an exploratory study, using open-ended interviews. From this a programme of systematic survey interviewing was developed and carried out with trainers and managers from a number of organisations. The criteria for judging effectiveness, and the factors leading to effectiveness, were elicited. These were built into a questionnaire survey of several thousand trainers, in an attempt to gain support for the interview findings as well as to elaborate upon them. Finally, case study research was carried out in several companies to explore relationships between factors leading to different levels of effectiveness.

--------------------------------------------------------

[1] Reports on this study carried out at the Slough College of Higher Education by T. Leduchowicz are available from Thames Valley Regional Management Centre, Slough, United Kingdom.

---

## 4.6 Some techniques of research

Many texts refer to instrumentation, measurement devices and methods of data collection. A more general term for these is "technique". Some other terms are very precise (such as "instrumentation") or involve the use of terms applied elsewhere (such as "data collection method"). We are talking about "how" we do it as opposed to "what" we do or "why" we do it. Brief descriptions of the most common techniques are given here - most are discussed more fully in texts on research methods.

Observation

This classical and natural technique simply involves looking at what is going on - watching and listening. We all do it, most of us badly because we do not know what to look for or how to record it. Work study practitioners are probably the most competent of observers - they have been trained to do it. So, too, are most researchers. Good observers have a wide scope, are alert and can pick up significant events. Technology can help, ranging from simple pen and paper, through tape recorders and cameras to video-tapes. Carried out quietly, unobtrusively, and shrewdly, observation is useful, if not powerful. It can tell us the difficulties encountered in running meetings; how workers relate to each other; or the effects of tea-breaks on worker activity levels - all of which have managerial implications. It does not allow much scope for probing and exploring relationships further, unless used with other techniques. Combinations of techniques are now quite common. Since, however, observation is "simple" (if time consuming), it can be used effectively to build up a general picture. It is, therefore, often a part of naturalistic research methods.

Another approach, known as <u>participant observation</u>, has been adapted by management researchers from cultural anthropologists. The researcher becomes part of the group or organisation being studied - usually by becoming a "proper" employee. The researcher participates in the activities of the group whilst taking note of the things being studied. It is less structured, but produces good insights into, for example, behaviour and relationships. This approach is less susceptible to the problems of the more structured ones - the events observed are real and therefore not so contaminated by the researcher. The group rarely knows that the participant is also a researcher.

Interviews

It is quite tempting to suppose that the interview was first "created" by the early observers who could not resist asking people why they were doing what they were doing. Whatever its origin, the interview is fundamental to management research. It allows for exploration and probing in depth and, if the money and time are available, in breadth as well. The questions asked might stem from periods of general observation - and this is to be preferred to just dreaming up questions in the bath! Interviews can be unstructured and free-ranging, a general discussion, picking up points and issues as they emerge and pursuing them in depth; or they can be structured around questions and issues determined in advance, based on theoretical principles, preconceived ideas or prior (exploratory) investigation. If the questioning is non-directive and free from biased or loaded questions, if the interviewer is a good, attentive listener (and adept recorder), and if the interviewee is open and candid, the results can be effective. However, problems of time, cost and sampling related to research objectives may mean that a full-scale interview programme is not possible or necessary. For example, a researcher who wishes to develop a job appraisal form may need only a few "pilot" interviews. If detailed views on the attitudes of managers to newly trained personnel were required, a wider programme of indepth interviews could be used. Remember, too, that for some purposes (e.g. where a "testing of views" is required), group interviews have a role to play. Whilst they may be more difficult to handle, they may provide more useful insights than if the same people were interviewed separately.

Regardless of the type of interview, the means of recording information must be thought through in advance: whether to tape-record unstructured group interviews or to take notes; how to design an interview schedule (a "questionnaire" completed by the interviewer) for structured interviews with maximum ease of recording information but minimum effect on interviewees - e.g. a feeling of "not being listened to" when writing copious notes. As with all research, advance thinking and planning reduces later difficulties.

## Questionnaires

Whilst undoubtedly the most used technique - or more correctly, instrument - of researchers in the behavioural and social sciences, questionnaires do pose problems. The major difficulties are associated with response rates, bias and flexibility. Since questionnaires are important to the survey researcher (as are interviews), the effect on the results of someone not responding must be considered. Who are they? What are their characteristics? Would they share the views of those who did respond? Even when "reasonable" response rates (however defined) are achieved, these problems still exist. Furthermore, the resulting data may be biased. Bias might be due to respondents anticipating the answers they think the researcher wants, or putting down "socially expected" answers (on the basis of what is "good", or would be the "right sort of thing to say"), or simply as a result of finding some form of pattern to, say, the first ten questions and assuming the pattern must be repeated. These and other difficulties can be reduced by careful design and piloting of the questionnaire. Flexibility, however, is not so much a design problem (although it can be considerably reduced by poor design) - it is much more a function of the research questions being asked. Answers might range from factual information (e.g. date of birth), through simple "yes/no" replies (e.g. do you smoke?), to scale-type responses of the agree-disagree form (e.g. training is a waste of time!) with a number of possible responses in-between. Often, however, the person filling in the questionnaire would like to say "yes - but!" and has no opportunity to do so. The qualifying "but" may be important - and an interview would allow it to be explored. If thought is given to the major drawbacks and to the way in which the data are to be analysed, there is every reason to expect fairly reliable and valid results. If preceded or backed up by interviews or observations, many additional benefits can be derived as well as difficulties minimised.

## Other techniques

Many other techniques exist, some of them variations on those described here (e.g. the "diary" technique is a form of questionnaire/self-observation log), others developed for specific purposes. They will not be discussed here since most of them require considerable experience in their design and use. They can be found in many texts, from which special references (e.g. to sociometry, testing, scaling and projective techniques in psychology) can be obtained.[1] Often such techniques are limited in their application and will probably have restricted value for the management researcher.

4.7 Further reading

In a guide like this, it is not appropriate to go into the detail of methods and techniques of research. Whole texts are devoted to this, and a lot of material exists. Readers interested in expanding their knowledge will find useful the annotated bibliography in appendix 1 at the end of this book. Whilst also dealing with other aspects of research, it contains several texts on research methology. It is structured to help readers sort out the most useful texts.

---

[1] See, for example, G.C. Helmstadter: Research concepts in human behavior (New York, Appleton Century Crofts, 1970).

# HOW RESEARCH CAN BE ORGANISED    5

## 5.1  The basic dilemma

The organisation of research in a management institute reflects many of the issues concerned with the organisation of any business enterprise, especially those which include production and R & D. Such issues also exist within R & D organisations. Bridging the gap between the generation of new knowledge and ideas and their use in production is no easy matter. As one eminent writer has so ably put it:

> "Organising a professional school ... is very much like mixing oil with water: it is easy to describe the intended product, less easy to produce it. And the task is not finished when the goal has been achieved. Left to themselves, the oil and water will separate again. So will the disciplines and the professions. Organising ... is not a once-and-for-all activity. It is a continuing administrative responsibility, vital for the sustained success of the enterprise."[1]

This dilemma - the choice between integration and differentiation along specialised job/functional lines - remains. Whilst the theory and practice of organisation design has advanced since the late 1960s, there does not

---

[1] H.A. Simon: "The business school: A problem in organisational design", in *Journal of Management Studies*, Feb. 1977.

appear to be any unique, universal way out of this dilemma. The organisation of research within a management institute can be guided by contingency theory. This suggests that the way to organise research depends upon many factors; the size of the management institute, the extent or amount of research, and the institute's major activities. In addition, experience from other types of organisations helps us analyse this organisational problem.

This chapter is concerned mainly with the internal organisation, but at the end we shall consider the need for establishing organisational linkages with the wider research environment, in terms of managing the boundary between the institute and the external research stream. First, we shall look at the issue of the organisational-task fit.

## 5.2 The need for organisational-task fit

The work of Morse and Lorsch[1] suggests that enterprises must be designed to ensure a proper fit between the task and the structure to execute that task. As the task varies, so will the appropriate organisation structure and the variable which influence the individual's sense of "competence motivation". Thus, effective production units are organised and managed quite differently from successful research laboratories. This is illustrated in figure 7.

In management institutes, many tasks are routine (e.g. the planning and administration of courses/programmes, day-to-day finance) and can be organised and managed as suggested by quadrant (4) of figure 7. On the other hand, activities such as research, and the development of new programmes, take on the requirements of quadrant (2)! Attempting to produce a common organisation approach to handle the two is like "mixing oil and water ..." So where to start?

## 5.3 Where are you now?

Determining the best way to organise research has to start with an assessment of where you are now. First

---

[1] See J.J. Morse and J.W. Lorsch: "Beyond theory Y", in Harvard Business Review, May/June 1970.

**Figure 7  Relation of task, organisation and managerial approach**

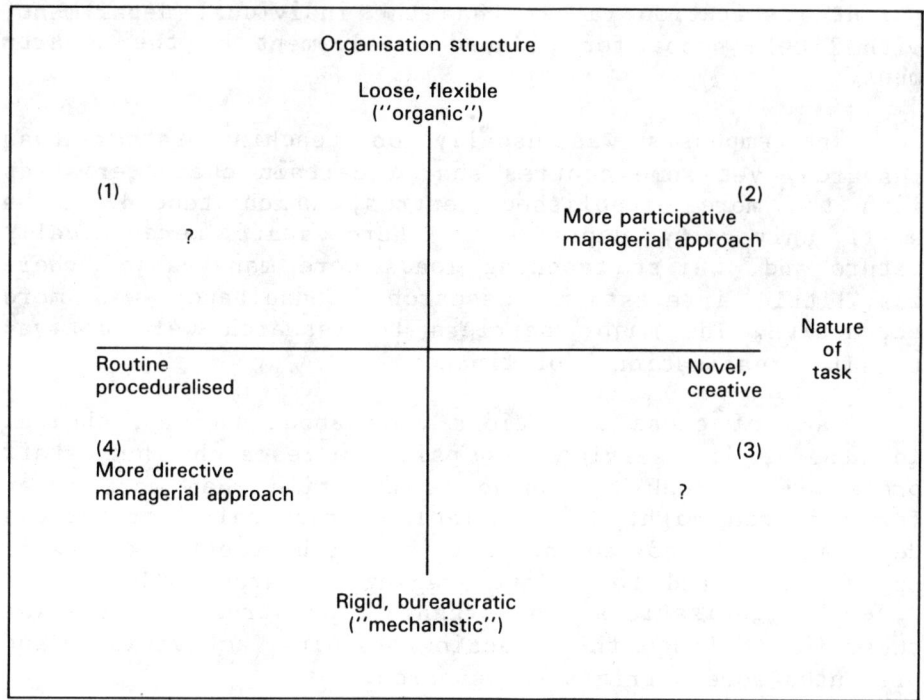

assess how big the institute is, how much research is taking place, and the key objectives for research. A survey of management centres in the United Kingdom shows that different organisational patterns exist in relation to these variables. Five fairly different categories emerged.[1]

Category 1 - Teaching departments undertaking little or no research (young and established)

The young had only been recently set up or greatly expanded and were struggling for identity. Teaching pressures were high. Little departmental autonomy existed.

---

[1] Based on B. Barry, V. Shackleton and P. Lansley of Ashridge Management College: Management and industrial relations research in British academic centres, paper given to the fifth annual conference of the European Foundation for Management Education, Berlin, 1976. (Published in Management International Review, 1978, Nos. 1 and 2).

Development was erratic and radical and governed by the parent institution rather than the individual department, with little scope for planned development by the department.

The emphasis was usually on teaching rather than research, yet some centres shared certain characteristics with the more established centres, which tended to be small university departments. Here staff were usually mature and, whilst teaching loads were manageable, there was little interest in research. Consultancy was more attractive. The major barriers to research were motivational, organisational or financial.

Many of these situations came about through choice. In others, lip service was paid to research, but staff preferred to look far ahead to the time when more money for research might be available. Practically orientated departments hoped to attract research-orientated staff, but few appeared to be encouraging research within their present organisations. The organisation structure here was thus dictated by the teaching/training activities, and presented some barriers to research.

## Category 2 - Teaching departments undertaking unsponsored research (small and large)

Both types experienced the pressures against research activities cited above - the attractions of consultancy, large teaching loads, motivation, costs and inexperience. These centres had developed from positions similar to those in category 1.

Many polytechnics fell into the "small" subgroup. Their entry into research was recent and had been achieved in the face of the difficulties mentioned. This was aided by a flexible attitude towards teaching and research by the heads of departments, such as being prepared to provide time off from teaching for research and of putting a minimal constraint on the areas researched. There appeared to be a greater orientation towards applied research with some obvious teaching/training use. Here we see emerging some of the characteristics of quadrant (2) of figure 7.

Some university departments were also in this group; their progress had been aided by a more liberal use of institutional funds. The larger centres were composed entirely of university departments. Some were "small business schools" where research had always been an accepted part of their work and which relied on institutional funds. Others had secured long-term grants and convenants to support research into unspecified areas, or were involved in research as a result of their major involvement in postgraduate courses. In addition, these centres differed from those in the "small" group by having a majority of staff engaged in research. Generally such departments were attempting to establish funded research, the most common route being to recruit a research "manager". Here we see the emergence of a separate organisation structure of research - and an important financial dimension. The transformation process from category 1 to 2 was affected by individual motivation and organisational flexibility.

Category 3 - Teaching departments undertaking sponsored research

These are mainly university centres, some of which had developed from category 2 through individuals pursuing their research interests. In some cases, fairly large sums of money had been put aside to support the initial stages of research, with the aim that the research would become self-supporting. In other cases, generous time allowances were provided to facilitate the writing of research proposals by teaching staff whilst, in others, supported research had been developed through consultancy work.

The transformation from category 2 to 3 had more to do with the persistence of teaching staff becoming involved in research, identifying supportable research areas and developing/negotiating research contracts. There is, however, the problem of maintaining such organisations. Many staff appeared to want to consolidate their research activities by becoming full-time researchers either in their existing departments or elsewhere, or to return to unsponsored research. Research assistants had trouble finding stable career opportunities, their tenure being limited by the length of the research projects. If there was no continuity in research, their employment was generally terminated. Some centres, however, were remarkable stable. They tended to be large centres where the impact on research of an experienced researcher, and sometimes his "entourage", was less than it would have been on a small centre where one team might represent the total research effort.

Some centres were attempting to develop into research centres. Others found their present condition satisfactory: these tended to be heavily involved in postgraduate studies, where a direct research input to teaching was feasible. These centres had comparatively low morale, due perhaps to the pressures of bridging research and teaching and to the uncertainties which resulted from this organisational dilemma.

## Category 4 - Departments employing both teaching and research staff

These were mainly university departments aiming to establish research in its own right. Few had developed far from category 3. The exceptions were those that had identified the need for a research activity and had recruited established researchers from other centres. Some had developed from category 3 through the provision of funds and fellowships for researchers, while others had developed on the basis of long-term covenants and grants. The organisational dilemma remains, but is softened by the availability of considerable resources.

## Category 5 - Departments solely employing researchers

These were mostly independent institutions and large university centres, set up to undertake research, and were well established. Growth came from reputed excellence, from past experience in relevant fields and a greater market awareness than was found in the other centres. For some, internal support from a parent institution had been vital in their establishment. Long-term planning was a reality, and such centres effectively ran as small businesses. The pressures were mainly financial, but they did not hinder the development of ideas. The provision of careers for researchers, changing from traditional "reactive" approaches to more pro-active ones, and entering new areas of research were areas of concern. On the other hand, the basic organisational dilemma was eased, if not eliminated, since staff were not trying to combine different roles or seeking to co-exist with other groups of staff.

## 5.4 The structural component: organisational alternatives

Studies such as these suggest alternatives for organising research in management institutions. Since most institutions will be seeking to develop their research capacity from a category 1 situation, the key considerations are (i) how big do you wish research to grow, (ii) how fast do you wish to get there, and (iii) what resources (financial and staff) will be available to aid the attainment of your research goals? Armed with answers to these questions, you can choose from among the alternatives.

The important factors to consider when deciding how to organise research include the following:[1]

- the research goals the institute wishes to pursue: in terms of <u>outputs</u>, e.g. to do substantive research, to develop new researchers, to contribute to teaching/training activities of the institute, to provide research-based services to client enterprises; <u>system objectives</u>, e.g. to ensure the research unit's survival, to increase the growth rate of research; and <u>product objectives</u>, e.g to improve the quality of research, to increase the range or content of research. In some research organisations, especially the larger, more formal ones, system objectives tend to dominate product objectives;

- the strategy employed to achieve these objectives;

- the type of research the institute adopts;

- the nature of the environment in which it operates;

- the relationships with the external environment, especially to maintain and develop its knowledge and skills, to gain access to sources of data, and to obtain finance to support research;

- the personal characteristics of the researchers.

---

[1] See, for example, the paper by A.W. Pearson of Manchester Business School, R & D Research Unit, in the seminar report <u>Strategies for management research and development in Europe</u> (Manchester Business School, 1972).

**Figure 8   The basic organisational framework — little or no research**

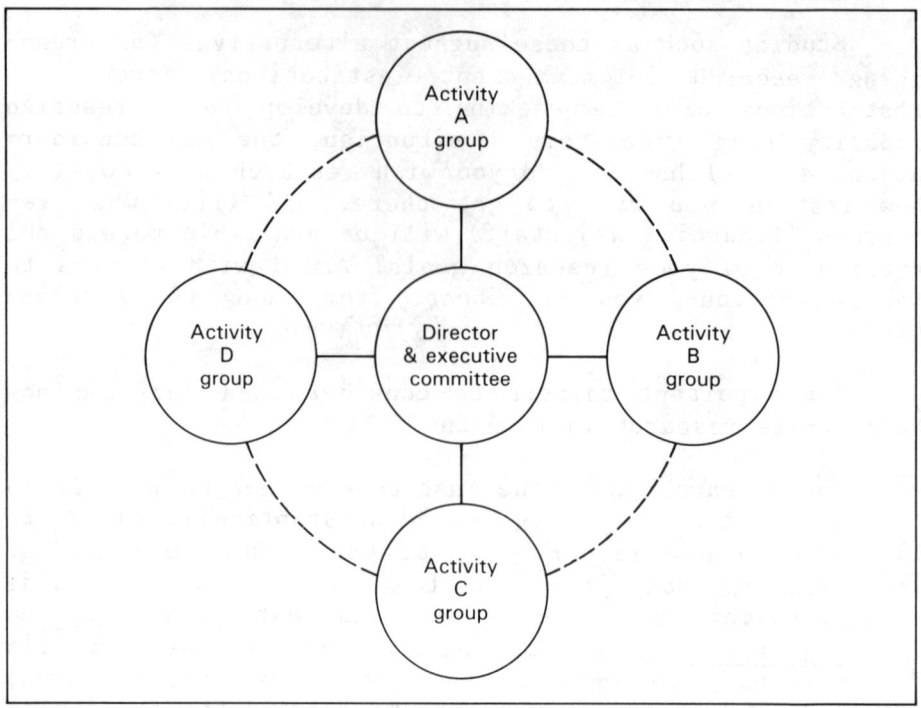

The last point is particularly important. Usually, researchers have different values, different time perspectives and orientations, and different capacities to operate within certain organisational frameworks from staff who are mainly involved with training and administration. Relatively open, flexible approaches to the organisation and management of research are needed.

Basic organisational framework

As a guide to comparing the alternatives, a basic organisational framework has been developed. This is shown in figure 8 and is based on departments or institutes undertaking little or no research. The key components are:

- a director (or dean or head) who is in charge of the institute, probably operating through an executive committee (or faculty, board or similar body);

- several "activity" groups of staff members. An "activity" may be task-based (e.g a "short courses" group or "consultancy" group) or discipline-based (e.g. academic subject groupings), or a combination of these. Few institutes are big enough to effectively operate a "matrix" structure, i.e. task groups with their own leaders supported by subject/academic groups, again with their own leaders. This matrix structure is now prevalent but presents major difficulties of authority and control;

- a direct authority relationship between the director and the activity group leaders (solid lines);

- an indirect relationship between activity groups (dotted lines). Although some interchange of staff can take place, the groups are relatively autonomous.

Alternative ways of organising research can be thought of as variations on this basic structure.[1]

Individual research - integrated yet differentiated

This form is based on the institution's existing structure, whatever that may be. There may be a director, or head of centre, with senior staff responsible for key activity areas such as short courses, advisory services, qualification programmes, and consultancy services. Research is seen as part of a staff member's role, and is thus "integrated" with other activities. It is "differentiated", since each staff member often has different research interests unrelated to those of other members. Often, researchers operate in isolation from each other. Without support from the institute, the research activity may die. Support may be provided internally by nominating a member of the executive committee to take charge of research. The director often takes on this responsibility. An active and enthusiastic lone researcher will establish a network of external, supportive contacts. If this is not reinforced internally, the researcher may be attracted to more promising pastures. The key relationships in this form of organisation are shown in figure 9.

---

[1] See also M. Kubr (ed.): Managing a management development institution (Geneva, International Labour Office, 1982). Ch. 5.

**Figure 9  Individual research — the lone researcher model**

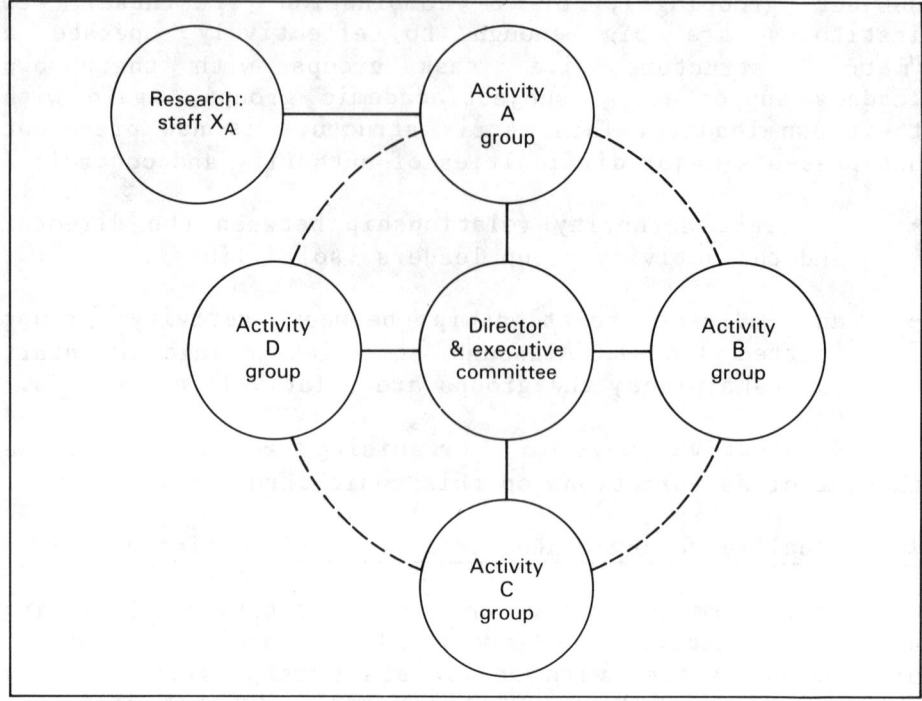

Team research

An important element of support is access to other researchers or staff interested in the research topic. A way of achieving this is to organise research on a "team" basis, using single and/or multi-groups of researchers/ staff, as illustrated in figure 10. Staff from one or several groups are brought together to form research teams. These teams have their own leaders (elected by the staff or nominated by the group leaders/director). Where several teams exist, team leaders may meet under the chairmanship or guidance of the senior staff member responsible for research. This is often formalised as a research committee. In addition to providing greater internal support, team or group-based research fosters greater awareness of research opportunities, develops a momentum for continuing research and provides opportunities for developing large-scale programmes of research. There is a danger of producing feelings of divided loyalties amongst the staff. They often experience a conflict of interest between their normal group tasks and research. A close

**Figure 10  Team research — single or multi group model**

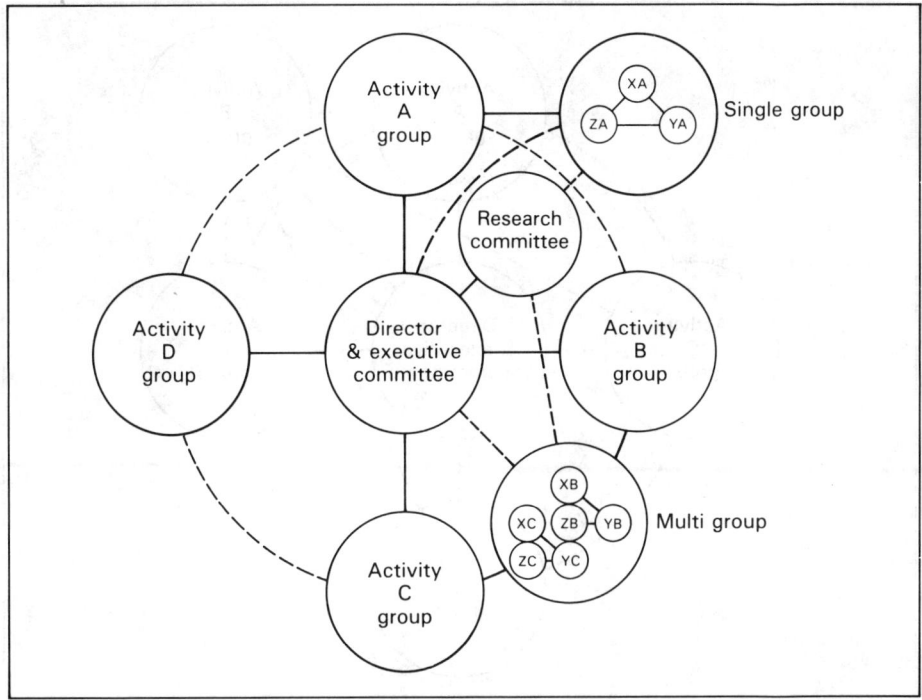

relationship between research topic and the main group activity can reduce such conflicts. For example, staff working on tailor-made programmes for local industry would probably be interested in research into the effectiveness of different approaches to training managers. Team research increases the chance of relevant research being carried out because it reduces members' tendencies to pursue their own flights of fancy. It also helps integrate research with other activities. Research assistants are more likely to find a stimulating environment in which to work than if they are isolated with (and, sometimes, from) a lone researcher.

Research units
─────────────

Some management institutes formalise team research by establishing a separate research activity, as illustrated in figure 11. Here research is viewed as a key activity along with the others (e.g. in-company courses, qualification programmes). The senior member of staff will be the group leader or head of unit - the titles used are direc-

125

**Figure 11 Group research — the separate research unit model**

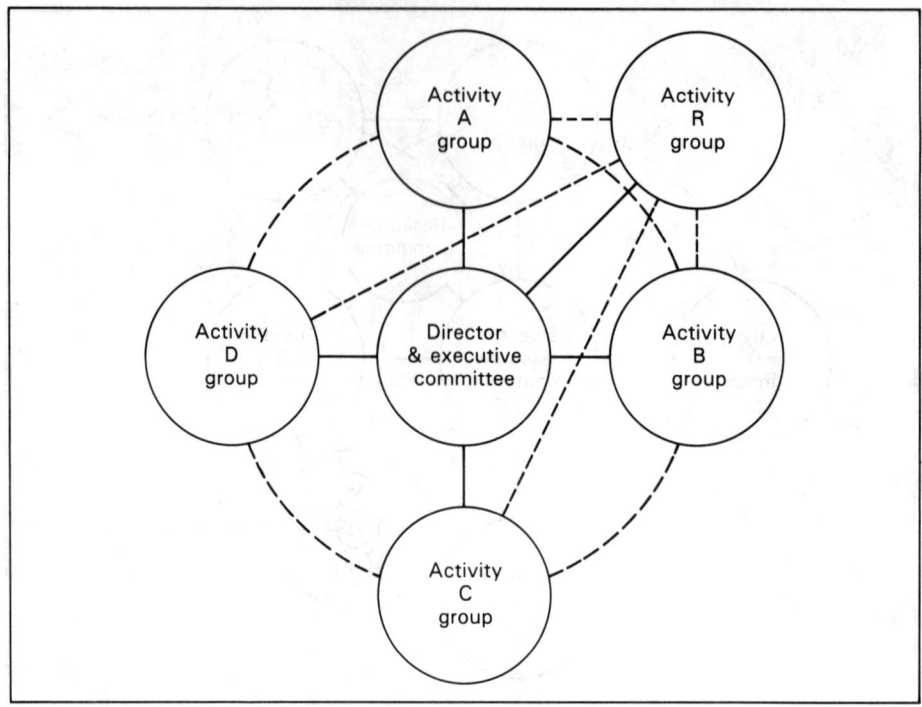

tor of research, research co-ordinator, etc. The key person may be a member of the executive committee, thus linking research and the management of the institute. The research unit will have its own members of staff, on contracts funded from within and/or from external research grants. Staff from other activity groups may become temporary, part-time or full-time members of the unit, thus providing links with other groups. The more autonomous the research units become, the more research is seen as differentiated from the other activities. Research then risks becoming isolated from other activities.

The strength of the research unit approach, however, lies in building up cohesive research activities which can provide a direct service to industry. Careful management of the centre's activities, the timely use of staff seminars, the involvement of research staff in training activities, and the interchange of staff within the unit all help overcome the problems of separation. Where a research committee is used, benefits can be gained by having among its members staff from other groups.

**Figure 12  Institutionalised research — the research institute model**

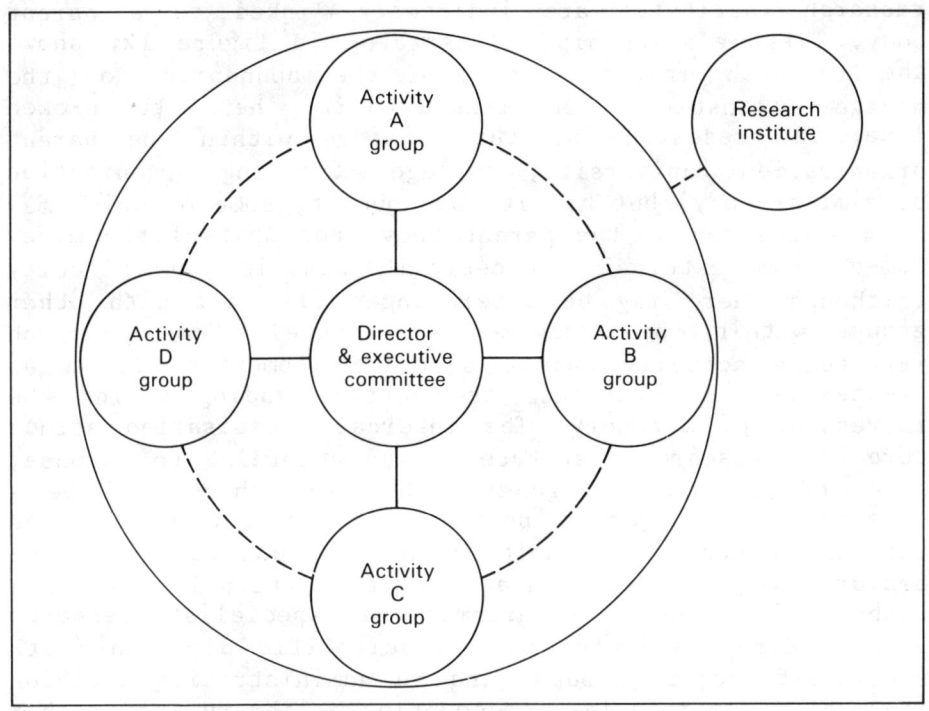

This approach makes heavy demands upon an institute's services. There will be pressure for secretarial support. Whilst the salary costs will usually be met from research funds; space, desks, chairs, typewriters, etc., usually have to be acquired from internal budgets. Library and information facilities will be required. A better range of journals and books, access to indexing, abstracting and search services will all be required. Small units can get these services from central library provision. Large units may require decentralised services. The illustration in figure 11 becomes more complicated as the research unit grows and a different form of organisation may need to be considered. The research unit may be transformed into a department or separate research institute.

The research institute

There are many examples of separate research institutes. Two examples are the Institute for Social Science Research at the University of Michigan and the Tavistock Institute of Human Relations in London (the latter being autonomous of any university/college organisation). Such research institutes are indirectly linked to a parent body. This relationship, illustrated in figure 12, shows the research institute outside the boundaries of the management institute, but linked to it - hence the broken line. The research institute resides within the parent organisation (university, college, training organisation or similar body) but has its own budget, some of which may be supplemented by the parent body. But most of the money comes from external sources. It has its own faculty (although there may be interchanges of staff with other groups within the management institute). Some research institutes actually appear separate, sometimes known as "letter head" institutes, the letter heading giving the impression of autonomy. The internal organisation structure of a research institute varies according to purpose, size and autonomy. In general, however, there will be a director, a management board or council (sometimes an internal management committee and a council comprising senior staff and representatives from external bodies), a number of research programmes or specialist research groups. Some institutes have a scientific division (with specialist/project groups) and an administrative division (including secretarial, accounting, library and other support services). There may also be an advisory service group, which offers (for a fee) guidance and consultancy on research matters to external organisations. An example is given in figure 13.

## 5.5 The managerial component

Management is important for research, just as in any other activity. It is important because it can resolve the integration-differentiation issue. Managing researchers is different from managing other types of staff. Researchers have different perspectives and approaches from those in managerial positions. Let us contrast these, first by looking at four important ways of considering managers,[1] and then at a "typical" researcher orientation.

---

[1] Based on ideas presented at a management research lecture by Charles Margerison of the Cranfield School of Management.

**Figure 13 Example of organisational structure of a management research institute**

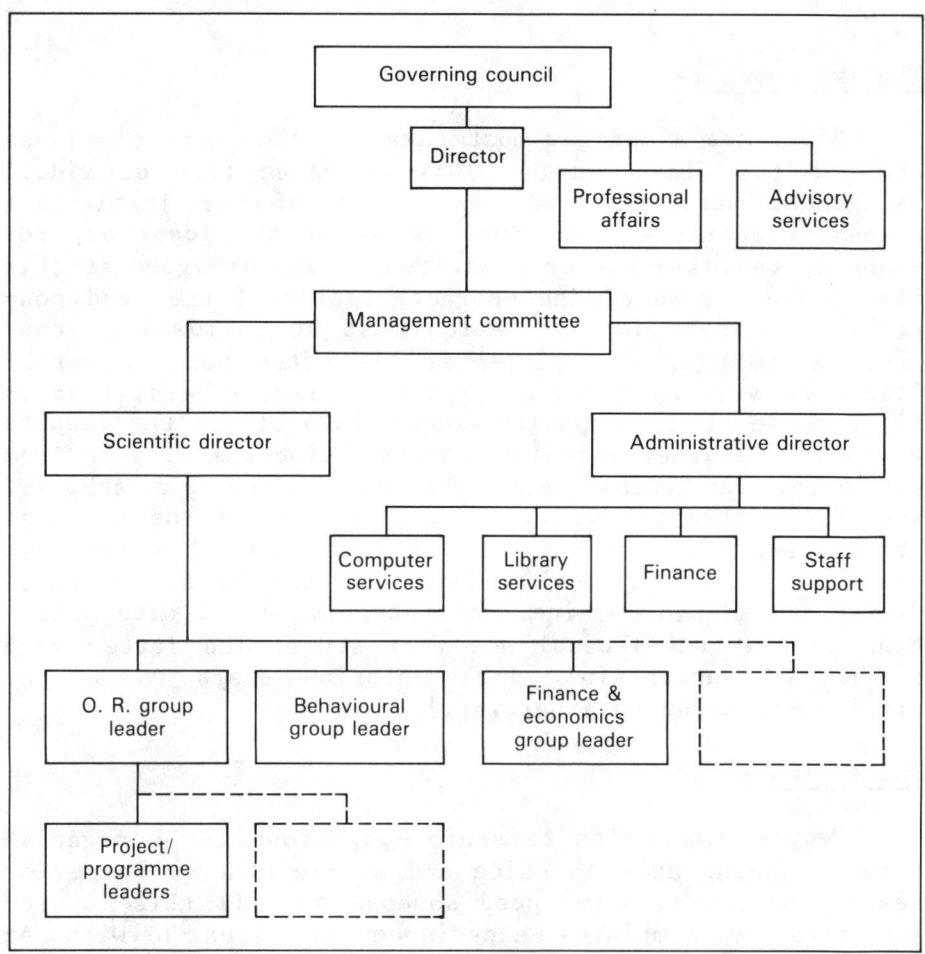

## The controllers

Management is largely concerned with making sure that things happen on time, resources are available, budgets are not overspent and targets are met. Staff who are good at this are often promoted to senior positions. They are good at fixing dates and schedules, and making sure that programmes have trainers and rooms allocated to them, and that finance is available to meet expenses. Charts and diagrams adorn their walls. Experience, however, shows that controllers are sometimes too rigid. Everything must be scheduled - even creativity! Whilst control of research is vital, it has to be limited to the directive role of quadrant 4 in figure 7, but that is not a research situation.

## The implementers

Sometimes a manager must take up other people's ideas and put them into action. This is often true of middle management positions and of members of the institute's executive committee, who must implement the ideas of, for example, the director or dean. People who are good at this also possess some of the characteristics of the good controller: indeed, implementation must be followed by control. A "managerial implementer" is often able to establish good working relationships with researchers, primarily because of his capacity to put into effect the outputs of their research. This may overcome problems arising from not being an "ideas" man, thinker, or even a scholar. Indeed, "managerial scholars" rarely achieve the organisational success of those in charge of research who remain aloof from the internal affairs of the unit, or those "integrators" who combine administrative skill with attention to the intellectual needs of staff. The latter seem to be very successful. Implementation seems to be the vital administrative expertise.[1]

## The advisors

People often rise to senior positions in an organisation by being able to guide and advise others. Large research institutes often need someone to fill this important role by combining experience in research with an ability to act as an academic sounding board. Junior members of staff often need to be able to discuss problems, ideas, approaches, with such a person. Sometimes the director or research co-ordinator provides this support. Can a busy executive adequately perform this role? Will his office door be open sufficiently often for staff to be able to talk things over? Large research organisations need to ensure that project or programme directors can fulfil these requirements. This has implications for the

---

[1] For a very interesting research study into these aspects, see S.D. Sieber: Reforming the university: The role of the social reseach centre (New York, Praeger, 1972).

selection and promotion of staff to senior positions. Academic excellence alone is insufficient and possibly destructive. Senior staff who believe themselves the only sources of good ideas can frustrate the creativity of researchers.

## The explorers

A fourth type of staff are those who continually search out things, who delve into the new, uncharted areas. They often find it difficult to organise their own affairs effectively. Administration is alien to their interests. They much prefer to develop new ideas. Some ideas may be taken up and implemented, usually by others who can see their value and can put them to practical use. Without the help and support of a dedicated secretary or assistant, the "explorer" would get lost in his own conceptual world. The benefits of their work would be lost. We need such geniuses (for often, this is what they are) but not as managers of researchers! Whilst researchers may identify with them on academic and intellectual levels, they become frustrated in their attempts to get things done, to get decisions made.

## Meeting researchers' requirements - an integrated approach?

Clearly, a balance is required between the hard-nosed controller of minute-by-minute activities and the academic pilot who likes exploring but whose hands never seem to be on the controls. This can sometimes be found in one person. Where it is, considerable benefits will accrue, not least because it avoids the potential conflict inherent in a dual role situation. Where it does not, the dual role system can provide the necessary balance through a deputy. Thus, a director who is the controller-implementer might have a deputy who combines the attributes of the adviser with those of the explorer or implementer. However, the balance is often highly sensitive to political considerations and influences. Here conflict often arises.

A successful integrated approach to managing research involves:

- administrative expertise (gained prior to assuming responsibility for research);

- sensitivity to academic and intellectual requirements of staff;

- an emphasis on collaborative reseach;

- bridge-building between researchers and other professional staff;

- a low emphasis on personal research;

- experience outside the field of research;

- innovative and developmental orientations;

- gaining access to sources of power and finance;

- concentration upon a few key goals;

- (relative) freedom to act.

These allow a culture and organisational climate to develop in tune with the basic <u>orientations of research staff</u>. It gives researchers freedom to explore, but within defined boundaries; it finds resources for research, but only so long as there are some signs of results being achieved and outputs gained; it shields research staff from the seemingly petty requirements of an administration-bound parent organisation, but only if they show at least minimum tolerance for administrative requirements; it allows flights of fancy to be pursued, providing they are sympathetic to the director's fights (and flights?) in the corridors of power. In short, it will be a loose, flexible, organic organisation managed in a firm but participative manner - i.e. quadrant 2 of figure 7 in section 5.2. It will be one characterised by a "normative" compliance relationship of staff with the enterprise. Their goals will largely be shared with those of the institute, often derived from their main discipline base or their professional and scientific community. Thus a more scientific and integrated leadership is vital to the success of the research endeavour. Such leaders must also be able to influence the rewards researchers attain, both financial and professional, if they are to continue to receive the compliance necessary for the research endeavour.

The leaders must also ensure that the research group is open to information and ideas from outside and help those who generate ideas within to become known externally. A key director or senior researcher must occupy what has been termed a "boundary spanning" role.[1] People in this role are able to bring in new ideas, have many contacts both inside and outside the institute (e.g. through professional bodies and other centres in the research stream), are competent researchers, and are able to gather and communicate complex information to all sorts of people. They are important for the development of ideas for new research and setting up contacts with potential funding and user bodies. Whilst they may spend much time out of the institute, their absence is usually a sign of continued effectiveness.

## 5.6 The servicing component

Particular services are needed as the research activity grows. Individual researchers may make fewer demands than research teams or units, but their needs are similar. These may be met from the parent organisation, while large research units provide them themselves. The nature of the services required will vary. For example, a large operations research activity may require considerable statistical and computing services, whereas a qualitative, interview-based study makes heavy demands on secretarial services. Here we shall briefly describe the most common services. The nature and extent of the research programme will determine which ones, and to what extent, will be needed.

### Information services

Most research requires access to basic technical, scientific or statistical information. For example, a researcher may wish to know certain economic facts, or trends in employment patterns, or to acquire standardised tests or questionnaires. Many sources of such information exist. Governments, professional bodies and research

---

[1] See M. Tushman and T. Scanlon: "Boundary spanning individuals: Their role in information transfer and their antecedants", in Academy of Management Journal, 1981, No. 2, pp. 289-305.

institutes produce such data in report form. Indices of tests and their purposes are regularly published. A good librarian can track them down, and make sure they are available in the library if regular use is to be made of them. A telephone call to the appropriate government department, or other body, may produce the necessary one-off set of data. It is desirable to have on the staff someone who has experience of such information services, especially if the library cannot do it. An experienced researcher will be able to point out the way for less experienced members of staff.

Library services

A well-stocked library with knowledgeable staff is essential. Many libraries of management institutes are geared to the needs of students and course members on training programmes or qualification courses. Books will range from introductory academic texts through collections of readings to practical, "do-it-yourself" approaches. Journals are often practical and professional, with few academic journals. This is not adequate for research. The stock of books must include texts on research methods and reports of major research studies, and the journal range needs to include academic works which contain up-to-date reports of research findings. In addition, certain references, abstracts and indices will be needed. The more conventional retrieval tools (e.g. printed indices, card catalogues) are limited in scope and demand more time and effort to get the information. The library will also need registers of research being carried out elsewhere for identifying under-researched areas, locating related research and establishing a potential research network. Selectivity in these matters will be important: one large business school in the United Kingdom has over 400 on-line sources alone! This does not imply that all institutes must have massive resources in order to carry out research. What must be available, though, is a minimum set of reference materials, some good texts on research methods, and information on and access to other sources and resources in other institutes. Establishing cooperative linkages with others in the research environment, building networks of research interest groups with staff from other institutes, and ensuring that the person operating the "boundary spanning role" does so effectively, are all good ways of identifying where the resources are and generating the political will to share them or make access readily available.[1]

## Computing and statistical services

Many types of research, from survey research to quantitative research in OR, economics or finance, generate data which require large-scale data manipulation and the application of statistical tests. Large research centres and institutes have their own computer and associated facilities. Smaller research endeavours need the facilities of the parent organisation. In such cases, it is preferable to have access via your own terminals, rather than having to wait upon the availability of central services. A range of computer programmes are available - for example, SPSS (Statistical Package for Social Sciences) is widely used in management research. Most medium-sized computer departments have such software available. It is important to develop good working relationships with statisticians and computer programmers interested in the special problems encountered by researchers in other areas. Quite often, this is where they gain much job satisfaction and recognition. Desk-top computers (such as APPLE and PET) are now extremely valuable to management researchers. As with many areas, this is one where some basic training and experience will prove invaluable.

## Secretarial services

Research depends on communication, whether about intended research (e.g. a research proposal) or research findings (e.g. a research report). A good research secretary is familiar with research work, is able to deal with inquiries satisfactorily, quickly develops initiative, and helps provide quick, responsive services. Careful filing and cataloguing of research data can be effectively met by someone (or, in a large centre, a group of secretaries) "dedicated" to research work. Word-processors dramatically ease the production of questionnaires (e.g.

---

[1] This section has been kept very brief since it is hoped to examine the subject in detail in another volume in the ILO Management Development Series, devoted to information and documentation services of management institutions.

where slightly different versions are required to go to different subsamples) and the editing of reports. Even mailing questionnaires is facilitated by the capacity to store and retrieve names and addresses.

Reprographic services

It is vital to have access to photocopying and printing facilities. Questionnaires, reports, tables of data, articles (for research use only, of course!) and the like will be needed in quantities from one to several thousands. Again, the smaller units will have to rely upon the services provided by others, either internally by the parent body or externally by commercial organisations. Small and inexpensive desk-top copiers can meet urgent, low quantity requirements. Special services, such as photo-reduction (e.g. to reduce pages of a questionnaire), or technical/artwork design (e.g. for covers of important prestigious research publications) can often be obtained commercially, or through another department of the parent body (e.g. a department of art and design). The costs of such services are not trivial, and control has to be exercised.

5.7 The financial component

Research relies upon finance. The careers and livelihoods of researchers and support staff depend upon a steady, continuous flow of research funds. This places considerable strain upon senior staff and directors of research, who must continually scan the environment for research funding opportunities and set in process research funding negotiations. But where are the sources of research funds? Clearly, the answer depends on the particular national context, but some general sources can be identified.

Internal sources

Some institutes fund research from their own budgets. This can be achieved in several ways. One is to establish a budgetary provision for staff time to carry out research. Relief will be given from normal duties, usually to enable part-time research. Full-time research can be encouraged through the use of sabbaticals. Both cost money: extra (sometimes temporary) full-time staff to pick up the duties, overtime for existing staff, or the use of part-time appointments. A second way is to set aside a certain amount each year for the appointment of research assistants. A third is to negotiate a percentage allocation from earned revenue (e.g. from in-company programmes, consultancy, conferences and seminars) for research. However the internal funds are found, proper accountability for their use must be established. This can be achieved through the normal administration system or by delegating responsibility to a senior staff member in charge of research.

Government agencies and funding bodies

Some countries have many bodies which provide money for research. Sometimes this is done in what may be called the "responsive" mode: you apply to a particular body for funds, and it responds. In other cases, the funding body invites researchers to apply for funds, or commissions research from particular researchers or teams. This is a "pro-active" or "initiating" mode. In each case, the funding body expects detailed, costed proposals.

The types of funding bodies vary enormously. Government departments often promote research; research councils exist to disburse public research monies in areas of interest (e.g. disciplines such as science, agriculture, etc.); foundations exist to promote causes and some include management research in their lists; and charities abound, but only a few of them provide funds for research purposes. Obtaining funds from such bodies is rarely easy. One must study their priorities and areas of interest, for example by writing for their latest annual report. One needs, too, to contact those who allocate funds. An informal discussion over the telephone, or a personal visit, is often encouraged (creating a network and becoming known is useful). Formats of research proposals vary - some bodies have special forms, others do not. The exact requirements are easily determined through normal channels of contact. Few proposals are successful first time - revisions are often requested. Whilst this can be disappointing, determination usually produces results.

Industrial and commercial organisations

Institutes and members of staff with good reputations sometimes attract research contracts from the general "market place". A particular company may be impressed with a training programme run by a management centre and decide to initiate some research into, say, dominant managerial styles and how they can be influenced by training. Some large companies commission a good deal of research. Whilst there are no guidelines for securing funds from such companies, it is important to cultivate the institute's client organisations. Involving senior managers in seminars, research lectures and advisory committees can foster relationships from which research might spring. Such research funding can pose problems. The results are usually confidential and it may be difficult to publish them and thus gain further visibility and an enhanced reputation. Most companies will consider requests for publication of findings, sometimes in anonymous form, sometimes with the name very prominent. The important research at the Hawthorne plant of Western Electric, at Glacier Metals, at Volvo, among many others, has focused attention on these organisations. It is difficult to generalise from one study and another company is unlikely to contract the same research. The use, however, of funds from other sources can help to overcome this, and enable a useful body of comparative data to be built up.

Assessing the finance required

Estimating the cost of a proposed research project requires experience. There is no magic formula. The important factors are:

(1) <u>Staffing</u>. Where full or part-time research staff are required, estimate the time involved, and their cost. For example, the number of interviews that can be carried out by one person in a day ranges from two to five, depending on the scope of the interviews. Knowing the scope, and how many interviews are to take place, enables the workload in "work days" to be calculated. Other activities, such as designing and piloting questionnaires, can be estimated. Using computers for modelling can create problems in estimating time required, but usually an experienced computer specialist can help. All of the project activities (see, for example, illustration 4) can thus be

converted into time estimates. Calculating salary costs plus salary overheads, such as pensions and insurance, becomes a matter of arithmetic.

(2) <u>Staffing support</u>. Most research requires secretarial, clerical and technical support. The procedure here is the same as for that in (1) above. The problem is not usually that of calculating how much time (and hence, cost) will be incurred, but more of the sort illustrated by the question "How do we obtain one-sixth of a technician?" When several projects are in progress or being proposed, a "whole" person can be shared, and the costs allocated between projects.

(3) <u>Equipment</u>. Even established research units need extra filing cabinets, typewriters, calculators, computer software, tape-recorders, and other specialised equipment. Some funding bodies will not accept such cost items and will expect the institute to provide them. Check first, and if in doubt, include them. They can always be disallowed, but if they are not there in the first place, they cannot be accepted. The costs of such items can be determined from catalogues or local stockists.

(4) <u>Materials</u>. Research makes heavy demands on paper, envelopes, report binders, computer cards, specialist textbooks and the like. These can be listed and costs obtained as in (3) above.

(5) <u>Travel and subsistence</u>. This includes travel by train, car and all other forms of transport and meals/accommodation when away. Again, research work can create undue demands on the institute's normal budget for travel and subsistence. Such costs can be estimated by assessing, for example, how many journeys will be required to complete an interviewing programme (knowing, of course, the locations, or using an "average" figure), and the meals/accommodation allowances this would incur.

(6) <u>Telephone and postage</u>. In large surveys, these can be quite costly, but can be estimated fairly readily. Knowing the sample size, number of mailings and telephone calls (and expected durations) will yield a figure reasonably close to the actual.

(7) <u>Printing and reprographic services</u>. Reports, papers, training materials, questionnaires, etc., will be needed for, or produced as a result of, the research. Their lengths can be estimated, and approximate costs determined by an internal reprographic unit or external printers.

(8) <u>General</u>. There will invariably be other items to finance from the research budget. Some projects may involve visits of specialists, use consultants on technical problems, organise special seminars or conferences, increase general administrative overheads, and so on. Each project proposal must be analysed thoroughly to detect those activities which will have a significant cost implication, or bring the project to a halt if resources are not obtained.

(9) <u>Contingencies</u>. There will always be unknowns, and knowns which are difficult to cost. Inflation is an example of the latter. Most funding bodies allow a contingency sum for inflation; some may not be happy with the "unknowns". Again, try it out, or find out.

These costings can then be put together to establish the order of finance required if the research project is to take place. For example, the costings from an actual (and successful) proposal are given in illustration 18, updated for inflation, and extended to cover certain items not originally costed. It will be noted that direct salary costs amount to about 80 per cent of the total. This is not unusual in management research.

---

Illustration 18: <u>Example of costings for a research proposal</u>

This example comes from a proposal for a study of the industrial relations policies of six companies in different industries in one country. It is based on the employment of a full-time research worker, and is extended from the original.

<u>Salaries</u>                                              US$            US$

- Research officer for 3 years

|  |  |  |
|---|---:|---:|
| (at $16,000 per year including overheads) | 48 000 | |
| - Secretarial assistance (3/4 of a secretary at $6,000 per year, including overheads, pro-rata) | 13 500 | |
| - Inflation allowance | 6 000 | 67 500 |

Equipment
(not allowing for resale values)

|  |  |  |
|---|---:|---:|
| - 4-drawer metal filing cabinet | 140 | |
| - Electric typewriter | 1 600 | |
| - Typist's desk and chair | 300 | 2 040 |

Materials

|  |  |  |
|---|---:|---:|
| - General stationery | 600 | |
| - Envelopes and labels | 140 | |
| - Computer cards and paper | 300 | 1 040 |

Travel and subsistence

|  |  |  |
|---|---:|---:|
| - 6 visits to Institution A (400 miles) | 240 | |
| - 10 visits to each of 6 organisations (average 50 miles return) | 1 800 | |
| - Train fares (20 journeys at average cost of $20) | 400 | |
| - Meals (30 at $2) | 60 | |
| - Accommodation (20 overnight stays at $30 per night) | 600 | 3 100 |

Telephone and postage

|  |  |  |
|---|---:|---:|
| - Calls to Institution A | 8 | |
| - Calls to organisations | 72 | |
| - 2,000 mailings at 20 cents each | 400 | |
| - Contingency | 50 | 530 |

Printing and reprographic services

- 1,500 questionnaires (10 pages
  at 4 cents/page)                              600
- 50 reports at $4 each                         200
- General papers (5 x 100 at $2 each)  1 000          1 800

General administrative overheads

- Back-up facilities                          1 000
- Other staff time                            8 000          9 000

TOTAL FUNDS REQUIRED                                         85 010

# USING THE RESULTS OF RESEARCH  6

For some management development professionals research is an end in itself. It is an enjoyable activity in which to express and give vent to an inquiring mind. For others, it is an opportunity to gain research qualifications and research experience. These are important but, for the management community, secondary reasons for doing research. Society must benefit not only from greater knowledge but also from an improved capacity to do things. Research is a decision-making process, as is management. There is a need to ensure by deliberate action that research findings are made known to and used by the managerial community and by fellow management trainers and teachers, to contribute to our general capacity to make and implement effective decisions. This chapter discusses how this can be achieved.

## 6.1 A framework of research utilisation

A framework will help us analyse how to encourage the use of research. Our framework includes three main elements:

### Generating knowledge

The research process is geared primarily towards the generation of knowledge and ideas. Some types of research seek to apply or use existing knowledge and ideas. There is, therefore, an overlap between certain aspects of the research process and both the generation and use of knowledge. It is a fundamental characteristic of progressive civilisations that scientific endeavours exist and that they produce a knowledge base on which society can draw for the improvement of its peoples. Managers and trainers also need such knowledge. Often, however, they require a more tested set of ideas with which to work. Generating knowledge is primarily the function of so-called "pure" researchers, but all those involved in the research process add to the stock from time to time. They need to disseminate, to publish their findings if they are to be used.

Testing knowledge

Quite often, the findings of research cannot be directly used. They must be tested in potential areas of application, and developed to be used. These are the development and applied research processes. We know, for example, much about motivation. Many concepts exist, but could not be applied until people such as Herzberg and his colleagues had tested and developed the concepts into alternative techniques for job design. This testing, development and evaluation of ideas involves the invention, design and production of products or packages. This process is well known in engineering and is appropriate to the field of management. Applied researchers, curious trainers and innovative consultants operate in this area. Education itself can be a test bed, too.

Applying knowledge

Development engineers often have difficulty getting production managers to accept, use and produce the products and ideas they have developed and tested. Many reasons for this exist, not least of which is a lack of involvement in the development process. Similarly, managers and trainers cannot apply the techniques, packages and principles developed from research unless they know of them, see their relevance and have the experience and skill to put them to good use. Overcoming these "barriers to innovation" involves the promotion and demonstration of the new techniques (the "diffusion" stage) and generating enough awareness and interest in them so that they can be evaluated, and put to work (the "adoption" stage). This in turn throws up new problems or areas for research or development. Consultants and trainers frequently operate at this end of the process.

**Figure 14  Summary of the utilisation process**

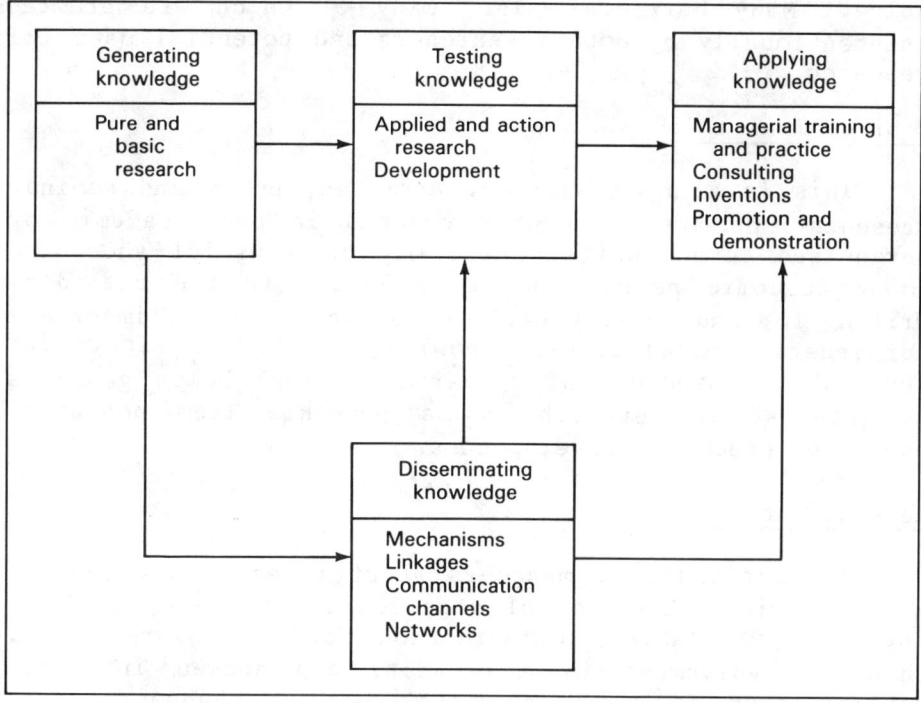

The process is complicated, yet rests on a simple notion: <u>hidden knowledge is useless knowledge</u>. Developers, testers, trainers and consultants who do not know of the ideas produced by researchers cannot do anything with them. The <u>dissemination of research findings</u> is crucial to their utilisation. The responsibility for making the findings known rests with researchers. However, they cannot be held responsible for a lack of keenness on the part of managers and others - or can they? This important question will be discussed later in this chapter. These key elements can be linked in a framework for utilising research findings as shown in figure 14.

6.2  <u>Barriers to using research</u>

Many things can go wrong in getting research findings put to good use. At one extreme is the absence of a method for potential users to become aware of what exists; at the other, a lack of any problem which research can help

145

solve. Many barriers exist, many of which are erected unintentionally by both researchers and potential users of research.

Poor communication

This is a major barrier. Articles, books and seminar presentations are frequently couched in over-academic or jargonised terms. Whilst these may be a useful shorthand among academic peers, they mean little to the outsider. Writing for and talking with fellow academics is important for generating and testing knowledge, but does little for application. Exposure of research findings helps generate an interest in research and a pressure from potential users for practical developments.

Lack of interest

The attitudes of managers about research are another major barrier. Poor use of research results from lack of interest. Suitable communication and exposure (e.g. through involvement in a project) can awaken interest. Anti-research attitudes are difficult to change but may yield to a good demonstration of how research can help. Some managers, trainers and consultants may simply not understand what research is all about. In some countries, there is no research tradition in the culture. If "scientific" research is not accepted, the results of management research will be even more difficult to apply. Again, exposure may help remove the impediment.

Nature of management institutions

Some schools and centres are locked into the knowledge generating game. For them research is an end in itself - a vocation. As long as research is carried out and reputable publications achieved, little else matters. It takes a good developer, trainer or manager to penetrate the "walls" of such institutes. Promotions based on academic excellence add to the problem, as do selection criteria which lead to a homogeneous academic staffing structure. If application and publication of findings are spurned and do not lead to the desired rewards, they are not likely to be sought. A more flexible policy is needed.

Inappropriate mechanisms

Research relevant to managerial needs must be identified and brought together. The means for doing this do not always exist. In fields such as medicine, third parties form an essential link in the mechanism. The highly qualified professional engineer scans the environment for good ideas; the salesman talks with doctors and relays back views and needs. This helps to "pollenate" the plant, giving flower to fruitful dialogue and co-operation. We need more of this in the management field - consultants, trainers and members of professional bodies constitute the third party, rubbing shoulders with members of the research and managerial communities. This can be formalised, for example, through setting up special professional interest groups.

Mistrust

Managers and academics do not always trust each another. Some managers have dealt with arrogant and conceited academics in the past, or with staff who were inexperienced. Academics have met ignorant, stubborn and hard-nosed managers whose only interest is in making money and solving burning practical problems. Such experiences are hard to forget, and, although rare, generate myths that divide managerial and academic communities. Researchers have to demonstrate that they can deliver practical solutions. Some mistrust will always exist. Let's recognise it and get on with the job where we can.

Knowing where to look

Some managers, keenly interested in seeking the aid of research in their work, make little progress because they do not know where to look. The range of sources is broad: from journals and books through research registers to seminars and individual researchers. Those engaged in management research need to be visible to the managerial community (e.g. through publishing in "practical" magazines). Those who train managers have a golden opportunity to help research along by providing seminars on the role and relevance of management research and where to find it.

Time span

Research findings take a long time to become known and accepted. It takes several years before they get published, several years more before they really come to the attention of potential users and several years more before they are accepted as part of a credible stock of knowledge. There is then a period of testing, development and evaluation of techniques or packages deriving from the findings. Little wonder some staff give up after the publication stage. Patience and persistence are required - and so, too, are some short cuts. The consultant has good opportunities for trying out ideas before they become generally accepted. This also offers a competitive marketing position vis-à-vis others in the field. Researchers and consultants can form a powerful axis in quickly establishing the utility of research.

Little funding of applied research

Often the sponsors of research are research councils and similar bodies which promote knowledge generation. More and more, however, in other fields (physics, engineering, aeronautics) funding of applied work is very visible. A similar need exists in management in particular, and in the behavioural sciences in general. This happens in many countries, and in many developing countries the specialist research training given to Ph.D. students is too theoretical. Additionally, in such countries, the shortage of good academics makes it difficult to find staff with an appropriate research orientation. Research staff there must submit more applications to fund applied work. Clients often sponsor applied or action research but confidentiality often prevents it becoming known to others. Some clients, though, try to expose their work to the wider community. This should be encouraged.

Lack of time

Managers often complain they lack time to read research reports and journals or to get involved in research. Day-to-day problems are so pressing that research is seen as a luxury. Similarly, academics busy with research, teaching and administration are rarely inclined to promote their work or seek opportunities to apply research to managerial problems. Clearly, a balance is needed.

## 6.3 Factors conducive to research

Fortunately, some factors facilitate the application and utilisation of research. A recent study of research by British social work organisations[1] identified four types of factors.

### Structural factors

These concern the organisation of the client or user institution. They include: support or commitment of chief executives; legitimation of the research by top management; function of research within the organisation; access of researchers to top management and operational staff; specialised research and application units; specific links between research and operational tasks (e.g. liaison groups); balanced research units (i.e. "pure" plus "applied" researchers); viable research unit size and continuity; general organisational support for research (e.g. time to think about it, good communication channels); supportive external environment (e.g. public opinion, political climate, economic resources).

### Process factors

Process factors concern the processes of research and research utilisation. Among these factors are: participation of relevant operational people in defining research problems, carrying out research and formulating recommendations; active dissemination of information and recommendations to appropriate people; translating recommendations into specific activities, setting up special groups, seminars, etc., to discuss findings and application; appropriate use and allocation of time for research work.

### Climate factors

Positive attitudes and good relationships between people facilitate the use of research. These include: active "listening" by researchers; researcher style that

---

[1] See R. Rothman: Using research in organisations (Beverly Hills, California, Sage Publications, 1980), and especially the summary of the major factors made in the final chapter of the book.

is responsive, respectful and non-threatening; researcher interest in operational matters, organisational processes and politics; researcher attitudes which encourage communication with operational staff; participation of researchers in organisational meetings; interpersonal contact in practical situations; researchers who are interpretive and supportive in communications; vigorous promotion of research findings and recommendations; friendly managerial attitude towards research, including advocating the value of research findings, providing psychological support to researchers; managers inviting researchers to participate in decision-making processes, focusing their attention on specific organisational problems and ensuring continuity of research staff.

Outcome factors

These factors have to do with the reporting and products of research. Some of the key factors associated with reading and using research knowledge are: reports being relevant to organisational/client problems; reports showing "credibility" (i.e. they are capable of being believed, in that they are sound as well as practical); style of presentation that communicates well with potential users; reports that are sensitive to the psychology and politics of organisational life and tailored to different audiences and purposes they must meet (e.g. through multiple forms of reporting).

These are a daunting set of factors to contend with. Not all are relevant to a particular utilisation issue. Check through them and establish which are important to your programme for research utilisation. The factors to be addressed are presented in checklist form in figure 15.[1]

---

[1] For comparable approaches to improving learning-interaction processes and project implementation see two working papers of the ILO Management Development Branch: K. Turumasi: <u>Training needs of rural development managers and local training institutes to meet the needs in Ghana</u> (Geneva, International Labour Office, 1980; mimeographed), and J.B. Wallace: <u>Improving project implementation: A credible institution approach</u> (Geneva, International Labour Office, 1982; mimeographed).

**Figure 15  Checklist of factors generally associated with effective management research utilisation**

|  | Yes | No |
|---|---|---|
| 1. Is the research problem-centred? | ___ | ___ |
| 2. Do the research staff involved relate to the managers concerned as credible, helpful sources of support and information? | ___ | ___ |
| 3. Do the managers concerned have a strong personal interest in research? | ___ | ___ |
| 4. Have the managers been involved with the research? | ___ | ___ |
| 5. Does top management support the use/application of research findings? | ___ | ___ |
| 6. Will much of the knowledge/information to be used be generated locally (i.e. in the firm rather than taken from textbooks)? | ___ | ___ |
| 7. Are all relevant parties involved in the project on a fairly continuous basis? | ___ | ___ |
| 8. Do regular opportunities exist for interaction between managerial/operational staff and researchers? | ___ | ___ |
| 9. Are there regular channels of communication between users and researchers? | ___ | ___ |
| 10. Are there strong internal mechanisms for applying knowledge, linked with strong external sources of ideas? | ___ | ___ |
| 11. Will actual use/change/application be carried out by user-client staff? | ___ | ___ |

If more answers are "yes" than "no", a reasonably good basis for using research will exist. If the "no"s outnumber the "yes"s a good deal more groundwork is needed.

Note that these factors apply also to the use of research within a management institution. Replace the words "managers", "managerial", "operational" with "trainers", "teachers", "consultants", or "administrators" and you have a checklist applicable to your own institution.

## 6.4 Areas in which research can be used

The findings of management research can be used in many circumstances. Research aimed at solving a specific, unique problem has little utility beyond the problem it solves. Those who are responsible for popularising and applying research must concentrate on identifying the most appropriate uses. The following areas represent a wide scope for utilising research.

### Systems improvement

Organisations thrive on systems. We use them to manufacture mousetraps and to land men on the moon. Research can contribute to the design, development, implementation and modification of a system.

Some examples of <u>where</u> research has been used are:

- the identification of barriers to installation of computer systems and the factors influencing office design;

- analysis and design of wage payment systems based on findings of studies into wage drift, etc. (e.g. Lupton's work at Manchester Business School);

- design of coal-getting work systems in which social and technical factors are integral to the design (e.g. Tavistock Coal Mining Studies);

- design and improvement of jobs and work organisation systems for better satisfaction and quality of work (e.g. Herzberg's research on job motivation);

- predicting consumer behaviour, developing effective pricing systems, location of retail outlets (e.g. Ackoff's study including observations of petrol stations in the United States);

- changing organisational structures, communication patterns, etc., for improved organisational effectiveness (e.g. Likert's work on survey feedback);

- development and improvement of incentive schemes related to methods of working (e.g. the classic Taylor experiments);

- application of linear programming model to operation systems of manufacturing industry (e.g. study of Egyptian coke industry by the Institute of National Planning, Cairo).

Some illustrations of <u>how</u> systems can be improved thanks to research are:

- by providing comparative information of practices in different organisations and industries (e.g. types of payment systems in use);

- by describing the characteristics of system behaviour in order to improve design decisions (e.g. batch production systems versus mass or semi-mass production systems);

- by contributing to the development of system simulations for experimenting with new designs before a major change is implemented (e.g. different forms of management information systems);

- by providing models and data on which predictions and alternative states can be based (e.g. performance of the firm as an economic system).

The possibilities are numerous. Managers must describe their problems to researchers and researchers must promote their findings vigorously. Links between the two can be provided by "boundary spanning individuals", i.e. people who are able to speed up technical innovation by spotting good ideas and useful research findings, and introducing them into the organisation. If researcher and "boundary-spanner" can be brought together, a fruitful working relationship can develop. To achieve this, the researcher may need to become a "boundary-spanner" too.

<u>Self-development</u>

Research is an important process of self-development for those involved in it - researcher and manager. It sharpens critical intellectual and conceptual capacities, many of which are called upon in problem-solving and decision-making situations. The skills of problem identification, definition and resolution can be enhanced through carrying out research. The results of research can contribute to the development or enhancement of personal knowledge. The findings of a literature search add breadth whilst the study of a particular aspect of management and organisation adds depth to understanding. Self-development does not stop at personal knowledge: a capacity to act is important. Research aids this, not only through gaining skills, but also through gaining confidence in the application of skills to managerial and organisational problems. For example, a staff member may be asked to carry out a study of causes of employee sickness: a literature search will add to the researcher's general knowledge. A programme of in-depth interviews with employees off work will increase skill in collecting data and generating alternative solutions. Putting the recommendations into practice is a rare opportunity that should be grasped to improve confidence. The improved knowledge, skill and confidence will enhance the researcher's ability to teach through live, relevant and personally acquired case materials, examples and ideas.

## Consulting

Many management consultants gain considerable benefits and reputations from research they had undertaken. Names such as Herzberg, Reddin or Lippitt readily spring to mind. Their research findings were widely publicised, often in a wide range of outlets spanning the academic and practical. The interest generated in their work, and their capacity to develop findings and ideas into practical approaches (e.g. training packages, diagnostic questionnaires), led to considerable consulting work. Important and well-publicised findings can lead to more opportunities for research through increased personal credibility. The increased personal knowledge improves the capacity to recognise, identify and solve problems. Together with the extended diagnostic and analytical data-gathering skills acquired through research, they contribute immeasurably to consulting skills.

It is, however, not necessary to do research oneself in order to use it in consulting. What is important is to be able to read the literature and consulting reports, pick out relevant findings, and adapt these for application in consulting work. Some academics are good at this - they are translators and popularisers of research, as well as capable researchers.

Training

Research can aid training in many ways. It increases our knowledge of how managers learn. If the way managers learn can be related to what they need to learn in order to become effective, then an important contribution will have come about. Research thus contributes in the identification of training needs. Using a research-based approach (e.g. interviews, questionnaires), findings concerning trainees' major problems at work, knowledge gaps and attitudes, can be used as part of the learning material, as well as for identifying the appropriate content and structure of the training programme. If these same findings are compared with interview/questionnaire data obtained after the programme has been completed, a more effective evaluation is possible. This pre- and post-evaluation of training takes the shape of experimental designs used in other fields (e.g. medicine). A control group may not be available, but at least some evidence will be gained regarding the utility of the course to improve subsequent training. Using research in training requires a participative approach. If training is to work properly, participants must "own" their learning, i.e. be involved and active rather than preached at, and passive. Similarly, they must "own" the research findings by having helped to generate and use them, and by developing and agreeing on a post-training action plan or strategy. This means we do research with, rather than on, the training programme participants and that they control how the findings are used. In general, the use of research findings in training presupposes a commitment to a research approach, except, of course, where they contribute solely to the knowledge base or teaching input. The use of research as a training method is growing.

Management institutes can help company trainers use research effectively in five ways:

(1) Help the trainers to decide where to focus their research, e.g. through drawing up a checklist of major problems, difficulties, nuisances. If their bosses, peers and subordinates do the same, and share the results, a useful set of research areas will be generated. Then help them by looking at which alternatives are most likely to benefit from research. A review of the literature will reveal existing relevant research. Put them to work on

solving the problem or help them develop their own research project.

(2) <u>Mutually define the research problem and shape the proposals</u>. This helps generate a feeling of participation. If you do the research and "hand over" the research findings in a report, a low level of commitment to using the findings may be present. Involvement generates ownership, and ownership develops a need to do something with the findings.

(3) <u>Mutually agree on a research strategy</u>. If you are contracted to carry out a training research project, you will need to be involved with company personnel in setting out the strategy. This helps identify politically sensitive areas and other potential barriers to research progress and utilisation.

(4) <u>Set up a steering group</u>. This extends participation and ownership and provides support for the project, a sounding-board or testbed for the findings and access to information sources.

(5) <u>Agree on a future strategy based on the research findings</u>. A steering group can help set out what can be done with the findings, how action can be taken and who should take it. If an evaluation of this action (i.e. an assessment of what effect or influence it has) can be carried out, the research process will have been seen through to its logical end. Sadly, this happens too rarely.

Teaching
---------

Distinguishing between "training" and "teaching" can sometimes be helpful. Training is concerned with equipping a person to carry out a specific task, job or function. Teaching is more concerned with equipping a person to take on more general work, to take part in "management" (as compared with, say, managing a sales force in a particular company). It is more knowledge-based. Research takes on different forms when it is associated with the classroom.

There are as many ways of using research in teaching as there are creative, imaginative teachers and researchers. Experimentation with the processes, methods, techniques and outputs of research coupled with the needs, objectives and practices of management teaching improves learning. To do this, a teacher need not be an expert researcher, but must be imaginative and creative. Here are some suggestions:

(1) <u>Feeding in research results</u>. The most common approach is for teachers to relay to course members the outcomes of their own or someone else's research. If your research is related to the topic under discussion, bring it into the debate. This brings the topic alive and gives it a personalised and immediate impact. This is especially true when case studies, based on research findings, are used in class.

Using other people's research is less personal but still makes the subject more interesting. Well-planned reading is required to be up to date on the research. The significant points can be used to illustrate the theory, concept or principle being presented. To reduce the risk of rejection by the course members, relevance must be demonstrated. This can be achieved by splitting the course members into small groups of, say, four to eight people and asking each group to discuss their experience of the concept under consideration. After reporting back, the research can be fed in and compared with the groups' experiences.

An example of feeding in research results can be taken from the study of behaviour in organisations. It is well known that many factors influence the way people in organisations behave. A number of theories exist, too. One, "contingency" theory, argues that behaviour depends upon the factors present and the way in which they interact. As a prelude to a discussion on this, get course members to list, individually, the factors they feel influence their own behaviour at work (pay, the boss, the job, etc., appear in the lists) and to put these in order of importance (i.e. the most important has most effect on behaviour). Now put the class members into groups to agree a common list of most important factors and ask them to write their lists on flip-charts. Afterwards, put up the factors which research shows as important. There will be similarities <u>and</u> differences, but the research will have been compared to experience.

(2) <u>Doing research on course members</u>. A much under-utilised source of research data are the people we teach. For many research purposes, they constitute a biased sample, since they are self-selected and highly motivated. So, for research aimed at being "representative", they can be poor samples unless matched with other (non-course) groups. Often, however, we are interested only in judgements about something, or reactions to particular ideas or approaches. Here, course members can be of great help. In addition, we may be interested in the education process itself - how attitudes change over the period of the course; how particular views of work relate to standards of achievement on the course; how numeracy skills are influenced by the method of teaching; and so on. These can be looked at, studied, and experimented with whilst course members are present. The results can be fed into teaching in several ways: one is to highlight changes in the course design or teaching methods. But a word of caution: it can be overdone, leading to frustrated course members.

An example of this approach concerns behaviour in groups. When using certain social-skill development exercises, it is useful to have observers. If armed with a well-designed checklist, they can record behaviour of different levels of success. Call in the forms at the end of each session, analyse, record, feed back, and accumulate over time. In this way, you can build up a useful body of data. It can even be published!

(3) <u>Using research-based course work</u>. An effective way of demonstrating the usefulness of research and improving learning is to use research methods as part of the learning process. The most appropriate place is as part of the course work requirement. Projects or dissertations constitute an excellent research opportunity.

The approaches depend on the subject being taught. In finance, for example, it is possible to get each member on a part-time course to investigate the financial reporting system, the type of accounts used, the purposes to which they are put, etc., in his or her own organisation. Each set of data can be compared on a group basis and written up for presentation at a seminar. The lecturer can then present his own views and general comments on this area. Other research-based course work might use survey questionnaires or interviews (as in marketing - standing in a shopping precinct asking questions of every 25th shopper adds reality to many market research concepts) or other approaches.

(4) <u>Using research instruments in class discussion</u>. It is not necessary to do research in order to use the products of research. Much research in the behavioural and social sciences produces tested instruments, questionnaires, checklists and rating scales. Some of these are lengthy, complex and sophisticated, and are not suitable for teaching. Others are short, or include sections which are self-contained. These can be used to stimulate class discussion.

A typical approach during an hour and a half's session would be: introduce a topic, giving background and general ideas about it and hand out the device or instrument relevant to the topic. Course members fill it in; responses are collated and put on board or flip-chart; invite discussion, based on individuals comparing their results with the collated results; draw conclusions from the discussion, related to the theory, and summarise.

These approaches can also be used in combination. The research instrument developed for use "on course members" can also be used "with course members" to generate class discussion. The questionnaire designed by course members as part of their research-based course work can be built into a continuing research study. The results of that study can be fed back to various courses. However they are used, considerable learning benefits accrue.

Further research
---

Some forms of research contribute to our knowledge of the world through <u>theory building</u>. Theories take time to develop and become established. There has to be continual interaction between theory, research and practice. A theory may be proposed and its attributes tested through research. The findings may be applied to problems. The outcomes of both theory-testing and application help improve the theory. Challenges to that theory may be presented by the findings of other researchers. This may lead to it being replaced by an alternative theory, or to it being modified and refined to accommodate the new findings. The new, or refined, theory will then be the subject of further research.

Original research may be <u>replicated</u>. Studies are repeated in order to determine in which situations they do and do not hold true. Replication is important in management research because of the wide variations in the conditions in which managers operate. Thus, Fiedler's contingency theory of leadership and Herzberg's two-factor theory of work motivation have been extensively replicated. The findings from one replication have been used to refine or help interpret those of another. Although replication means "to repeat", it does not mean to be blindly repetitious, regardless of the findings of former research.

Findings can also be used to <u>develop or suggest hypotheses</u> as a prelude to theory building. Some forms of exploratory research (e.g. "grounded theory" approaches) aim solely at revealing potential answers to research questions. These then form the basis of confirming or hypothesis-testing research. Although such answers or hypotheses will be tentative, they stimulate healthy debate and further research in the academic community. This process generates both new thinking and established theory, and is part of the vital interaction between theory and research.

Vital interaction also takes place <u>between research and practice</u>. The findings of one research project may stimulate development work or applied and action research. For example, action research is common in organisational development. Many techniques and much of the content of OD action research have come from prior research studies.

Finally, research helps <u>develop and train tomorrow's researchers</u>. An important means of achieving this is the research degree. Students pursuing higher degrees through research often base their work on the findings of eminent scholars. Whilst the students' research may not produce earth-shattering results, it adds to our knowledge and enables the student to acquire skills for conducting research - perhaps later as an eminent scholar.

## 6.5 Disseminating research findings

Getting research findings known is critical for their utilisation. Academics and practitioners have a <u>duty to ensure dissemination takes place</u>. As figure 14 shows, dissemination links the generation of knowledge to its

**Figure 16 The dissemination process**

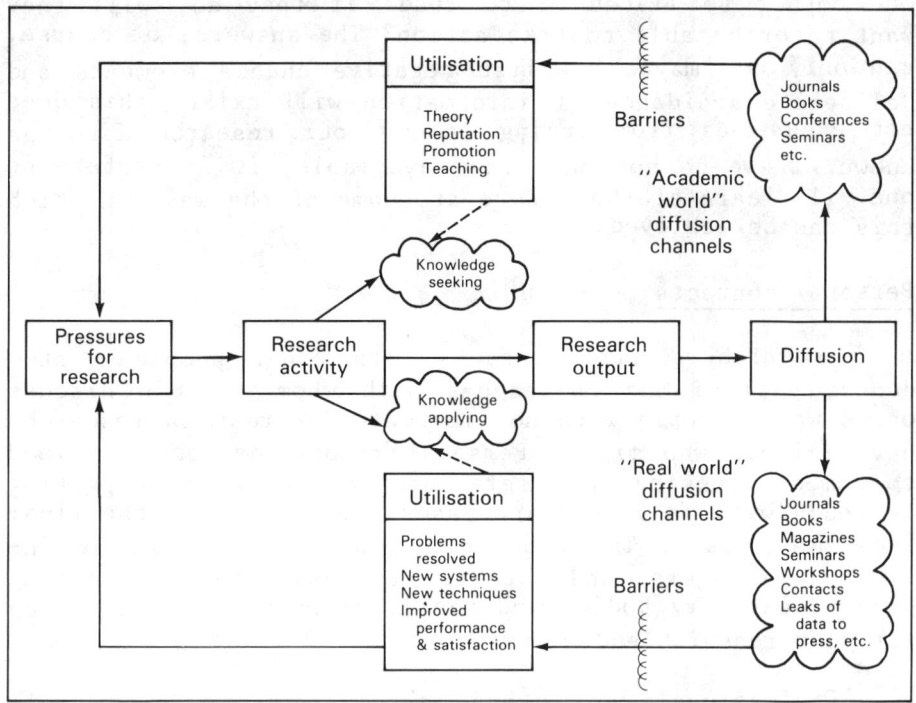

testing and application. It is important yet difficult to achieve.

The difficulties associated with dissemination are illustrated in figure 16. <u>Pressures for research</u> have to be communicated to potential researchers. This may come about through previous research. But are findings written up? Where are they reported? Who will read them, and take action on them? Pressures also come from other sources (e.g. managers, trainers) as noted in the section on identifying research needs. But what channels exist for them to be made known? <u>The research activity</u> generated in response to these pressures may or may not be appropriate. Whatever <u>research output</u> is achieved will not only be limited in its utility by its relevance to the research, but also by the way in which <u>diffusion</u> takes place. Two different but overlapping (in the sense that, for instance, some journals try to do both) diffusion channels exist - one for the "academic world", the other for the "real world". What factors determine which channel a researcher will use? Can the information flow down both?

Even if both are used, will it prove effective? Will anyone bother to listen or to read? If they do, will they want to or be able to take action? The answers, of course, can only be "maybe"! Whilst negative chance elements and deliberate avoidance of information will exist, this does not excuse us from trying to get our research findings known. If we do not make them available, it is certain no one will learn of them. Here are some of the ways in which this can be achieved.

Personal contacts

Researchers have contacts with other people – students, clients and colleagues with whom one can discuss one's work. People with no immediate interest in research have friends who might. Personal recommendations can lead to someone looking up a reference to your work or getting in touch with you. This increases the chances of the findings being used. The process can be strengthened by involving managers and others in committees, steering groups, advisory bodies and the like, which you can set up for your research endeavours.

Professional bodies and associations can often help disseminate research findings. For example, they can:

- publish results of research;

- pool resources to meet common problems;

- provide seminars and workshops;

- act as a clearing-house;

- stimulate interest in evaluation and research;

- consolidate training research.

Seminars

Management institutes with a research capacity should run research-based seminars. Where research is carried out by students, progress seminars should be held. Where research is seen as a staff development activity, seminars on research topics can be organised. For example, one institute has held seminars recently on:

- managing research for a higher degree;
- designing investigations;
- research in industrial relations;
- managerial behaviour and performance;
- the future of management education;
- problems faced by small businesses;
- management training needs;
- auditing management development;
- approaches to management development.

Each seminar had a research base, reporting findings of current or recent projects. Some were conducted by the institute's research staff, others by visiting seminar leaders - some of national and international repute. Seminar participants were mostly academic staff members and a few students carrying out research for higher degrees. Some seminars, such as those on industrial relations, managerial performance and small businesses, were attended by managers from selected client organisations. At the end of a research project, when the information has been analysed and a report of findings is available, managers or senior representatives of organisations taking part in the project are invited to a presentation of the findings and discuss implications for managerial practice, education, training or research. This is a valuable way of disseminating the findings. Those who attend can also be introduced to a wide range of the institute's programmes.

## Conferences, workshops and professional meetings

Some managers and academics who know of your work may be involved in organising programmes for conferences, workshops and professional meetings. Such people are always looking out for new and interesting speakers. If you are invited, use it as an opportunity to tell others about your work.

Academic and scientific conferences usually advertise for contributors through what is known as a "call for papers". Potential contributors are asked to submit an outline of their proposed papers. A committee or panel decides which papers are to be presented. If successful, the applicant has a good opportunity to make his findings known to a large number of people. The papers for such conferences are often published in book form, thus adding to the potential for dissemination. So, scan the journals and look out for "calls for papers", and cultivate contacts with members of professional bodies or associations. The more visible you are, the more likely it is that you will be asked to speak or present a paper.

Television and radio

Telecommunications also provides opportunities for research findings and scientific endeavours to reach into the homes of millions of people. Eminent scientists have their own TV and radio programmes; ordinary academics are interviewed for their research-based views on a current topic. Getting on TV or radio requires publicity, either in the popular press (newspapers) or through a marketing or public relations member of the institute's staff.

Publications

This traditional and widespread means of disseminating findings has many forms, each of which has differing audiences and effects.

(1) Journals and magazines. These can be grouped into three main categories. The first are the "popular" outlets. These are journalistic in style, often with a glossy, commercial finish. They are excellent vehicles for reaching a wide audience of practising managers. Unfortunately, many academic institutions frown on staff publishing in this outlet. The second category, "pragmatic-professional", journals are often associated with a professional institution or society. Their style is less journalistic than the popular outlets. They publish research-based papers by academics for practising professionals in simple, jargon-free language. The third category, "academic", publishes papers for fellow academics in a specialised, sophisticated language, often unreadable by the non-specialist.

These categories reflect the utilisation process depicted in figure 16: new knowledge is often first reported in academic journals; the results of knowledge testing, development, and so on, in pragmatic/professional journals; and managerial applications in popular journals. The boundaries are flexible, but help define the audience which will be receiving your research papers. The time to get into print in journals varies from a few months to between one and two years. They none the less represent one of the best ways of quickly disseminating research findings.

(2) <u>Books</u>. These range from ultra-academic to popularised accounts. Publication in book form takes longer (typically one to two years) but is a more permanent and visible means of dissemination. The frustrations of finding a publisher are many, unless a publishing agent is used who takes about 10 per cent of your royalties. It is best to develop a combined publications strategy - journal articles and a book. A well-planned book aimed at students and the practising professionals can achieve considerable effects in getting research findings known and used. Academic books depend on other writers reading, interpreting and popularising your research before it reaches the managerial community. They mainly inform other academics of your work, giving them an opportunity to judge its merits and perhaps repeating some of the research.

(3) <u>Research registers</u>. Some organisations (such as government agencies and research funding bodies) publish registers of current and completed research. These usually contain the title of the project, a description of main aims and methods, duration and funding, for current research. Entries for completed research often contain reference to published material derived from the research and areas of potential applicaton. Eligibility for inclusion depends on whether the register is for recipients of research grants from a particular agency, on the field of reseach covered by the register and on other factors specific to the register. One thing is clear: if you do not tell the publisher of the register about your research, it is unlikely to be included. Research registers are mainly referred to by other researchers either before developing research proposals or during their literature search.

(4) <u>Research reports</u>. Research projects should end with a full research report, which may eventually be made publicly available. In addition, progress reports at various stages of the project may be produced. Whilst intended primarily for internal use, they play an important part in the exchange of knowledge between interested parties.

## Developing a publications programme

Many institutes set up their own publishing activities, i.e. to develop a channel of dissemination over which they have direct control. This is not done in competition with other outlets (books, journals), although it may become competitive. Rather, it is complementary. For example, the Publications Division of the Indian Institute of Management, Ahmedabad, was established specifically to facilitate the dissemination of knowledge. It grew from a small case clearing-house, and now not only produces and distributes cases, but also publishes monographs and books written by the staff and offers a reprint facility for articles by staff. The Thames Valley Regional Management Centre in the United Kingdom has established its own imprint, called Thamesman Publications. Its publishing programmes include working papers, occasional papers (based on management research lectures given by invited eminent speakers), monographs (providing thoughtful practical guidance and advice in a particular area) and general publications (produced to a high standard on topics relevant to the work of the Centre, its staff and its clients, and printed externally).

Such publications offer opportunities for the research and ideas of staff and external speakers to become known to an audience specified by the institute. They can be made self-financing by charging realistic prices.

# DEVELOPING THE RESEARCHERS     7

The point was made in chapter 1 that not everyone is capable or interested in doing research. This situation has to be recognised and accepted if a balanced, healthy approach to management development and research is to be maintained. It is unfortunate that so many universities and other institutes insist that all staff <u>must</u> undertake research. If all staff have been selected on this basis, then the insistence is fair. However, many staff are appointed for other, more primary reasons, e.g. they are good teachers or consultants. To force them to do research can cause them to become bad teachers as well as bad researchers. Where an interest is shown in research, by all means develop the capacity to do it. This chapter is concerned with how this can be done.

Our starting-point is an analysis of the requirements of the "good" researcher. We can then apply our knowledge of selection and development approaches. But first, a cautionary note. Generating a research capability and developing competent staff is not easy in some countries. Staff resources are often limited, which implies that research is the last thing that anyone gets around to. There may be, too, a lack of tradition for research in general. If research is not something that educational and other institutes have experience of, then encouraging research in less traditional areas such as management will be difficult. Again, as we have seen before, a problem-centred approach to research may be needed, yet most staff of a calibre to do research will have undertaken a specialist, discipline-based doctoral study. They will, no doubt, wish to pursue their specialist interests. Coupled with small, narrow academic markets and communities, the Ph.D. staff members may be quite isolated from business problems. The end result is that research may be awarded the lowest priority among the key functions of training, consulting, information and documentation and research. Some ways to overcome these problems include:

- identifying the realities of effective management technologies on the local scene;

- having a concerted effort with the institute or between departments and schools to promote research;

- recognising that a commitment to research is necessary, and backing it;

- involving members on training programmes and courses for generating research opportunities;

- spelling out the research needs, capabilities and resources;

- making efforts to integrate research with teaching;

- seeking to attract a highly trained researcher to get things going.

If these efforts are made, then it is much more likely that attempts to develop researchers will pay off. But what sort of person is a competent researcher?

## 7.1 The competent researcher

It is tempting to identify the "competent" researcher by looking at examples - in the fashion of the "great leader" studies. As with leadership, the end result might be a long list of personal attributes which fit all possible situations, or a shorter list which fits only one. Just as leaders emerge for certain situations, so researchers develop in response to certain research opportunities. Certain kinds of researchers seek out particular opportunities. We might, therefore, conclude that it is useless to attempt to identify the "competent" researcher. On the other hand, we can consider the kind of work carried out by researchers, and develop our analysis from there. This approach is adopted here. One word of caution, though: the nature of research work varies and leads to varying competence requirements. The nature of the research work chosen here will reflect the general research role. Specific roles - and hence competencies - may be different.

## The research role

What are researchers expected to do? This may sound a silly question - we have, after all, worked through six chapters of this book assuming an answer. If we know what research is, we surely know what researchers do! This is not necessarily the case. We have for years had definitions of management, yet only recently have academics started to look at what managers actually do. Perhaps a similar study is needed of management researchers. Without such a study, we can establish at least the main elements of the research role from an analysis of the activities of a researcher.

Most researchers start by thinking about a problem or area of interest. In doing so, the researcher is doing conceptual and analytical work based on substantive knowledge of the field, using a creative and inquiring mind. It may demand a capacity to think in a multi-phasic way: to handle at one time diverse and seemingly unrelated ideas. The fruits of this activity represent some form of research problem. Work is then carried out in designing an appropriate method for exploring or researching the problem. This requires a knowledge of research processes, methods and techniques.

Putting the research design into operation is a major activity. It calls upon skill not only in the technical but also in the social aspects of research. People have to be persuaded to take part in research - to talk during interviews, to fill in questionnaires. Access to a company may have to be negotiated before research can begin. Negotiations about research funding may be crucial to the research getting started at all. All these activities depend on certain political, social and interpersonal skills.

The researcher must then collate the information and analyse it, perhaps using sophisticated statistical techniques. Interpretation of the findings will follow, bringing to bear on the data certain judgemental and decision-making capacities. The entire work must be written up, and persuasively communicated to different people - some, no doubt, hostile to the research. Implementation may follow, calling for the further use of social skills and previous experience of the managerial world.

Throughout it all, the researcher must manage time and other resources. Problems, disappointments and frustrations will be experienced, sometimes to such an extent that a desire to give up will be felt. Overcoming, and responding to, these feelings draws upon personal resources of emotional resilience and temperament, backed up by the urge to do research.

Performing such a role makes big demands on a researcher. It requires competence in many areas, some of which do not always fit naturally with each other. The stereotyped example of the introspective, eccentric scientist unable to relate effectively with other people may be an extreme case. It is one, however, to which many researchers approximate in certain of their behavioural characteristics. Most staff can handle the requirements of this complex role, and can be developed to do so. Let us now examine these requirements in detail.

Competence requirements

The foregoing analysis suggests several areas of competence. These can be classified according to their basic similarities.

(1) <u>Knowledge</u>. The researcher must possess knowledge of the substantive research area (e.g. finance, management learning, organisational performance). This is a prerequisite for identifying, analysing and understanding the research problem. He or she will also need a general knowledge of organisational and management thinking and principles. This is "contextual" knowledge on which to anchor the concepts and ideas used in the research. Knowledge of research processes and methods is needed, in order to choose the most appropriate strategies and techniques.

(2) <u>Technical skill</u>. This is needed to carry out research activities. The researcher must analyse problems, use appropriate mathematical techniques, design questionnaires, operate a tape recorder and write reports. Com-

petence makes it possible for the researcher to act. It bridges "knowing" and "doing". Practice is essential to develop the skills.

(3) <u>Conceptual skill</u>. Whilst linked with knowledge, this refers to the mental and intellectual capacities of the researcher. To develop a researchable problem, the researcher needs to think clearly and creatively about concepts and ideas, and to integrate them successfully, to have an inquiring mind, to interpret data and ideas soundly and make judgements about them in relationship to the research problem. We either possess competence in these areas, or we do not. It is difficult to acquire it: it is easy to draw it out and develop it if the potential is there.

(4) <u>Orientation</u>. A member of staff does not become a competent researcher by simply possessing the relevant skill and knowledge. He may feel an urge to do research; a persistence to carry it through with sufficient emotional resilience, an interest in the operational area of the work (e.g. training, managing), which will provide motivation for the research. Such orientations can be identified and encouraged. They are difficult to develop in staff who hold strong opposite views.

(5) <u>Experience</u>. Experience gained prior to carrying out the research forms the base for a project. Researchers often need direct experience (as compared with textbook knowledge) of managerial or organisational work, preferably related to the area which forms the topic for the research. This is particularly important for applied and action research. Then there is a need to have some experience of research itself. This may have been gained through a research training programme or direct involvement in research under the guidance of an experienced supervisor. These two sets of experience (of work and of research) create confidence and competence in carrying out a major project.

(6) <u>Work habits</u>. As with most jobs, research activity can be helped or hindered by certain work habits and practices. For the researcher, the main helpful habits are concerned with being methodical, logical and orderly, paying attention to detail, and organising time and commitments sensibly. Researchers unable to organise data, records, appointments, materials, etc., are likely to face

difficulties. A very competent secretary can help, but a badly organised researcher is likely to forget to tell the secretary about important meetings, schedule dates, and so on. Experience will show the need for sensible work habits: training in the use of diaries, managing time and other people, can help develop the basics.

(7) <u>Behaviour</u>. This is often the effect of the previous requirements. How a researcher behaves - what he does - is influenced by knowledge, skill and orientation. Some of the key behavioural characteristics concern communicating ideas and information to a varied audience, handling with sensitivity and tact personal, social and political relationships, using initiative and being motivated, and seeking out ways to use, apply and develop research findings. Some of these behavioural characteristics can be acquired through training (e.g. interpersonal skills), some through experience (e.g. utilising research), whilst others are really part of the individual's make-up.

Not all researchers will possess these "ideal" characteristics and not all research requires them. The requirements form a core around which others will develop and from which the researcher can select for a given situation. We need to be able to identify their presence or absence.

## 7.2 <u>Identifying the "competent" researcher and research training needs</u>

We shall adapt the characteristics outlined above into a profile and then ask the following basic questions:

(1)  Which characteristics do we require from our researcher?

(2)  To what extent does the person in question possess these characteristics?

A simple way to answer these questions is to use a checklist similar to the one shown in figure 17. In column (R) enter a number, say on a scale of one to four, about the <u>requirements</u> of a research task. In column (P), put numbers that reflect your assessment of the <u>person</u> in question (e.g. an applicant for a research post, a member

**Figure 17  Checklist of main elements of researcher competency**

| Main elements | Required (R) | Possessed (R) |
|---|---|---|
| **Knowledge** <br> 1. Understanding of substantive area <br> 2. Organisation and management background knowledge <br> 3. Background knowledge of research process <br><br> **Technical skill** <br> 4. Identifying/analysing problem situation <br> 5. Technical research skills <br><br> **Conceptual skill** <br> 6. Conceptual creativity and clarity <br> 7. Sound interpretation and judgements <br> 8. Inquiring mind <br> 9. Integration of diverse concepts and ideas <br><br> **Orientation** <br> 10. Persistence <br> 11. Emotional resilience <br> 12. Interest in operational area of research <br><br> **Experience** <br> 13. Managerial work experience <br> 14. Research work experience <br><br> **Work habits** <br> 15. Ordered, logical approach <br> 16. Organisation of time and commitments <br><br> **Behaviour** <br> 17. Communicating ideas and information <br> 18. Personal, social and political skills <br> 19. High motivation <br> 20. Ability to apply research findings | | |
| Rating for both (R) and (P): 1 = not at all; <br> 2 = a little; <br> 3 = moderately; <br> 4 = a great deal. | | |

of staff wishing to do research). The same scale to that used in column (R) can be employed.

If we compare column (R) with column (P), we can judge the likelihood of the person being a competent researcher. See if high scores under (R) are matched by high scores under (P). How many do not match? If the un-matched elements are ones where training can help, a set of research training needs will be identified.

If this exercise is carried out independently by several people, basing the ratings on selection interview data or personal knowledge of the person, a consensus can be reached concerning potential competence and training needs. The judgement will be subjective but will have been reached systematically. This helps avoid the grosser subjective feelings that distort effective decision-making.

## 7.3 Approaches to developing researchers

Approaches to develop competent researchers range from the passive (e.g. reading a book) to the active (e.g. actually carrying out a research project). Several approaches can be used in combination (e.g. reading a book to improve knowledge of research methods, and helping design a project in order to acquire technical skills). The appropriateness of an approach depends on the clear identification of needs. A systematic method, as outlined above, helps pinpoint what can be done. The how can be identified from among the following methods.

### Guided reading

This can be used by staff members who want to undertake research and possess the necessary conceptual skills, work habits and general behavioural attributes, but lack knowledge of research. A colleague experienced in research will be able to point out relevant reading material. This book, together with the sources listed in the bibliography in appendix 1, provides a "self-help" guide to the reader interested in learning about research. Reference to research in the staff member's field will provide more understanding of the design and execution of a research project. Some time spent in a library, working through back issues of relevant journals, will help locate good examples. But reading is not sufficient for developing

ing more than a knowledge and understanding of research. The acquisition of skill requires practice.

Research training seminars and workshops

These can go beyond individual programmes of readings (in terms of developing greater understanding and some skill), but require a group of staff keen to develop a research competence. The <u>seminar approach</u> typically involves an experienced researcher (from within the institute or invited from elsewhere) giving presentations either on research methods generally or on specific research. A presentation on the latter might describe why the research was carried out, how it was designed and executed, what were the major findings, and how the findings are being used. A discussion session should follow. If the institute has a postgraduate research programme, a series of seminars can be based on the students' requirements. Interested staff members should attend. Students who have successfully completed their postgraduate research studies can be invited to discuss their experiences. A typical programme of seminars, based on programmes organised by a number of management institutes, is given in illustration 19. The seminar programme provides for practice in technical aspects of research and has some characteristics of a workshop.

---

Illustration 19: <u>Typical research training seminar programme</u>

Each seminar is led by an experienced member of staff or invited guest speaker. It lasts for approximately three hours. Pre-seminar reading will be given out before each seminar starts.

<u>Aim</u>

The aim of this programme of seminars is to provide an overview of methods and issues in management research and an opportunity to get to grips with the practical aspects of doing research.

Seminar 1 - Introduction to research

The nature of research (e.g. social, economic, in

general); philosophical views and alternative research paradigms; levels of rigour and types of research; stages in the research process; outline of research methods.

Seminar 2 - Identifying the research need and problem

Deciding where to do research; evaluating the problem; translating the "real world" problem into a researchable topic; developing hypotheses or research questions.

Seminar 3 - Designing the research project

Approaches to design (experimental, quasi-experimental, survey-based, and "qualitative" designs); criteria of good design; matching the design with the research problem.

Seminars 4 and 5 - Data collection: The questionnaire

Types of questionnaires, purposes and functions; advantages and disadvantages; development, design and testing; examples of good and bad questionnaires; practice in designing a questionnaire.

Seminars 6 and 7 - Data collection: The interview

Types of interviews, purposes and functions; advantages and disadvantages; stages in the interview; preparing an interview schedule; practice sessions in conducting an interview.

Seminars 8 and 9 - Data collection: observation

Types of observational methods, purposes and functions; advantages and disadvantages; the roles of the observer; use of technical aids (e.g. recording, televising equipment); analysis of examples of research where observation techniques have been used.

Seminar 10 - Data collection: Documentary sources

Types of archival sources of information; limitations of data format; use of content analysis; preparing frameworks and codes for analyses; practice at analysing prepared material.

Seminar 11 - Analysing the data

Methods of data preparation and analysis; role and limitation of statistical tests; testing hypotheses, drawing inferences and making interpretations and judgements.

Seminar 12 - Utility of research

What to do with research findings; the role of research in problem-solving; applying results in teaching, training and consulting; barriers to effective use of research; ethical and political considerations of research and the role of the researcher.

Seminar 13 - Getting down to doing it

Getting the research project off the ground; establishing contacts; gaining access; organising time, commitments and materials; writing a report; communicating the outcomes.

The workshop approach will extend the time devoted to the development of practical skills. Often, the workshop will spread over several days of full-time study and activity. This enables more intensive and time-consuming activities to be undertaken. Workshops of, say, half-day duration can be organised. These will have to be limited to those specific activities which can take place effectively within the time constraints. An example of a workshop is given in illustration 20.

Illustration 20: Typical research training workshop

The workshop sessions will be led by staff and invited guests experienced in research or in the topic of the workshop session. Sessions will consist of lectures on the topic, an opportunity for discussion, and time for practice. Participants are encouraged to prepare and bring with them topics, issues or problems on which they would welcome advice and discussion. Their maximum number will be 12, to allow for maximum participation in an intensive workshop.

AIMS

The workshop will have the following aims:

- to increase understanding of the role and utility of research;

- to improve the knowledge and technical and conceptual skills of participants;

- to contribute to the development of appropriate attitudes and work patterns for pursuing research;

- to increase knowledge of and motivation to use the wider research community networks;

- to enhance the quality and quantity of research output.

DAY 1

0930 - 1030    Introduction to workshop; getting to know each other and each other's interests.

1100 - 1230    Management research and the social sciences: overview of role of research and different approaches (e.g. positivism and phenomenology) to and stages in research; nature of theory and data; epistemology.

1400 - 1530    Designing research investigations: different types of design (e.g. experiment, survey, cross-sectional, longitudinal); criteria of design; examples of good and poor design.

1600 - 1730    Exercise: design of investigation, based on a participant's research problem, in small groups.

Evening        Social gathering.

## DAY 2

| | |
|---|---|
| 0930 - 1030 | Continuation of exercise. |
| 1100 - 1230 | Presentation and criticism of designs produced during the exercise. |
| 1400 - 1530 | Data collection techniques: an overview. |
| 1600 - 1730 | Documentary and historical sources: discussion plus practice at content analysing and interpreting documentary material. |
| 2000 - 2130 | Observation: discussion plus practice using a pre-taped video film of a short management meeting. |

## DAY 3

| | |
|---|---|
| 0900 - 1030 | Interviews: discussion of types and problems; development of a short practice interview schedule. |
| 1100 - 1230 | Practice interviews plus tutor comments. |
| 1400 - 1530 | Questionnaires: presentation of approach to designing questionnaires; illustration through qeustionnaires used in previous research. |
| 1600 - 1730 | Practice design of simple questionnaire, plus discussion. |
| 2000 - 2130 | Talk on establishing and using research community networks. |

## DAY 4

| | |
|---|---|
| 0900 - 1030 | Analysing and interpreting data: an introduction to key approaches. |
| 1100 - 1230 | Practice at using a selected analytical tool or technique under guidance with pre-prepared research data; plus discussion. |

| | |
|---|---|
| 1400 - 1530 | Getting into print: opportunities, approaches and guidelines. |
| 1600 - 1730 | Analysis, in small groups, of particular management research articles (given out in advance for reading), plus discussion. |
| Evening: | Social programme. |

DAY 5

| | |
|---|---|
| 0900 - 1030 | Using research: introductory talk and discussion on needs, problems and factors related to effective research utilisation. |
| 1100 - 1030 | The politics of research: talk and discussion on client-researcher relations, negotiating access, safeguarding client and researcher interests, and how to withdraw from the research situation. |
| 1400 - 1530 | Workshop summing up and participant feedback: discussion of further training requirements and setting of personal action plans. Close of workshop. |

## The apprentice approach

Many workers in industry learn their craft by working as an apprentice to an experienced worker. Where the research training fits (e.g. where skill development and experience are required) and where just one or two people are involved, this is a good way to train researchers. It involves an experienced researcher "taking on" an apprentice, i.e. allowing the inexperienced staff member to join in the research process - watching what is done (e.g. how an interview is conducted), doing certain things (e.g. coding and analysing interview data), taking part in debates on the research and its findings. Combined with guided reading and participation, where possible, in some relevant research training seminars, this approach can develop knowledge, technical and certain conceptual skills, work habits and behaviour, and provide important experiences. It is an on-the-job approach to development.

## Direct research experience

A more intensive on-the-job approach is for the new researcher to undertake a complete research assignment. This form of development is often used in Ph.D. programmes, preceded by a thorough grounding in research methods. Many institutes adopt the programmed, project-based approach to research training at the doctoral level.[1] A different version is known as the "sink or swim", or "throwing in at the deep end" method. If the person does not drown, valuable skills will have been learned. In many circumstances, however, the risk of drowning is too great. It is best usually to combine different on-the-job experiences with prior guided reading and some experienced supervision. In this context, pursuing a higher degree through research has considerable benefits. So too does the setting of a specific development assignment - a piece of research that the institute wishes to have carried out (e.g. a survey of management training needs in local organisations), which can be carried out as a tangible, identifiable and meaningful project. Supervision of the project will be necessary but can be arranged easily. Where several staff members need research training, the project can be designed and managed on a group basis.

## Developing publishing skills

The communication of research findings to a selected target audience is an important means of initiating the research utilisation process. Mostly, we seek to achieve this communication by publishing the results of our research in journals, special reports or books. Doing this effectively requires certain skills which not all staff possess or find easy to acquire. These skills have to do with determining what we want to say, to whom we wish to say it, and in what form it can be said best. There are a number of key steps involved in doing this:

---

[1] Two helpful articles describing this approach are A.J. Lockett and R.D. Witley: "Teaching research skills by the project method: An example from the MBS doctoral programme", in Management Education and Development, 1977, No. 1, pp. 3-9; and D. Allen: "Research and doctoral training in management", in Management Education and Development, Winter 1980, pp. 201-205.

(1) determining the major and minor points of the message to be communicated;

(2) deciding on the audience (e.g. managerial, professional, academic, the population in general);

(3) identifying the most appropriate publishing form, e.g. book or journal; if journal, the relevant type (e.g. academic, professional, popular);

(4) writing, editing, submitting, revising and resubmitting the manuscript.

Each step is critical. None can be omitted or fudged. Many staff find it easy to work through steps (1) to (3), but lack the skills for step (4). Such skills involve setting out a clear structure for the material; marshalling the key material and information before writing commences; writing up the material using whatever language skills are possessed (these can be extended through experience); reviewing the manuscript from an objective standpoint (e.g. discussing it with colleagues); paying attention to detail, especially with regard to the publishing format used by the journal in which it is hoped the article will appear.

A number of institutes have developed writing or publishing workshops to help staff develop these skills. The aim is, usually, to guide the staff member through to the stage of having a manuscript written to a standard suitable for publication. A typical workshop programme is shown in illustration 21.

---

Illustration 21: Workshop on skills in publishing

Communicating the results of research is an important part of the research process. Publishing research findings, especially through journals and magazines, is a common way of achieving this. Certain skills are required by staff who wish to publish. This workshop is open to all staff who wish to develop such skills.

## AIM

- to demonstrate to staff the importance of publishing;

- to provide opportunities to acquire the necessary skills;

- to produce a manuscript in a state ready for submission to a journal editor.

## PROGRAMME

This will comprise three one-day sessions, spaced over three academic terms. Each workshop will be limited to six participants to provide for maximum individual tutoring. Before the workshop starts, participants must have identified an area on which the intended manuscripts will be based. They must also have read the pre-workshop material.

### Session 1 - Getting geared up to publish

This session will cover, on a lecture and discussion basis, the following:

- the needs publishing can satisfy (personal, professional, institutional);

- the process and stages of publishing an article;

- types of journal outlets;

- matching target audience, message and type of journal;

- determining an agreed topic for the development of a manuscript.

During this session, time will be devoted to a critical discussion of previously circulated journal articles, exploring the main message intended by the author, the manner of communicating that message, and the success with which that might have been achieved. Technical writing considerations will be drawn out.

### Inter-session activity

During the eight weeks separating sessions 1 and 2, participants will work on the development of a structure for their proposed articles. These will be typed and circulated to all workshop members and tutors two weeks before the start of session 2.

### Session 2 - Developing the manuscript

This session will be devoted to the presentation, defence and development of the proposed structures. The morning will be spent in plenary session discussing and criticising each structure. During the afternoon, tutors (of whom there will be three in attendance) will provide individual guidance on the development and revision of the structures. They will also discuss the next steps.

### Inter-session activity

During the 16 weeks between sessions 2 and 3, participants will write up their articles along the lines agreed at the end of session 2. Typed, draft manuscripts will be circulated two weeks before session 3 to all participants and tutors.

### Session 3 - Getting ready for publication

Each draft manuscript will be subjected to critical comment by tutors and participants in plenary session. Tutorial guidance will then be given on how the manuscript can be revised and made ready for submission to the chosen journal.

### Post-session activity

Participants will revise their articles and submit to journal editors. Copies of submitted articles should be made available to participants and tutors. The outcomes of the submissions will be monitored. If necessary, a fourth session will be arranged at which participants can report on successes, problems and failures and discuss further action.

> Workshop reading
>
> Participants will find the following references to be of help in thinking about and preparing their manuscripts: J. Barzum and H. Graff: <u>The modern researcher</u> (New York, Harcourt Brace Jovanovich, 1977), 377 pp.; and E. Harman and I. Montagress (eds.): <u>The thesis and the book</u> (Toronto, Toronto University Press, 1976), 88 pp. Sections on writing up research can be found in many of the general research methods texts. It is not essential that participants refer to these before the start of the workshop. They should at some time locate and browse through such texts.

## 7.4 Writing the research report

An important skill which every researcher must possess or should acquire is that of writing the research report. The research report is, more often than not, the <u>base from which other forms of dissemination develop</u>. It is the primary vehicle for carrying the results of the research project from the researcher to the client. The form of the report will, of course, vary with the nature of the client. If the client is an academic body or academic research funding organisation, the report may be expected to be written in conceptual terms, using appropriate "jargon" and statistical techniques. For the managerial audience, the report will usually be shorter, more punchy, concentrating on major outcomes and their implications rather than finer theoretical points. Sometimes, the audience will comprise both; in such cases either two reports are written or the report is structured and written in such a way that the major findings come over easily and clearly early on in the report, with back-up details and discussion on statistical and conceptual analysis. Some clients want the report in a format specific to their own requirements. This is especially so of some government departments. Other clients will be happy to receive the report in any format, provided it is clear and meaningful. Usually, it is best to discuss with the client the format of the report before starting to write it.

The nature of the reports will also vary according to their <u>purpose</u>. A <u>progress report</u> may be quite short and give only the barest of details. It will describe what has been done and what remains to be done, and say whether the research plan and targets will be achieved. It may also discuss any problems encountered, how these were overcome, or how they affected the research project and its findings. An <u>end of project report</u> is more complete and fully describes what was done and what was found. The body of the text should contain only material central to the key argument being advanced. Subsidiary detail should be relegated to appendices. For major projects, where a great mass of detail has been accumulated, it may be necessary to split the report into volumes. The first volume should contain the key arguments and data; the second, all the subsidiary data not crucial to but supportive of the major findings.

## Contents of main reports

Here too, practice varies. Whilst the sequence of presentation may vary according to the audience, all main reports should contain the following (known as the logical structure).

(1) <u>Title page</u> - bearing the name of the institute and of the client, the full title of the report (which should be neither too long nor too short but contain sufficient key words to describe the research), the name of the author(s), and the date. If the report is to be confidential, or subject to copyright, this must be clearly stated.

(2) <u>Abstract</u> - a short (two pages or so) summary of the overall report. One way of producing the abstract is to describe in one paragraph each major section of the report.

(3) <u>List of contents</u> - a statement of what appears where, with sections or chapters coming first, followed by lists of tables, charts, illustrations, appendices, bibliography. Each should give sufficient information for the reader accurately to locate a particular section or subsection, table or appendix. In long reports, the list of contents may take on the form of an index so that the reader does not wander aimlessly looking for key material.

(4) <u>Introduction</u> - a statement of the key objectives of the research and the background. The latter should contain the reasons or interest for pursuing the research and acknowledgements to those people who have influenced it or taken part in it. In some reports, it may be better to have a separate acknowledgements section, especially if the list is long. This should appear after the abstract.

(5) <u>Review of literature</u> - this does not always form part of the report, particularly if the report is for a business client. However, little management research stands on its own. There is nearly always something relevant to draw on. Where there is not, it is important to say so. In this case, this section may be quite short but should contain sources of material and information referred to.

(6) <u>Methods used</u> - this section must state clearly what was done and how it was done. This is important. If other researchers are to follow up the work or replicate it, they must know in detail the methods and techniques employed. If such information is not given, doubt may be cast on the validity of your findings, or even whether they are real!

(7) <u>Findings/results</u> - probably the longest section of the report, containing an organised logical presentation and discussion of the major research results. This section presents and explains the data but does not draw conclusions from them. It should be organised to help the reader relate the findings to the various stages and methods employed in the research design. Data included should only be those that are important in helping the reader understand the problem and hypothesis, and findings. All other data should be given in appendices, and clearly referred to. Tables should be presented as close as possible to the relevant descriptive material, and numbered in sequence. Discuss each key point or finding (or set of related findings) in a separate subsection. The tables can follow each subsection.

(8) <u>Implications and conclusions</u> - a discussion of the meaning of the research findings, e.g. for managers, for management trainers, etc. It should contain no new evidence and no new references to the literature, except where the latter confirms or denies implications and con-

clusions reached. It must contain a statement of the key inferences (inductions or deductions) drawn from the findings. These should be related quite clearly to the original problem, hypothesis or theoretical formulation.

(9) <u>Recommendations</u> - a statement of future actions which, in the researcher's opinion, might be worth pursuing. They may concern future research, the development of theory, or the practice of management in relation to the problem studied. In certain cases, e.g. where the project has studied a particular business problem, it may be preferable not to present recommendations, but to use the report as the basis of a seminar or workshop with the client in order to produce mutually agreed, acceptable and workable recommendations. If alternative actions are proposed, some evaluation of each will be needed.

(10) <u>Summary</u> - where an abstract is used, a summary may not be necessary. Where it is, it should contain a brief, clear statement of the major findings, conclusions and recommendations. It should stand on its own and not need support from the rest of the report.

(11) <u>Appendices</u> - should include all complex tables, statistical texts, primary data, supporting documents (e.g. questionnaire), forms used, fieldwork guide notes, etc. Interested readers can then pursue their scrutiny of the report to a much more detailed level.

(12) <u>Bibliography</u> - if the study makes use of other people's work or secondary sources of information, a bibliography will be required. This should not take the place of footnotes used within the report, which can give additional information or explanation about another study. The material should be presented in alphabetical order by author's name, and date order for each author where more than one piece of work is cited. Sometimes it may be desirable to number each entry, and use numbers only in the text. Or the text reference could be of the form "Smith (1982)". The reader can then readily look this up in the bibliography.

<u>Other formats</u>

There are other formats for writing research reports, apart from this so-called logical format. There is the psychological format where the logical approach is reversed. The conclusions and recommendations come first (after the introduction) and the findings are presented later. This an arrangement widely used in what might be called popular reports, e.g. for business clients. Typical contents of a popular report would be:

- title-page,
- list of contents,
- research project objectives,
- methods used,
- conclusions and recommendations,
- findings,
- appendices.

This style is simple, clear and free of jargon and complicated statistics.

A third approach is what might be called the chronological or historical format. Here, the report is organised along the time sequence or historical dimension of the study. Because research does not always proceed in an orderly way, such reports can cause confusion. There is also the difficulty of pulling together important data or themes. Because of these problems, this is the least desirable report format to use.

Principles of effective report writing

Writing the report is more than knowing what to put in it and in which order. It is also concerned with how to write it. This is a much more difficult problem to tackle because styles vary from one language to another, from one culture to another. There are, however, some general points that should be borne in mind:

Make sure all the data are to hand. Nothing stops the flow of writing more than the lack of organised data at a crucial point in the report. By the time you have found the missing data, you may have lost the theme or argument you were following.

<u>Have a clear report structure in mind</u>. You cannot just sit down and write a report. You need a structure - a title plus section headings and subheadings. List these on a piece of paper, then check that you have sufficient information or material to write up each section. If you don't, go and get it. Fill out each subsection with key contents. This makes writing easier.

<u>Follow a logical, or simplistic, procedure</u>. The logical procedure requires that the earlier sections be written first. This makes sense if you have the material in a logical, sequential manner. If you don't, write up whatever sections you have material for, treating each one separately. This is the simplistic approach. You will then need to edit and rewrite thoroughly to make sure the report hangs together, with the necessary cross-referencing.

<u>Follow the "write - revision - rewrite" process</u>. The first draft will seldom be satisfactory. Pass it on to a few colleagues and ask for their views on it. Where key points emerge, revise the appropriate sections, edit the rest and rewrite as appropriate. If necessary, revise the structure. First attempts tend to be poor - all drafts can be improved. There must, however, be a limit - all reports can be endlessly rewritten. One edit and rewrite is usually sufficient.

<u>Be clear and simple</u>. Lengthy, wordy reports full of jargon are a bore to read. The reports that achieve greatest impact are those that make their point and present their findings simply and intelligibly. Sometimes it is difficult to avoid using conceptual labels (or jargon). This is fine, as long as simpler words do not exist. If they do, and the conceptual tags are important, use both to get the meaning clear. Break up the text with diagrams, illustrations and tables - a report containing nothing but words can be tedious to read.

<u>Seek help</u>. There will usually be others around with experience of writing reports. Seek their help. If there is no one around, consult some of the excellent literature that exists. There is much to be gained from a single review of appropriate texts on writing reports.

7.5 Careers in research

Many management institutions are unable to develop research because they lack career opportunities and career structures for researchers. With the exception of large research centres, few opportunities exist for a progressive research career. Research work is characterised by short-term contracts, uncertainty over future employment, lack of continuity between contracts and projects, low organisational status and pressure to move into teaching or other posts which offer more job security. Staff carrying out research on different contractual terms face different pressures and problems. Let us examine some of these problems.

Contract researchers

Staff are often appointed to help carry out a project (under guidance from an experienced supervisor), for a period of time with financial support from an external body. Their work ends when the contract expires. Employment, therefore, is erratic and career progression difficult, unless they are able to move to better-paying, more senior posts elsewhere. The institution can offer employment and career progression only if it can secure funds (internally or externally) for further projects. This poses problems of timing: it is difficult to secure external funding to start a second project the day after completion of the first. This can be eased if the institution can set aside some of its own financial resources in a research fund. Even with such continuity and bridging support, contract researchers rarely have a sensible career structure and progression. Sooner or later the funds will be exhausted and they must either leave or secure a permanent post which usually takes them away from research.

Research assistants

Some institutions provide for research within their range of permanent posts usually by appointing a research assistant to carry out research under the guidance of a member of staff. Such posts are often treated as "trainee lectureships": indeed, the research assistant may be required to teach _and_ do research. Since both activities are usually new experiences, the researcher feels competing pressures in deciding which should have priority. Because career progression is normally through teaching, research suffers. This results in poor research and frustrated research assistants. There is a need to develop a research career structure parallel with the lecturing structure, with cross-over possibilities built in so that staff are not trapped in one or the other. This may be easier to achieve in academic institutions than in other management institutions.

Staff also doing research

A third form of research staffing is where members of staff, who are usually in permanent positions, carry out research as part of their work. Career and promotion issues will arise if research and publishing are not considered important criteria. Where teaching, training, consulting and administration are given greater weight, staff will not pursue research-based careers. Research is no soft option to teaching or administration, yet the promotion criteria adopted by some institutes make it look as if it is. Excellence on several dimensions may be required to justify promotion; the dimensions used should be at least open to discussion, with a degree of choice as to, say, which three out of five will be used. Good research should be rewarded in the same way as good teaching or good administration. If research is to be encouraged, it must be seen to count for something and to be rewarded. If it is not, staff will either be reluctant to pursue research, or will indulge in only that form of research which has direct personal appeal.

Career structures

Different countries, and different training sectors and institutes within a country, will develop career structures to suit their own needs. Some will not bother; others will recognise the problems but only pay lip service to their solution. It is possible, however, to develop a general career structure for researchers as follows:

Level 1 - junior researcher - comprising

        (i) research officer, appointed on short-term contract,

(ii) research assistant, appointed on normal establishment, but initially on a two-year probationary period.

Level 2 – <u>researcher</u>, such as research associate, appointed either as permanent member of staff or on three-to-five-year contract. Junior researchers would be able to move up to this level, subject to satisfactory reviews.

Level 3 – <u>senior researcher</u>, such as associate or fellow, appointed on permanent or normal contractual basis; a person of considerable research experience.

Level 4 – <u>principal researcher</u>, such as reader, on permanent appointment; exhibiting considerable research and research management skills as well as a growing reputation.

Level 5 – <u>chief researcher</u>, at head of department or professorial level, with responsibilities for initiating, developing and managing research and setting research and academic policy.

Staff would be able to be promoted from level 1 through to level 5, subject to posts being available and to being judged satisfactorily against the relevant criteria. It is possible to allow for transfers from this structure to the same or more senior level on the normal lecturer/trainer/consulting structure.

Designing, installing and operating such a structure is not easy. Problems of compatibility, fairness, equity and comparability arise. These can be managed and are preferable to the difficulties faced when no proper structure exists. Benefits will accrue: researchers will see the possibility of achieving long-term goals that characterise most research, leading to higher levels of commitment and motivation; research that cannot be finished within the project period will not be left uncompleted; researchers will be able to concentrate on writing up and disseminating research findings rather than on looking for another job; senior colleagues will spend less time recruiting researchers, good researchers can be encouraged to stay; and, above all, research will stand a chance of becoming more than a political and financial football - it may come to be recognised for the key, important part it can and does play in achieving the goals of management education, training and development.[1]

---

[1] This seems to be clearly recognised by a number of management institutes. See, for example, S. Alvi: "An overview of research for management training", in <u>Pakistan Management Review</u>, Second quarter 1980, pp. 83-90.

# CONCLUSION: GUIDELINES FOR ACTION    8

We have come a long way from our initial questions about "Why bother with research?" We have looked at the research process and at management research; described how to assess what to research; explained some important methods of carrying out research; considered how research can best organised; analysed the ways of effectively using the results of research; and discussed methods for developing researchers. In the final analysis, however, it all depends on the institutional context within which you are trying to develop research and to disseminate and use its results.

## 8.1 Some conclusions concerning policy

Carrying out research can be a lonely activity in an institution where little research is under way and where there are few other researchers with whom to talk. Most other staff will have their own work to get on with: classes to teach, training programmes to run, meetings to attend, consulting assignments to finish, and so on. The researcher may not share any of these. Even the project supervisor may have little time to spend in discussion with the researcher. Results can take months or years to achieve, and in the process of reaching them, there is the isolation that occurs when getting down to the detailed slog of analysing data. All this can add up to feelings of loneliness, frustration and a desire to quit.

The institutional context - the researcher's working environment - is all-important in promoting an atmosphere, a culture, conducive to good research. Researchers share similar motivational requirements to all of us. They want to know that others in the institute not only recognise they exist but also regard them and their work as important; they need to talk over ideas and problems; they need contacts and friendly working relations; they want to know how they are doing. In short, they need the kind of feedback and stimulation to do a good job that most other people need.

Creating an environment that is conducive to effective research is not easy; neither is it impossible. Research into organisational behaviour, structures and contexts has provided some important pointers on how to achieve a supportive, constructive and motivating environment.

Commitment at the top

It is essential that research is seen to be supported by those in charge of the institution. It must form part of the overall philosophy and policy for its work. Lip service is not enough. Staff must know that a genuine commitment is given to supporting relevant research. There must be a policy and an objective for research. Without these, it will develop in an aimless, wandering way.

Identification of key people

The commitment must be translated into tangible effects, i.e. something that staff can actually see as a result of the institute's policy towards research. A highly visible and effective way of lending credence to research policy is to appoint a senior member of staff to take charge of research. Such a person will perform the "boundary spanning role" referred to earlier, and provide a natural focal and contact point for researchers. He or she will be responsible for developing research and providing the momentum for continuing it. The identification with research of a senior member of staff is an important means of developing a supportive research atmosphere.

Integrating processes

Research often develops in isolation from the main activities of the institute. This may be healthy for the growth of research for its own sake but damaging to the

creation of an integrated set of activities within a
management institution. Certain organisational arrangements (e.g. appointment of research staff to existing
units) will help better integration than do others (e.g.
establishing a separate research unit). If research is to
be organisationally separated, as discussed in chapter 5,
then specific integrating methods will be called for.
These include regular seminars or programmes; involving
staff members in steering committees for research projects; staff memberships on the institute's research committee; staff participation in research projects; allocat-
ing time for staff to carry out research. Whatever organisational arrangements exist, these methods will help
ensure that research is seen as an important part of the
whole portfolio of activities.

Relevant resources

It is easy to pay lip service to the need for research. It is less easy to take the necessary action to
bring it into being. Appointing researchers requires
financial resources. Some institutes stop at this. It is a
mistake, and one that is likely to waste staff. If the job
is to be done properly, researchers require a place to
work in peace and quiet; easy access to a telephone; secretarial and technical support services; research information sources via a well-equipped library; access to computing facilities, and so on. These support services are
essential if researchers are to do research: without them,
the researcher becomes a wasting - and frustrated - asset.

Feedback and recognition

People like to know where they stand and how they are
doing. Researchers are people, and share these needs.
Regular reviews of progress, combined with advice on
future plans and comment on achievement to date, help form
supportive attitudes about research and its role in the
institute. Where such reviews emphasise the implications
of the research findings for the work of the institute,
research staff become more conscious of the need for
application and utilisation. Encouraging the use of research in designing training programmes, for example,
gives meaning and relevance to its pursuit.

Regular review of research policy

The establishment of a research policy should not be treated as a once-only event. If it is so treated, staff may take it for granted: worse, they may ignore it altogether, thus bringing it into apathetic disrepute. It will be seen only as a token gesture to the political expedience of being able to say "Yes, of course we have a policy for research." Experienced policy-makers recognise that real policies may have to change to take account of changing circumstances. Thus, a policy for getting research started will not be appropriate later when a vigorous research activity has been generated. Policies must be reviewed, they must be seen to be reviewed and, preferably, staff should be involved in the review process. Such an involvement will not only breathe life into the policy but produce energy for its effective implementation.

## 8.2 How to improve dissemination and application

However hard we try to improve the dissemination and use of research findings, there is always room for further improvement. Experience of recent years suggests a number of possible areas where improvements could be made or specific action taken. The list presented here represents some thoughts on the kinds of actions that may be needed. It is not assumed that all management institutes and countries will be found wanting in these respects. The list will, it is hoped, provide some stimulus to thinking about what is needed and why.

More pragmatic journals

Often there is a need for translators of academic research output into managerial language. A "Harvard Business Review" type journal may be needed, based upon a well-known and accepted research institution, and supplemented by existing pragmatic journals. A "Management Research Digest" sponsored by a professional body, employers' organisation and national research foundation would have a credible appeal. In developing regions, such journals may be established as regional since most smaller countries may be unable to afford one. In addition, a regional journal helps to transfer experience and research findings among countries.

More specific use of research in teaching

Managers taking MBA courses should be more exposed to the nature and output of management research than is often the case. Some teachers do this, but many peers simply present concepts and principles with little research foundation. Validating bodies might be urged to consider this as an important criterion for approving courses where it is currently not employed. In nonqualifying courses (short programmes, in-company training), a subtle introduction of research output might encourage more managers to become interested in using research.

More direct funding of research

Industry and government can influence the utilisation of research by providing more financial support for applied developmental work. In some countries, special funding is made available. Whilst such initiatives are welcome, they only scratch the surface of a very large pond. A planned programme of applied research in important areas of work, linked with credible academics, could be of significance.

Organisational innovations

Research on knowledge utilisation shows that organisations which innovate are those that use knowledge effectively. Internal utilisation teams backed by a strong R and D function and involving members of the academic and managerial communities achieve successful research-based innovations. The stages usually involve diagnosis of need; awareness of research outputs; selection or adaptation of solutions; pilot implementation, evaluation and decision; full-scale implementation; and institutionalisation (or disappearance). We need to develop ways of encouraging such approaches to innovation.

Greater use of the action research approach

As we have seen, action research involves both researcher and client working on problems, using research data as it is generated to improve the functioning of the organisation. This is much more likely to produce real action than research which ends in a report that may contain recommendations for action.

## Cluster grouping approach to research

Better application and use of research appears to be achieved where management centres organise research on a group basis. This affords opportunities for knowledge-seeking and knowledge-applying research to coexist and develop from common problems. It provides a basis for developing a knowledge and resource base linked with teaching and consultancy, and for initiating participative research with the managerial community.

## Joint seminars and conferences

Some institutes bring academics and managers together to discuss research findings and issues, but not methods and processes. Such events are easy to organise, do not require vast funds, and result in useful interaction and exchange. It is an important mechanism for helping to transfer knowledge.

## Utilisation teams

Several centres can set up "utilisation teams". Such teams might require external funding over a long period of time (at least five years). The teams would identify specific areas of valid knowledge and seek to push this through the R and D stream into practice. This provides a broad frontal attack on the problem. The teams need to involve members of the organisations willing to take part in the work. Members should preferably be regular teaching and research staff - not brought in. Where possible, a participative and collaborative approach should be adopted, using managers as researchers in order to improve the chances of the research getting used.

## A national forum

A means of encouraging research is to establish a national forum for research utilisation. Key professional, academic, industrial and research funding bodies are powerful forces for bringing about and sustaining such a forum. Its form should not be prejudged, but one option is to set up an institute for management research to fund and encourage applied research. It would organise study groups around the country, comprising academics, professionals and managers, to examine areas and potential for utilisation. It would bridge the two communities.

> Illustration 22: **Qualities of professional behaviour**
>
> 1. Focuses on the problem-solving approach to consulting and change; guided by data, not hunches.
>
> 2. Helps develop independence in others, and does not foster dependency.
>
> 3. Is able to "practise what is preached" in the field of his or her specialised knowledge.
>
> 4. Diagnoses situations rather than merely treating symptoms.
>
> 5. Possesses sufficient self-understanding so that personal considerations do not get in the way of helping.
>
> 6. Is able to communicate in an open fashion.
>
> 7. Admits mistakes and learns from failure.
>
> 8. Has developed interest and skill in working with people in a non-controlling manner.
>
> 9. Is willing to experiment and innovate.
>
> 10. Has developed a personal philosophy about working and about developing people.
>
> 11. Is capable of saying "I don't know", and is willing to learn and to change.
>
> ------------------------------------------------------------
>
> Taken from G.L. Lippitt: "Evaluating consulting services", in _Consultation_, Fall 1981. See also M. Kubr (ed.): _Managing a management development institution_ (Geneva, International Labour Office, 1982), Ch. 4.

<u>Becoming more professional</u>

Researchers will have to become more professional,

not only at doing research but in handling organisational problems. The qualities of the actionoriented researcher are different from those of the academically remote researcher. Illustration 22 suggests some of these qualities.

A study of utilisation

It may be appropriate for some systematic work to be done on the use of management research. A useful start could be made by seeking out innovations, changes and applications directly or indirectly deriving from research, exploring the effectiveness with which this happens and identifying the causal factors. Such research would also throw light on the principles put forward earlier in this section. It may be necessary for a research funding body to take an initiative in this field in order to make any headway.

8.3 How to use this book to improve research in your institution

A guide such as this can only go so far in helping to improve research. It can generate enthusiasm; it can add to knowledge and understanding of research and its methods; it might generate ideas for research topics, or for organising research; it will give guidance on how to do things. What it cannot do is to actually do any of these things for you. You and your staff need to get the action going. This book can be used as part of this process. It can form the background reading and basis for workshops or seminars aimed at generating or enhancing a research capacity.

But clearly not everyone will approach this task from the same starting-point. Some staff and institutes will need to go further than others. There are at least four major, different starting-points:

1. Starting from zero, in a situation where no research is taking place and no staff have research competence. In such a situation, someone senior must have the enthusiasm to get research started. He needs to acquire or develop some competence in the staff of the institute.

2. Starting with some competence, in a situation where there is no research but one or two staff members

have acquired research competence elsewhere. An enthusiastic senior staff member is still necessary but now has some material with which to start work. He now has to identify appropriate projects and get the staff interested.

3. <u>Starting with a base</u>, where some staff have some competence and are doing a little research. Here the requirements are to expand both competence and research, and ensure that it is organised effectively. There will be a need, also, to look to the effective dissemination and use of research findings.

4. <u>Maintaining a highly developed capacity</u>, where the research competence is high and well spread among staff, and research is of good quality and quantity. The main needs in such a situation will be to improve the effective dissemination of findings. There will also be a need to develop new staff as they join the institute, but this should pose few problems.

Whatever the particular starting point, chapter 7 ("Developing the researchers") should be used as a basis for designing any proposed workshop, seminar or developmental activity. The rest of the guide can then be used selectively, subject to the starting-point. For example, if you are starting from zero, most chapters will be relevant (apart from chapter 7) for those undergoing the development activities. Thus, if a workshop is proposed, each chapter could form the basis of a session. Read before the session, the ideas in the chapter can be isolated and picked up in discussion and practice sessions. For example, chapter 1 ("Why bother with research?") could precede a session during which a discussion took place on the needs for and purposes of research in the institute. Reaching agreement on these would prove a valuable starting-point. Similarly with chapter 2, and so on, working progressively through the guide. The sessions can be concentrated within a full-time period or spread out over time, offered on a half-day or full-day basis. The latter, i.e. part-time, approach would allow the training and development to be integrated with the other work and responsibilities of participants. This might help bring about a more supportive attitude towards research.

The following table provides a summary of material in the book which might be relevant to workshops related to each of the major starting points.

| MAJOR STARTING-POINT | RELEVANT CHAPTER | | | | | | | |
|---|---|---|---|---|---|---|---|---|
| | 1 | 2 | 3 | 4 | 5 | 6 | 7 | 8 |
| (1) From zero | * | * | * | * | * | * | * | * |
| (2) Some competence | * | * | * | - | * | * | * | * |
| (3) From base | | | * | | * | * | * | - |
| (4) Maintaining capacity | | | * | | | * | * | - |

Knowing roughly your starting-point, read along the appropriate row and identify the chapters that are asterisked. Build these into the design of the workshop. A typical workshop for those starting from zero is suggested in illustration 23.

---

Illustration 23: <u>Workshop on how to improve research</u>

<u>Pre-workshop reading</u>: Introduction, chapters 1 and 3.

<u>Session 1 (1 1/2 hours)</u>: Discussion on needs for and purposes of research in the institute. Agree either set of relevant needs and purposes or a means of identifying them (e.g. via visits to companies, or a survey).

<u>Pre-session reading</u>: Chapter 2.

Session 2
(1 1/2 hours): Discuss and agree generally type or form of research most relevant to your institute and to the needs and purposes identified in session 1.

Pre-session
reading: Chapter 4.

Session 3
(1 1/2 hours): Review, explain and discuss different research methods.

Session 4
(1 1/2 - 3
hours): Practice session at designing an investigation, based on a proposed piece of research, preferably by one of the workshop participants.

Further sessions can be devoted to the design of investigations if sufficient workshop participants have reached this stage (see also chapter 7).

Pre-session
reading: Chapter 5.

Session 5
(1 1/2 hours): Discuss and agree upon way in which research in the institute is to be organised.

Pre-session
reading: Chapter 6.

Session 6
(3 hours): Discuss methods for disseminating research findings and getting them used. Analyse and criticise some past examples. Agree on an action plan appropriate to your institute.

Pre-session
reading: Chapters 7 and 8.

| Session 7 (1/12 - 3 hours): | Discuss and agree further development requirements and institutional support. Produce set of recommendations. |
|---|---|

In these ways, it should be possible to develop an institutional setting in which research will have its rightful place and where the development of researchers will be seen and known to be as important as any other form of staff development. In such an environment, the effective integration of research with training and consulting can take place, so as to maximise the use of scarce resources and gain mutual benefit from each other. In particular, research will become practically useful and will gain the practitioner's respect. Let us remember the price we pay for not tackling real-world problems in favour of poor academic philosophising, as ably summed up by Gardner:

> "The society which scorns excellence in plumbing as a humble activity and tolerates shoddiness in philosophy because it is an exalted activity will have neither good plumbing nor good philosophy. Neither its pipes nor its theories will hold water."[1]

---

[1] Quoted from B.M. Bass: "The substance and the shadow", in *American Psychologist*, 1974, Vol. 29, No. 12a, pp. 870-886.

# Appendix 1
# Annotated bibliography

1. Introduction

The literature on research methods and related topics in the management field is characterised by a paradoxical feature. On the one hand, there is a vast amount of literature to draw upon; yet, on the other, there is very little which is specifically addressed to management research. This may be because there is no identifiable activity which could be termed "management research". For the management student or staff researcher, this can cause frustrations. Combing the considerable amount of literature on social science research methodology for relevant texts and guides can lead to many blind alleys. Wasted time and effort, that could be put to good effect in developing the research itself, is begrudged. This bibliography should help reduce some of the difficulties. It is not exhaustive, yet contains over 110 entries. It is only a selection from the many texts and other sources which exist. Certain criteria have guided the selection. These are:

- in general, the material should be of recent origin (most of the texts have been published within the last ten years);

- most should have been seen by the author, in order that reasonable and fair descriptions may be given;

- most should have been selected at random from library shelves and reading lists;

- some would have a personal appeal for the author.

Because of the nature of the field covered, this bibliography can never be 100 per cent accurate, or complete - it is seminal rather than terminal.

2. Structure and use

No one structure can meet all the needs which might put it to the test. There are too many ways in which management and research can be classified for a "one best approach" to be possible. The structure used here has been devised in an attempt to guide readers to sources which may help meet their needs and queries. Typically, such questions as "What is research all about?", "What are the methods of research?", "Which methods are relevant to a particular area or subject?", "How can research be organised?", "How can the results of research be best used?", "Where can further information be obtained?", are raised by staff and students starting out on research. The structure adopted here should enable relatively easy access to literature relevant to these questions. This structure comprises the following:

- <u>brief review of key areas</u>

    - philosophy of science and research

    - methods and techniques of research by subject or area of interest

    - organising and planning research

    - effectiveness and utilisation of research

    - information sources

    - report writing.

- <u>alphabetical annotated bibliography</u> (by author) to some of the key material, related to the brief reviews and giving further details of what each source covers.

- <u>references to other material known to exist</u> but not seen and therefore not annotated.

It is recommended that readers commence using the bibliography with a quick reading of the brief reviews. This will highlight texts which may be of use to them. Reference can then be made to the annotated entries to establish more clearly the fit between needs and content. In this way, a minimum amount of search time and effort will be required. Needless to say, the author is not able to accept responsibility for texts acquired not meeting readers' needs. Differences of view and perspective are bound to lead to different judgements. This bibliography should, however, point people in the right direction.

## 3. Brief review of key areas

This section provides in brief some pointers to the directions readers might take in looking for help. It is not exhaustive, nor are the subsections mutually exclusive. The available texts overlap quite considerably in the topics they cover. The aim here is to provide some stepping-stones through the considerable mire of material.

### Philosophy of science and research

Many texts on research methods start with a discussion of the nature and philosophy of scientific endeavour. A good example is Helmstadter (1970). Such texts are helpful in providing a general backcloth or context to the role of research in developing scientific knowledge. They will not be adequate for those who wish to pursue in depth a study of the different philosophical perspectives in science and research. For these, a wealth of material exists. There are the classics, among them Popper (1963) and Kuhn (1970) for whom the great debate has partly been about the nature of verifiable (or valid) knowledge, i.e. when is an idea rejected - or "protected"?

These two have dominated recent discussions on the philosophy of science, as evidenced by Sparkes (1981). Others enjoy perhaps a more humble but no less useful place in philosophical thinking. Thus, for example, Diesing (1972) has something to say on methods in the philosophy of science; Evered and Louis (1981) bring us closer to the issues which affect organisational research; Handy (1964) addresses some of the philosophical and epistemological issues in behavioural science research and Herbst (1970) focuses on "behavioural worlds"; Hughes (1980) contrasts positivist and humanist approaches to social research; Reason and Rowan (1981) present arguments for the so-called "qualitative" philosophies; whilst Wilson (1972) gives a personal view of philosophy and educational research, and Zinman (1968) looks at the meaning of science. These, and others, provide a range of interesting discussions on issues connected with and insights into the nature, meaning and philosophy of science and research. In many senses, these issues and insights are rather neatly captured by Barnes (1979), who discusses privacy and ethics in social science research. This little book looks at whether people should have to answer questions about their private lives; what happens to the information so given; and who can use it and for what purposes. It puts into perspective many of the more "erudite" discussions on the philosophy of science.

Methods and techniques

General. A very good introductory text that is geared to business research is Rummel and Ballaine (1963). Others, such as Madge (1953), Beveridge (1961), Blalock (1970 - a good "primer"), Rosen and West (1973), Johnson (1975) and Seltiz et al. (1976) provide varying degrees of coverage. For fairly detailed descriptions, Helmstadter (1970), Diesing (1972), Kerlinger (1973), Emory (1976), Bailey (1978) and Clover and Balsley (1979) are useful sources. Kerlinger's book is particularly detailed, and not for the novice. For texts geared specifically to the business field, refer to those by Bailey, and Clover and Balsley, as well as Rummel and Ballaine.

Scientific method experimental design. Many texts (e.g. Bailey) describe the so-called positivistic, "objective" method of research. There are chapters on it in, for example, Clover and Balsley - chapters 2 and 4; Helmstadter - chapter 4; Kerlinger - chapter 23; and Madge - chapter 5. More comprehensive treatments are to be found in Campbell and Stanley (1966), Evan (1971), Goldstein (1979) - and for specific longitudinal studies of child development, Vroom (1971) and Zinman (1968). The article by House (1970) on scientific investigation is useful. A statistical treatment of experiments can be found in Box, Hunter and Hunter (1978).

Qualitative research. Again a number of general texts discuss qualitative research methods (for example, Helmstadter discusses historical research methods). This particular approach to research has attracted much attention in recent years and there now exist several texts which address the relevant methods and techiques. Good introductions are given by Bogdan and Taylor (1975) and Erikson and Norsanchuck (1977). Useful follow-up texts are those by Douglas (1976) and Webb et al. (1966). Phillips (1973) discusses the need/arguments for abandoning method, whilst Turner (1974) goes into ethnomethodology - neither text is for the beginner. The "classic" text is that of Glaser and Strauss (1967) which describes "grounded theory": a more recent book, probably to become the "new classic", is that by Reason and Rowan (1981), which provides a comprehensive set of readings/chapters by different authors.

Survey methods. Numerous sources exist, including the general texts (see, for example, Clover and Balsley - chapters 5, 6 and 7; Helmstadter - chapter 3; Kerlinger - chapter 24; and Madge - chapter 4, part C). A very good introduction is given by Oppenheim (1967) - Weisberg and Bowen (1977) and Hoinville and Jowell (1977) are also introductory but more comprehensive. Tull and Albaum (1973) present a "decisional" approach to survey work. A more recent and well-written guide for practitioners is by Reeves and Harper (1981) - also produced, in different format, as a student project manual. For more experienced survey researchers, the books by Belson (1981) and Schuman and Presser (1981) will be found helpful. Cook et al. (1981) provide descriptions of many approaches to the measurement of work experience.

Statistical analysis. There exists a wide range of texts from which to make a choice. As well as basic, general texts, there are those based on specific areas of work - e.g. marketing, psychology. Selecting appropriate material depends upon the subject area being researched and the researcher's current level of knowledge and skill in statistics. Many of the general research books contain chapters on analysis and statistical methods - Clover and Balsley, Bailey and Kerliner, have several. Researchers and staff with little knowledge of statistics would do well to start with basic texts, such as Langley (1970), Plews (1979) and Rowntree (1981). A good introductory book, which requires a basic level of mathematical knowledge, is Moore (1969). More specialised treatments are given by Bennett and Bowers (1976), on multivariate techniques; Camines and Zeller (1980), on reliability and validity; Caulcott (1973), on significance texts; Goldstein (1979), on longitudinal studies (but mainly for child development research); Irvine, Miles and Evans (1979), on social statistics; Nie, Bent and Hull (1970), on the statistics package for the social sciences; Schiffman, Reynolds and Young (1981), on multi-dimensional scaling; and Siegel (1956), on non-parametric statistics. In addition, the books by Box et al. (1978) and Erikson and Norsanchuk (1977) will be helpful to experimenters and qualitative researchers respectively. A very useful range of texts is provided in the Sage University Paper Series, "Quantitative Applications in the Social Sciences". As well as those already referred to, this series contains over 20 titles.

Specialist areas. A growing supply of specialised texts is beginning to emerge. Some examples will illustrate the type of material avaiable.

Education. Johnson (1977) provides a review of methods; Taylor (1973) looks at conceptual foundations and key issues; Verma and Beard (1981) cover nature, methods, tools and statistics; Ward (1973) maps out educational research resources; Evans (1968) gives good advice on planning small-scale research; and Wilson (1972) relates educational research to philosophy.

Evaluation research. Rossi and Williams (1972) and Rutman (1977) both deal with methods for evaluating social policy/social change programmes and are of relevance to some management evaluation research concerns.

Finance and economics. Good "methods" books are those by Abdel-Khalik and Ajinkya (1979) and Buckley, Buckley and Chiang (1976). Hofstede (1968) provides an interesting account of the methods and findings of a study of budgetary control. Some interesting "conference-based" books are Dopuch and Revsine (1973), which looks at accounting research between 1960 and 1970; the Federal Reserve Bank's report (1977) on business cycle research; Robicheck (1967) on financial research; and Sterling (1972) on accounting research method.

Marketing. A number of texts are available, influenced largely by market research requirements and practices. Good examples are Albaum and Verkatesan (1971) on scientific marketing research; Elliott and Christopher (1973), and Tull and Hawkins (1980) on research methods in marketing; and Livingstone (1977), who provides a guide for managers.

Organisation research. This is a field very much dominated by the social/behavioural science researchers. A good deal of literature exists, some examples being Clark (1972) and Foster (1972) on action research; Dunham and Smith (1979) on organisational surveys; Scott (1965) and Vroom (1967) on methods; Cook et al. (1981) on measuring work experience; and Fombrun (1982) on strategies for network research.

Social research. This is a well-covered field; many of the more general texts emanate from social researchers. Some examples of texts in this area are Bulmer (1978) on social policy research; Bynner and Stribley (1978) on principles and procedures; Carley (1981) on social indicators; and Lees (1975) on research for social welfare. Miller (1977) provides a detailed comprehensive coverage.

## Organising and planning research

Although not much seems to have been written on this aspect of research, there are some useful sources. Some are directly concerned with social science research, others with industrial R and D management. Some specific guidance on planning and alternative approaches to organising research is given by Bennett (1982).

The little book by Evans (1968) contains some useful pointers to the planning aspects of research. Several case studies of the organisation and impact of social research are written up in Shipman (1976). Though based on education research, they offer much of interest and use to researchers in other fields. Issues regarding the organisation of contract research are taken up by Hyder and Sims (1979), whilst Crawford and Perry (1976) provide an interesting review of social science research organisation in Europe. Some useful indirect sources - concerned with the management of innovation, research and development - are the works of Burns and Stalker (1966), Dean and

Goldhart (1980) and White (1975). There is much we can learn from experience gained in other contexts. We can learn, too, from experiences of research centres in universities: in this regard, Sieber (1972) has something interesting and helpful to say, based on a survey of research centres in schools of education.

Effectiveness and utilisation of research

This aspect of research seems to be receiving increased attention in literature and, it is to be hoped, in practice. An important emphasis is on the way(s) in which the research and research findings can be used in different facets of management education. Thus, for example, Bennett has written quite extensively on the use of research in management practice, teaching and training (1974, 1975, 1977, 1979 and 1980); Bennett and Gill (1978) consider the role of research in a management centre; Buchanan (1980) has written on the use of research in developing management skills; Cole (1981) sees a role for trainers in using attitude surveys, concerning the use of research in organisations; Van de Vall and Kang (1976) look at the use of applied social research in industrial organisations; Tushman and Scanlan (1981) consider the role of "boundary spanning" individuals in information transfer; and Williams (1982) provides insights into using personnel research.

The productivity of research and its utilisation is also considered on a broader front; Andrews (1979) provides data on the effectiveness of a number of research groups in Europe; Clark (1972) discusses models of knowledge utilisation; Crawford and Perry (1976) talk of translating social research into action; Farrow (1969) provides some examples; Gowler and Legge (1977) discuss impediments to implementation of research findings; Rich (1981) goes in some depth into knowledge use and production; and Zinman (1968) considers the social dimension of science. Other material is available - that mentioned here should form a good starting-point for a thorough literature search.

Information sources

The array of information sources for researchers is quite vast. There are abstracts, indexes, literature reviews, on-line computerised bibliographical and statistical information sources, to mention just a few. A good library, with an experienced librarian, will prove invaluable in locating the kind of information source sought after. All that will be done here will be to provide some illustrations of the kind of texts which tackle the task comprehensively. The Association of Commonwealth Universities (1978) provides information on research taking place in developing countries of the Commonwealth; the British Library (1980) produces an annual volume on social science research in British universities, polytechnics and colleges; Hall and Brown (1981) have written an international directory of on-line bibliographical data stores; Vernon (1975) provides good guidance to the use of literature in the business and management field; and Kubr and Vernon (1981) give extensive lists of institutions in management development (including research) in 140 countries and list key information sources in management development. Depending on the researcher's specific need, one of these should provide a good start-base.

Report writing

Many of the texts on research methods have good sections on writing reports. See, for example, Clover and Balsley (1979) and Emory (1980). There is an excellent section on writing in Barzum and Graff (1977) - some 124 pages. These texts refer, of course, only to reports written in the English language.

4.  Alphabetical bibliography

The annotated material presented in this bibliography is primarily concerned with research methods. In selecting appropriate references, the reader will find it helpful to refer to the guidance given in the previous section.

Abdel-Khalik, A.R.; Ajinkya, B.B. 1979. Empirical research in accounting: A methodological viewpoint. Sarasota, Flor- American Accounting Association. 125 pp.

> Aimed at writers and readers of research. Covers basic concepts and methods of verification/research design, plus useful section on analysis of specific articles and how to tackle reading of research accounts. Useful set of references at end of book.

Helpful reading for novice researcher (student or staff) and for those interested in gaining insights into research reporting in accounting.

Albaum, G.; Venkatesan, M. (eds.). 1979. <u>Scientific marketing research</u>. New York, Free Press. 415 pp.

Collection of readings emphasising research methodology and quantitative approach to marketing research. Covers meaning, planning, measurement, methodology, analysis and interpretation, and management in marketing research. Useful diagrams, helpful book.

Andrews, F.M. (ed.). 1979. <u>Scientific productivity</u>. Cambridge, Cambridge University Press; Paris, UNESCO. 469 pp.

Study of effectiveness of research groups in six European countries, covering 1,200 groups in varied disciplines, universities, public and private research institutes, and industries. Comprehensive review of factors relating to scientists meeting research goals. Important volume for those involved in planning, funding or managing research.

Association of Commonwealth Universities 1978. <u>Research strengths of universities in the developing countries of the Commonwealth</u>. London, 2nd. edition. 208 pp.

Describes areas of research, numbers of researchers and other data in brief summary form. Section of social, administration and business studies. Appendices give addresses and other useful information (e.g. scholarships).

Bailey, K.D. 1978. <u>Methods of social research</u>. New York, Free Press. 478 pp.

Comprehensive, detailed, basic text designed for undergraduate and beginning graduate in social research. Coverage includes: principles of social research (the research process, choosing the research problem, constructing social explanations, measurement); survey research methods (sampling, questionnaire construction, mailed questionnaires, interview schedules); non-survey data collection techniques (experiments, observation, ethnomethodology, document study, content analysis, simulations and games); data processing (coding and reduction, analysis, scaling, ethics, applications, theory constructing).

Barnes, J.A. 1979. Who should know what? Harmondsworth, United Kingdom, Penguin. 232 pp.

Concerned with social science, privacy and ethics. Looks at changes in conduct of social research since early nineteenth century, how power of scientists have changed and similar issues, including the ethical and political obligations scientists should meet when carrying out research and publishing findings. Extensive set of references.

Belson, W.A. 1981. The design and understanding of survey questions. Farnborough, Hampshire, United Kingdom, Gower. 420 pp.

Claimed to be for survey practitioners, buyers of survey research or research students. Plenty of guidance, examples and descriptions of methods by well-experienced author.

Bennett, R. 1974. "The role of research in management decision making", in Management Decision, Summer 1974, pp. 189-198.

Discusses common properties of management decision making and research, and how research can help the manager. Gives guidelines on when and how research strategies can be used.

———. 1975. "Using research in human resource development", in Industrial Training International, Nov. 1975, pp. 310-313.

Looks at the need for research in HRD, the nature of research, deciding where research should be focused - with a step-by-step approach.

———. 1977. "The anti-social scientist", in Management Today, July 1977, pp. 17, 20 and 24.

Argues for more research that is relevant to management, with guidelines on how managers can work out their research needs and gain benefit from the findings.

―――. 1979. Using research in training: Journal of European Industrial Training Monograph. Vol. 3, No. 5, Bradford, MCB Publications. 32 pp.

Written for trainers, HRD specialists, personnel managers and related practising professionals. Advice and guidance on understanding research process, deciding what needs to be researched, using the results and communication with researchers.

―――. 1980. "Using research in management teaching", in Management Education and Development, Summer 1980, pp. 95-105.

Shows how and in what way management teachers can use research processes and findings in their work; with examples and illustrations.

―――.; Gill, J. 1979. "The role of research in a regional management centre", in Management Education and Development, Dec. 1979, pp. 151-161.

Describes findings of research into role, objectives and attitudes to research in two regional management centres in the United Kingdom.

Bennett, S.; Bowers, D. 1976. An introduction to multivariate techniques for social and behavioural sciences. London, Macmillan. 156 pp.

Multivariate data analysis is growing in importance. This book will help many to understand how to do it. Covers factor analysis, rotation of factors, principal factor analysis, mutiple groups analysis, multidimensional scaling, discriminant analysis, and analysis of qualitative data. Requires basic knowledge of statistics and algebra.

Beveridge, W. 1961. The art of scientific investigation. London, Mercury Books. 177 pp.

>Interesting slant, reflected in the title, by a professor of animal pathology. Emphasising the point that research is really a matter of the mind (for all our hardware and techniques), it covers (in terms of chapter heading) preparation, experimentation, chance, hypothesis, imagination, intuition, reason, observation, difficulties, strategies, and scientists. Has photographs of some of the great scientists. Interesting general reading.

Blalock, H.M. 1970. <u>An introduction to social research</u>. Englewood Cliffs, New Jersey, Prentice-Hall. 120 pp.

>Readable, concise introduction written for student and layman. Explains basic issues encountered in doing social research. Covers principles of experimental design, exploratory and descriptive studies, explanation and theory, and measurement, in addition to considering the complexities and implications of social research. Very good primer.

The British Library. <u>Research in British universities, polytechnics and colleges</u>, Vol. 3: <u>Social sciences</u>. London, British Library, 1980 edition. 401 pp.

>Register of research, produced each year, of research in academic, government departments and other institutions. Titles of research plus addresses are given.

Bogdan, R.; Taylor, S.J. 1975. <u>Introduction to qualitative research</u>. New York, Wiley. 262 pp.

>Helpful for anyone interested in gathering so-called "soft" data, or in explaining management using a phemomenological approach. Covers conduct of qualitative research, appropriate techniques and methods, and how to write up the findings. Some good examples of research conducted using the qualitative approach.

Box, G.; Hunter, W.; Hunter, J. 1978. <u>Statistics for experimenters</u>. New York, Wiley. 653 pp.

>Written by statisticians, an "introduction" to the philosophy of experimentation and role of statistics, for experiments and researchers. Extensive treatment of different designs.

Buchanan, D. 1980. "Gaining management skills through academic research work", in <u>Personnel Management</u>, Apr. 1980, pp. 45-48.

>Short readable article discussing the role of part-time research in developing management skills, based on argument that many of the skills implicit in the research process are vital to effective management.

Buckley, J.W.; Buckley, M.H.; Chian, H.F. 1976. <u>Research methodology and business decisions</u>. New York, National Association of Accountants. 89 pp.

>Basic text or primer on methodology for people new to research, particularly in the finance area. Four main chapters covering a framework of methodology, criteria for selecting a methodology, scientific study and business decision problems, general remarks and applications. Useful selected bibliography on research methodology, science of decision making, and examples of research into business decision problems. Draws examples from other subject areas and disciplines.

Bulmer, M. (ed.). 1978. <u>Social policy research</u>. London, Macmillan. 373 pp.

>Collected contributions to important debate on research and social policy. Covers opinion polls and survey data, action research, social indicators; and relations between academic researchers and government values in policy research and institutionalisation of social research in government.

Burns, T.; Stalker, G. 1966. <u>The management of innovation</u>. London, Tavistock. 260 pp.

>Classic study of innovation and its management, in contrast to more stable, production management. Source of "mechanistic" and "organic" systems of management organisation.

Bynner, J.; Stribley, K.M. (eds.). 1978. <u>Social research principles and procedures</u>. London, Longman, in association with the Open University. 354 pp.

Collection of readings put together for the Open University's "Research methods in education and the social sciences". Five sections covering language of social research, research design, data collection, measurement, and data analysis and reporting. Range of readings is quite wide and will appeal to the researcher taking a broad interest in research issues.

Campbell, D.; Stanley, J. 1976. Experimental and quasi-experimental designs for research. Chicago, Rand McNally. 84 pp.

Discusses problems of experimental design, pre-experimental, true-experimental, quasi-experimental, and correlational and ex post facto designs. Examples drawn mainly from educational research. Still a helpful guide for the positivist.

Cabley, M. 1981. Social measurement and social indicators: Issues of policy and theory. London, Allen and Unwin. 195 pp.

Of interest to those involved in government and policy research of a social nature. Defines the field and the various social indicators. dicusses theory and models; policy-making process; social reporting in the United Kingdom, the United States and other countries, and the use of indicators at the urban level.

Carmines, E.G.; Zeller, R.A. 1980. Reliability and validity assessment. Beverley Hills, California, Sage Publications. 70 pp.

Short guide but requires knowledge of correlational analysis.

Caulcott, E. 1973. Significance tests. London, Routledge and Kegan Paul. 145 pp.

Assumes a basic knowledge of algebra and descriptive measures (means and standard deviation). Aimed at those with interest in sampling and interpretation of sample survey findings. Good glossary of terms and formulae.

Clark, P.A. 1972. <u>Action research and organisational change</u>. London, Harper and Row. 172 pp.

>For OD researchers but will have relevance to management researchers in the behavioural field generally. Good blend of description of approaches and case studies. Chapters in types of researcher, approaches to change, collaboration, valid knowledge, intervention strategies, and models of knowledge utilisation are particularly helpful.

Clover, V.T.; Balsley, H.L. 1979. <u>Business research methods</u>. Ohio, Grid Publishing, 2nd. edition. 385 pp.

>Good example of one of few research methods texts geared to business. Covers nature of research; scientific method; problems, hypotheses, and data; observation and experimentation; surveys and questionnaires; statistical inference and sampling; correlation, regression and trend analysis; use of tables, charts and graphs; and preparing reports. Useful appendices on statistical tables. Introductory yet comprehensive: more than just a basic text.

Cole, G. 1981. "Employee attitude surveys: A new role for trainers", in <u>Journal of European Industrial Training</u>, Vol. 5, No. 6.

>Describes role and use of surveys, areas of use, and how to conduct them.

Cook, J.D.; Hepworth, S.J.; Wall, T.D.; Warr, P.B. 1981. <u>The experience of work</u>. London, Academic Press. 353 pp.

>A compendium and review of 249 measures and their use for measuring work attitudes, values and perceptions. Nine sections: introduction and overview; overall job satisfaction; specific satisfactions; alienation and commitment; occupational mental health and ill-health; work values, beliefs and needs; perceptions of the job, work role, job context and organisational climate, leadership style and perception of others. Sources are well referenced. Helpful index of scales and subscales. Valuable source of material for researchers in OD, job design, leadership and many related fields of study.

Crawford, E., Perry, N. (eds.). 1976. Demands for social knowledge: The role of research organisations. London, Sage Publications. 276 pp. No index.

> Interesting collection of papers arising from seminar held in Cambridge to review progress on European Survey of Social Science Research Organisation. In addition to stimulating introduction ("Sketching a theory of social science research organisation"), it contains material which covers research organisations in its social context, the development of research organisations and institutions in the social sciences, studies in the production of knowledge by organisations, and translating social research into action.

Dean, B.; Goldhart, J. (eds.). 1980. Management of research and innovation. Amsterdam, North-Holland. 300 pp.

> Of interest to those (e.g. students, researchers and managers) concerned with effectiveness of R and D. Some of the papers on organisational and financial matters will interest directors of research institutes and centres.

Diesing, P. 1972. Patterns of discovery in the social sciences. London, Routledge and Kegan Paul. 350 pp.

> Organised in three parts: formal methods and theories, participant-observer and clinical methods, and methods in the philosophy of science. Very descriptive, with personalised arguments. Readable, and much referred to.

Dopuch, N.; Revsine, L. (eds.). 1973. Accounting research 1960-1970: Critical evaluation. Illinois, University Press. 194 pp. No index.

> Preceedings of conference on accounting research held in the United States in 1971. Broad coverage, interesting papers.

Douglas, J.D. 1976. Investigative social research: Individual and team field research. Sage Library of Social Research, Vol. 29. Beverly Hills, California, Sage Publications. 229 pp.

More for the sociological management researcher. Concerned with seeking out truth by getting at what goes on naturally, and how to go about it. Good chapter on team field research. The book is descriptive and does not require much knowledge of statistics. A drawback is the lack of an index.

Dunham, R.B.; Smith, F.J. 1979. <u>Organisational surveys</u>. Glenview, Illinois, Scott, Foresman. 179 pp.

Aims to provide managers and aspiring managers with expertise necessary to properly conduct and effectively use results of surveys. Covers purposes of surveys, how to carry out surveys, analysing and using survey results plus plenty of guidance and examples. Valuable book, especially for those concerned with assessing organisational health.

Elliot, K.; Christopher, M. 1973. <u>Research methods in marketing</u>. London, Holt, Rinehart and Winston. 248 pp.

For student and practitioner. Part I is on methods (very good coverage of, for example, research process, client-researcher communication, desk research, experiments, observation, coding and analysis): part II is a useful taxonomy of statistical methods.

Emory, C.W. 1976. <u>Business research methods</u>. Homewood, Illinois, Irwin. 483 pp.

Cross-discipline book for use in business and management schools, for student and instructor. Introductory but not basic. Coverage: foundations of research, research design, data collection, and analysis and reporting plus appendix on reference tools (e.g. bibliographies) and another giving selected statistical tables. Very good general text.

Erikson, B.H.; Norsanchuk, T.A. 1977. <u>Understanding data</u>. Milton Keynes, United Kingdom, Open University, 1977 (1979 this edition). 388 pp.

Introductory book on exploratory and confirmatory data analysis for social science students. Very useful for generation of hypotheses. Geared to OU courses but can be used on its own.

Evan, W.M. (ed.). 1971. <u>Organisational experiments: Laboratory and field research.</u> New York, Harper and Row. 274 pp.

> Collection of readings on use of experimental method as approach to study of organisations. Part 1 looks at some laboratory methodological problems; Part 2 carries selection of reports on laboratory experiments; Part 3 looks at problems of the field experiment; and Part 4 reports on some field studies. Of interest to courses in organisation theory and to seminars on research methods. Good source of examples. Difficult, close-packed, small-print text!

Evans, K.M. 1968. <u>Planning small-scale research.</u> Windsor, United Kingdom, NFER Publishing Co. 89 pp.

> Although written for people in general field of education, useful and interesting little book. Covers nature and types of research, preliminaries to research, planning experimental work, use of tests and questionnaires, the main investigation and reporting research.

Evered, R.; Louis, M.R.. "Alternative perspectives in organisational sciences: 'Inquiry from the inside' and 'inquiry from the outside'", in <u>Academy of Management Review</u>, Vol. 6, No. 3, pp. 385-395.

> Compares detached, objective "spectator" scientific method approaches ("inquiry from the outside") with experiential, involved, more qualitative approaches ("inquiry from the inside"). Very fair assessment of both plus guidance on how to combine both to good effect. Informing, stimulating, helpful. Good article.

Farrow, N. 1969. <u>Progress of management research.</u> Harmondsworth, United Kingdom, Penguin. 157 pp.

> Edited collection of articles that first appeared in <u>Business Management</u>. Although dated, contains something of interest for many management researchers (operational research, marketing, economics, management development) with final chapter on the problems of implementing management research.

Federal Reserve Bank of Minneapolis. 1977. <u>New methods in business cycle research</u>. Minneapolis, Federal Reserve Bank. 227 pp.

>Proceedings of conference held in the United States in 1975, including papers and comments. Covers topics such as time series approach to econometric model building and macroeconomic models. For the specialist.

Fombrun, C.J. "Strategies for network research in organisations", in <u>Academy of Management Review</u>, Vol. 7, No. 2, pp. 280-291.

>Describes three sets of strategies (modal, dyadic and triadic) for analysing transactional networks. Relative merits of each are assessed, and research directions suggested. Of interest to the experienced researcher wishing to pursue a network approach to organisational analysis.

Foster, M. 1972. "An introduction to the theory and practice of action research in work organisations", in <u>Human Relations</u>, Vol. 25, No. 6, pp. 529-556.

>Useful review covering historical perspective, definition, elements of theory and practice (including client system, change agent, change target, approaches to planned change). Several pages of references. Helpful article for those working in OD/change field.

Glaser, B.G.,; Strauss, A.L. 1967. <u>The discovery of grounded theory: Strategies for qualitative research</u>. Chicago, Aldine Publishing Co. 271 pp.

>Probably the classic of texts concerned solely with qualitative research approaches and methods. Puts over notion that theory should derive from data rather than being developed through conventional hypothesis-testing approaches. Based on social research, but many management researchers use the book. Covers generation of theory by comparative analysis, flexible use of data and implications of grounded theory. Shows how to do it.

Goldstein, H.; Legge, K. 1977. "Notes on some impediments to the implementation of social science research findings", in <u>Personnel Review</u>, Vol. 6, No. 2, pp. 57 and 58.

> Brief discussion of several aspects of the relationship between an organisation and the social scientist with reference to the use of relevant research findings.

Hall, J.L.; Brown, M.J. 1981. <u>Online bibliographic databases</u>. London, Aslib, 2nd. edition. 213 pp.

> International directory of bibliographical data stores available online. Such stores contain an estimated 70 million references, updated at the rate of 10 million per year. This directory is therefore a valuable tool for literature searches. Introduction provides an intriguing background to data bases. Good index gives easy access to management and related database references.

Handy, R. 1964. <u>Methodology of the behavioural sciences</u>. Springfield, Illinois, Charles C. Thomas. 182 pp.

> Deals with problems and controversies in behavioural science research method, including the philosophical and epistemological. Interesting material, but most of the issues will be dealt with in more modern texts.

Helmstadter, G.C. 1970. <u>Research concepts in human behaviour</u>. New York, Appleton-Century-Crofts. 448 pp.

> Good, introductory yet not basic text. Covers nature of science and research, methods of research, tools of research (e.g. library, measurement), and results of research. Requires familiarity with statistical terms but the procedures (e.g. factor analysis) are well explained. Although aimed at researchers in education, psychology and sociology, the management researcher will, in fact, find it relevant.

Herbst, P.G. 1970. <u>Behavioural worlds</u>. London, Tavistock. 248 pp.

Deals with four different techniques for studying single cases (i.e. behaviour of individual as opposed to a sample), namely, longitudinal time-independent, cross-sectional, longitudinal phase-transition, and longitudinal time-dependent. In three parts: generalised behaviour theory, principles of behaviour and analysis of cognitive and social structure. Based on argument that the "science" of physics is not necessarily the "science" of behaviour. Needs experience in philosophy/methods of science to gain benefits.

Hofstede, G.H. 1968. <u>The game of budget control</u>. London, Tavistock. 363 pp.

Report of research findings of study of budget systems in six manufacturing plants in the Netherlands. Discussions of (1) the research subject (from theoretical viewpoint); (2) the research design; (3) the research findings; and (4) implications of research.

Hoinville, G.; Howell, R.; and associates. 1977. <u>Survey research practice</u>. London, Heinemann. 228 pp.

Written by practising professionals, presents good coverage of survey research method, problems and pitfalls, and what to do about them. Straightforward, without complicated statistics.

House, R.J. 1970. "Scientific investigation in management", in <u>Management International Review</u>, Vol. 4, No. 5, pp. 139-150.

Helpful readable article, presenting very balanced view of approaches to management research. Uses the notion of "rigour" to assess different approaches. Three levels of rigour are put forward: (1) qualitative and narrative research; (2) survey/longitudinal/uncontrolled experimentation; and (3) classical experimentation. Appropriate methods are discussed in terms of an example (testing the management principle of span of control). Good, concise, useful article.

Hughes, J. 1980. <u>The philosophy of social research</u>. London, Longman. 142 pp.

Useful introductory book which describes and compares two key philosophies of social research - positivist and humanist approaches, or advocates of scientific method ("hard" research) and qualitative method ("soft" research) respectively. Whilst not specifically addressing the management researcher, is of relevance to many management researchers.

Hyder, S.; Sims, D. 1979. "Hypothesis, analysis and paralysis: Issues in the organisation of contract research", in Management Education and Development, Summer 1979, pp. 100-111.

Excellent discussion of issues relating to contract researchers, by two people who have experienced them at first hand. Included are short- versus long-term approach, isolation, career problems, role of the researcher and positive thoughts on how to approach the issues. Valuable reading for research directors and researchers alike.

Irvine, J.; Miles, I.; Evans, J. (eds.). 1979. Demystifying social statistics. London, Pluto Press. 390 pp.

Much needed, as the title implies. In five sections: (1) historical perspectives; (2) knowledge and numbers; (3) statistics and the State; (4) statistics in action; and (5) conclusion. Range of areas covered includes teaching of statistics; statistics on poverty, wealth, health; computerisation of statistics; opinion polls; social forecasting, etc. Good value.

Johnson, J.M. 1975. Doing field research. New York, Free Press. 225 pp.

For the sociologist. Covers: observation, research and objectivity in sociology; research setting; gaining access; developing trust; collecting data; recording and analysing. Rather like a long essay, but some useful ideas.

Johnson, M.C. 1977. A review of research methods in education. Chicago, Rand McNally. 471 pp.

Geared to research in schools, but relevant to other fields including management education. Selective coverage of nature, methods, types of research, analysis and reporting, but quite broad. Written specifically for courses and seminars in research methods.

Joynt, P.; Rytter, M. 1981. "Experimenting with experience", in *Journal of European Industrial Training*, Vol. 5, No. 7.

Describes research-based approach to management education as operated by the authors at the Norwegian School of Management.

Kerlinger, F.N. 1973. *Foundations of behavioural research*. New York, Holt Rinehart and Wilson, 2nd. edition. 741 pp.

Classic text on research design and methods. Based on "scientific" approach to research, covers virtually everything the so-called "hard" data collector will want to know, from design, through hypothesis to testing, analysis, measurement, report writing, etc. Not suitable for the beginner.

Kubr, M.; Vernon, K. (eds.). 1981. *Management, administration and productivity: International directory of institutions and information sources*. Geneva, International Labour Office. 305 pp.

A selective list of 2,300 management development and public administration institutions from 140 countries. Followed by a list of 1,000 key information sources covering management, and management training and research. Updated periodically.

Kuhn, T.S. 1970. *The structure of scientific revolutions*. Chicago, Chicago University Press, 2nd. edition. 210 pp.

A major essay on the philosophy of sciences. Assesses historical developments in history of science and identifies different paradigms (e.g. Newtonian mechanics). Proposes that science progresses by one paradigm replacing another. Thirteen sections, including "the route to normal science", nature of scientific revolutions, and progress through revolutions. One of the most influential works.

Langley, R. 1978. Practical statistics. London, Pan Piper. 400 pp.

Written by a lecturer in scientific method: aimed at non-mathematicians. Good coverage of principles and practice of statistical inference, with chapter on designing investigations.

Lees, R. 1975. Research strategies for social welfare. London, Routledge and Kegan Paul. 105 pp.

Helpful discussion of research approaches relevant to social welfare, covering experimental and action research, identifying needs/programmes, values and theoretical perspectives, as well as action research approach to different aspects of social welfare.

Livingstone, J.M. 1977. A management guide to market research. London, Macmillan. 173 pp.

Aimed at business executives and students of management and marketing. In two parts: (1) scope and methods (e.g. sources of data, surveys, basic quantitative methods, sampling); and (2) the market research survey (e.g. why bother, how to carry it out, how to export). Plain straightforward introductory text.

Madge, J. 1953. The tools of social science. London, Longman. 308 pp.

A classic – first published in 1953, ninth impression 1978. Covers language and logic of social science; has chapters on the use of documents, observation, interviews, surveys and experiment. Although dated, a practical book which describes the main techniques used by social scientists.

Miller, D.G. 1977. Handbook of research design and social management. New York, David McKay, 3rd. edition. 518 pp.

Aimed at being a "professional guide for teachers, researchers and students". Very comprehensive and detailed. Five parts: (1) general description of guides to research design and sampling (15 sections); (2) guides to methods and techniques of collecting data in library, field and laboratory (12 sections); (3) guides to statistical analysis (10 sections); (4) selected sociometric scales and indices (13 major sections); (5) research funding, cost and reporting. Author-index only. Data specific to the United States, will be unhelpful to others. Not for the beginner.

Moore, P.G. 1969. Principles of statistical techniques. Cambridge, Cambridge University Press. 288 pp.

Written by a business school professor for schools and universities. Good, introductory text.

Nie, N.H.; Bent, D.H.; Hull, C.H. 1970. Statistical package of the social sciences. London, McGraw-Hill.

Manual for one of the popular computer statistics programmes. Explains statistical procedures used as well as how to put the data on cards and through the computer. Programme itself offers wide range of facilities.

Oppenheim, A.N. 1967. Questionnaire design and attitude measurement. London, Heinemann. 298 pp.

Very readable, introductory book, full of good advice. Covers problems of survey and questionnaire design, wording of questions and statements, and quantifying questionnaire data. Discusses various techniques such as checklists, semantic differentials and rating scales.

Phillips, D.L. 1973. Abandoning method. San Francisco, Jossey Bass. 202 pp.

Concerned with sociological studies in methodology. Looks at issues of bias and invalidity in sociological research and questions assumptions of belief and world views in sociology. Concludes that abandoning method may be necessary for improving knowledge. Non-sociologists might find it difficult going, unless well-versed in "qualitative" methods.

Plews, A.M. 1979. Introductory statistics. London, Heinemann. 244 pp.

> First-level book, covering usual basic range. Plenty of good examples.

Popper, K.R. 1963. <u>Conjecture and refutations: The growth of scientific knowledge</u>. London, Routledge and Kegan Paul. 431 pp.

> Classic collection of essays by one of the great men of scientific argument/philosophy of science. Main argument is that theories must be testable, i.e. attempts made to refute or falsify them, if they are to be of scientific value. For the philosopher although its key messages are of importance to all researchers.

Reason, P.; Rowan, J. (eds.). 1981. <u>Human enquiry: A sourcebook of new paradigm research</u>. Chichester, United Kingdom, Wiley. 530 pp.

> A "must" for those involved in qualitative, "subjective" or so-called "soft" research, i.e. the opposite of positivism. Excellent material covering philosophy, methods, examples and directions. Probably best read after working through more introductory texts on qualitative research.

Reeves, T.K.; Harper, D. 1981. <u>Surveys at work</u>. Maidenhead, United Kingdom, McGraw-Hill. 258 pp. Hard cover and limp cover; different versions.

> This useful text is produced in two formats: one as a practitioner's guide for managers, personnel specialists, unions, management consultants; the other as a student manual. Basically common material, apart from different introductory chapters. Covers aims, design, entry to organisation, co-operation, exploratory studies, questionnaire development and design, secret ballots, drawing conclusions, survey management and planning, ethics, and use of results. Helpful selected further reading. Useful text.

Rich, R.F. (ed.). 1981. <u>The knowledge cycle</u>. Beverley Hills, California, Sage Publications. 222 pp.

> Collection of essays on knowledge use and production. In four parts: knowledge creation (knowledge in

society, an overview, selected bibliography); knowledge diffusion/dissemination (diffusion research, problem and solution, selected bibliography); knowledge utilisation (current issues, selected bibliography); and linkages (linkages between creation, diffusion and dissemination, selected bibliography). Useful source book.

Robichek, A. (ed.). 1967. <u>Financial research and management decisions</u>. New York, Wiley. 232 pp. No index.

Collection of conference papers. Examples of research in relation to financial management. Field will have advanced somewhat since 1967.

Rosen, L.; Welt, R. (eds.). 1973. <u>A reader for research methods</u>. New York, Random House. 360 pp.

For the general sociologist, although one chapter (out of 25) is on management. Readings cover data sources, management, analysis and research design. Marginal value for management research.

Rossi, P.; Williams, W. (eds.). 1972. <u>Evaluating social programmes</u>. New York, Seminar Press. 326 pp.

Concerned with the theory, practice and politics of evaluative research. Broad coverage, mainly examples/studies, ranging from method through philosophy to application. Relevant to social researchers/ social work agencies.

Rothman, J. 1980. <u>Using research in organisations</u>. Beverley Hills, California, Sage Publications. 229 pp.

Study by an American professor of research utilisation process in British social work organisation. Presents many propositions, backed by research findings, as to how research utilisation can be facilitated. Excellent summary of these in final chapter. Much food for thought for all who seek to improve use of research findings. Practical checklists at the end of each chapter.

Rowntree, D. 1981. <u>Statistics without tears</u>. Harmondsworth, United Kingdom, Penguin. 200 pp.

Primer for non-mathematicians. Good starter for those with no background in statistics. Ranges from descriptive statistics, through samples to analysing relationships (correlations and regression).

Rummel, J.F.; Ballaine, W.C. 1963. <u>Research methodology in business</u>. New York, Harper and Row. 359 pp.

Excellent general introductory text providing elementary insight into research methodology - good "first book" to read. Covers nature of research, how to choose a research problem, planning and organising research projects, collecting and analysing data, and writing up the report. Strongly recommended as a basic text.

Rutman, L. (ed.). <u>Evaluation research methods: A basic guide</u>. Beverley Hills, California, Sage Publications. 241 pp.

Readings range from planning evaluation study through randomised quasi-experimental designs to benefit/cost evaluations. Clear and well set out. Oriented towards social science/social policy research.

Sage Series. <u>Quantitative applications in the social sciences</u>. A Sage University Paper Series, methodological works providing introductory explanations and examples of various data analysis techniques for social sciences. Assumes a limited background in statistics and mathematics.

Series now runs to at least 22 short books (less than 100 pages) in paperback.

Titles include:

<u>Analysing panel data</u>, by G.B. Markus.
<u>Analysis of covariance</u>, by A.R. Wildt and O.T. Ahtola.
<u>Analysis of nominal data</u>, by H.T. Reynolds.
<u>Analysis of ordinal data</u>, by D.K. Hilderbrand, J.D. Lang and H. Rosenthal.
<u>Analysis of variance</u>, by G.R. Iversen and H. Norporth.
<u>Applied regression: An introduction</u>, by M.S. Lewis-Beck.
<u>Canonical analysis and factor comparison</u>, by M.S. Levine.
<u>Casual modelling</u>, by H.B. Asher.
<u>Cohort analysis</u>, by N.D. Glenn.

Discriminant analysis, by W.R. Klecka.
Ecological inference, by L.I. Langbein and A.J. Litchman.
Exploratory data analysis, by F. Hartwig and B.E. Dearing.
Factor analysis, by J-O. Kim and C.W. Mueller.
Interrupted time series analysis, by D. McDowall, R. McCleary, E.E. Meidinger and R.A. Hay, Jr.
Introduction to factor analysis, by J-O. Kim and C.W. Mueller.
Log-linear models, by D. Knoke and P.J. Burke.
Multidimensional scaling, by J.B. Kruskal and M. Wish.
Multiple indicators: An introduction, by J.L. Sullivan and S. Feldman.
Operations research methods, by S. Nagel and M. Neef.
Reliability and validity assessment, by E.G. Carmines and R.A. Zeller.
Tests of significance, by R.E. Henkel.
Time series analysis: regression techniques, by C.W. Ostrom, Jr.

Schiffman, S.S.; Reynolds, M.L.; Young, F.W. 1981. Introduction to multidimensional scaling: Theory, methods and applications. New York, Academic Press.

> Multidimensional scaling (a mathematical procedure for systematising data by presenting the similarities of objects spatially) is an important technique. This book describes six major MDS computer programmes, and deals with basic concepts, methods, applications and theory. Knowledge of statistics desirable to gain most from this book. Not for the novice.

Schuman, H.; Presser, S. 1981. Questions and answers in attitude surveys: Experiments on question form, wording and context. New York, Academic Press.

> Valuable book for those involved in survey research in a big way. Beginners would do well to start with a book such as that by Oppenheim before tackling this text.

Scott, W.R. 1965. "Field methods in the study of organisations", Chapter 6 in J.G. March (ed.): Handbook of organisations. Chicago, Rand McNally.

> Concise review of the range of possible research methods, particularly related to organisational change and development.

Selltiz, C.; Wrightman, L.S.; Cook, S.W. 1976. Research methods in social relations. New York, Holt, Rinehart and Winston, 3rd. edition. 624 pp.

> Excellent text, particularly for those concerned with research in social and behavioural fields. Subjects covered: why do research?, logic of analysis, selecting and formulating a research problem, research design and methods, measurement and data collection/processing, analysis and interpretation, report writing and ethical issues. Appendices on sampling and questionnaire/interview procedures. Popular text on research methods courses.

Shipman, M. (ed.). 1976. The organisation and impact of social research. London, Routledge and Kegan Paul. 155 pp. No index.

> Six original case studies in education and behavioural sciences are described by the key researchers involved in them. Covers longitudinal studies, school-based studies, and policy studies. Cases describe origins, organisation and implementation, including research design, problems and basic thinking behind the research.

Sieber, S.D. 1972. Reforming the university: The role of the social research centre. New York, Praeger. 229 pp. No index.

> Report of a study of research units/centres in schools of education in the United States. Chapter on research methods used is good example of research design. Remaining chapters discuss findings, which will be of no interest to anyone managing a research centre. Fascinating chapter on "the managerial scholar". Don't be put off by the book's title.

Siegel, S. 1956. Nonparametric statistics for the behavioural sciences. Tokyo, McGraw-Hill. 312 pp.

> Excellent - has stood the test of time. Presents a range of techniques for testing hypotheses where certain parametric characteristics are not present. Well-structured, good explanations.

Sparkes, J. 1972. <u>Research methodology in accounting</u>. Houston, Texas, Scholars Book Co. 163 pp. No index.

    Papers and comments from an accounting colloquium. Mix of academic and practitioner papers, inside and outside accountancy field. Content ranges from accounting research design through behavioural science methods to practitioner's view. Very small, close-packed print.

Taylor, W. (ed.). 1973. <u>Research perspectives in education</u>. London, Routledge and Kegan Paul. 238 pp.

    Main focus conceptual foundations and organisation/management of educational research, plus key questions/issues: does not deal with techniques or methods. Relevant to educational policy and practice considerations. Three parts, covering: resources, organisation and staffing; disciplinary perspectives; research and practice. Draws in reference from several countries. Of interest to education management researchers.

Tomberg, A. (ed.). 1978. <u>Eusidic database guide</u>. Oxford, Learned Information. 130 pp.

    "Eusidic" stands for European Association of Information Services - the Guide lists broad range of bibliographical files, i.e. databases of references. Over 1,000 listed. Contents cover business, economics, law, public administration and social sciences as small part of wide range. Useful for literature search purposes.

Tull, D.S.; Albaum, G.S. 1973. <u>Survey research: A decisional approach</u>. New York, Intertext. 244 pp.

    Useful follow-up text to some of the more general reading (e.g. Rummel and Ballaine). Contains good descriptions of different approaches to research and has useful chapters on sampling, measurement and scaling, and analysis.

Tull, D.S.; Hawkins, D.I. 1980. <u>Marketing research: Measurement and methods</u>. New York, Macmillan, 2nd. edition. 796 pp.

Extensive treatment, at introductory level, of decisional research. Examples and illustrations of application. Should be of use to student and instructor. Twenty chapters ranging from role of marketing research through methods and techniques to ethics.

Turner, R. (ed.). 1974. *Ethnomethodology*. Harmondsworth, United Kingdom, Penguin. 287 pp.

Selection of readings in four parts covering the name and uses, theorising as practical reasoning, practical reasoning in organisational settings and methodological bases of interaction, focusing on demonstrations/examples of research using the ethnomethodological approach. Reader will benefit considerably by pre-knowledge of this approach.

Tushman, M.L.; Scanlan, T.J. 1981. "Boundary spanning individuals: Their role in information transfer and their antecedents", in *Academy of Management Journal*, Vol. 24, No. 2, pp. 289-305.

Report of investigation of alternative mechanisms for importing information into organisations, indicating the key role of individuals who are connected both internally and externally.

Van de Hall, M.; Bolas, C.; Kang, T.S. 1976. "Applied social research in industrial organisations: An evaluation of functions, theory and methods", in *Journal of Applied Behavioural Science*, Vol. 12, No. 2, pp. 158-177.

Long but interesting paper concerning the "transformation of social science intelligence into organisation policies". Suggests, among other things, that qualitative research methods have greater impact on utilisation.

Verma, G.K.; Beard, R.M. 1981. *What is educational research?* Farnborough, Hampshire, United Kingdom, Gower Press. 244 pp.

Argues that research is important in the learning-teaching situation and that teachers should consider themselves as producers as well as consumers of research. Covers nature of educational research, methods and tools, key statistical concepts, research and the teacher, with examples and a glossary of educational research terms. Management teachers may find it helpful.

Vernon, K.D.C. (ed.). 1975. Use of management and business literature. London, Butterworth. 327 pp.

Useful source of information for researchers in management field. Part 1 deals with the literature, the library and the bibliographical tools; Part 2 with forms of business information; Part 3 with subject surveys of the literature. Points people in right directions. Good source book, e.g. for lists of core journals, key business school libraries in the United Kingdom, United States and Europe, directories, bibliographies, indices, and so on.

Vroom, V. (ed.). 1967. Methods of organisational research. Pittsburgh, University Press. 211 pp.

Based on seminar held in 1964, covers organisations in the laboratory (i.e. lab. experiments), field experiments, comparative studies, and computer simulation models for organisation theory. Advances made since mid-1960s, but still interesting.

Ward, A.V. 1973. Resources for educational research and development. Windsor, United Kingdom, NFER. 131 pp.

Maps the resources field in the United Kingdom, which will have changed - useful and interesting report.

Webb, E.J.; Campbell, D.T.; Schwartz, R.D.; Sechrest, D. 1966. Unobtrusive measures: Non-reactive research in the social sciences. Chicago, Rand McNally. 225 pp.

Interesting and novel. Describes unusual research methods, from the social to the physical. Should be read by all "qualitative" researchers, and a few others.

Weisburg, H.F.; Bowen, B.D. 1977. An introduction to survey research and data analysis. San Francisco, W.H. Freeman. 234 pp.

Helpful and readable book, requiring an understanding of basic statistics and explaining others. First part is concerned with survey design and covers the meaning of survey research, sampling procedures, designing questionnaires, interviewing, coding and interpretation. Part Two focuses on data analysis, including use of computers and a useful range of statistics, from single to variable statistics to statistical control.

White, P. 1975. Effective management of research and development. London, Macmillan. 295 pp.

Well-written and clear presentation covering R and D generally; structure of R and D organisations; sources of research effort; choice of portfolio; control of project; efficiency and productivity; staff selection/development and management; lab. planning, technical assistance and leadership. United Kingdom oriented.

Williams, A.P.P. (ed.). 1982. Using personnel research. Farnborough, Hampshire, United Kingdom, Gower Press. 250 pp.

Collection of specially written chapters by people involved in management research. Emphasis is on how to use research rather than how to do it - on using research tools to help solve problems. Fifteen chapters, the first introductory. The rest are in four parts: discovering problems; weighing up alternatives; evaluating programmes and structure; effective use of personnel research. Wide range of topics covered, by academics, managers and specialists.

Wilson, J. 1972. Philosophy and educational research. Windsor, United Kingdom, NFER. 133 pp. No index.

Unusual but interesting. Discusses research in education - a personal view, argued with force with reference to the literature. Further reading given.

Zinman, J. 1968. Public knowledge: The social dimension of science. Cambridge, Cambridge University Press. 154 pp.

Written by professor of theoretical physics, this essay covers the meaning of sciences, what is and is not science, scientific method and argument, role of the scientist, community and communications, and the role of institutions and authorities. A personal view. Interesting general reading.

5.  Further references

It has not been possible to annotate all the available material. Apart from the fact that this would be a monumental task, not all the material has been seen, and a good deal of the texts overlap. This section contains a selection of further references taken from a variety of reading lists. In some instances, full information was not available.

Bell, C.; Encel, S. (eds.). Inside the whale: Ten personal accounts of social research. Oxford, Pergamon, 1978.

_____; Newby, H. Doing sociological research. London, Allen and Unwin, 1977.

Berdie, D.R.; Anderson, J.F. Questionnaires: Design and use. Scarecrow Press Inc., 1974.

Borg, W.R. Educational research: An introduction. London, Longman, 3rd edition, 1979.

Borger, R.; Cioffi, F. (eds.). Explanation in the behavioural sciences. Cambridge, Cambridge University Press, 1970 (1975).

Blalock, H.M. (ed.). Casual models in the social sciences. Chicago, Aldine, 1971.

_____. Social statistics. Tokyo, McGraw-Hill Kogakusha, 2nd. edition, 1972. An introductory text.

Brenner, Marsh and Brenner. The social context of method. London, Croom Helm, 1978.

Brown, S.C. Philosophical disputes in the social sciences. Brighton, United Kingdom, Harvester Press, 1979.

Burrell, G.; Morgan, G. Sociological paradigms and organisational analysis. London, Heinemann, 1979.

Clark, A. *Experimenting with organisational life*. Plenum Press, 1976.

Davis, G.J. *A systematic approach for managing a doctoral thesis*. Brussels, European Institute for Advanced Studies in Management, 1972.

Denzin, N.K. *The research act in sociology*. Chicago, Aldine, 1970.

Ehrenberg, A.S.C. *Data reduction*, New York, Wiley, 1975.

Festinger, L.; Katz, D. *Research methods in the behavioural sciences*. New York, Holt, Rinehart and Winston, 1965.

Fransella, F.; Bannister, D. *Manual for repertory grid technique*. Academic Press, 1977.

Friedlander, F. *Alternative modes of enquiry*. Ohio, Case Western Research University, Department of Organisational Behaviour, 1977.

Eden, C.; Wheaton, G. *In favour of structure - - -*. Bath, United Kingdom, Centre for the Study of Organisational Change and Development, 1980. Working paper 80/06. 18 pp.

Gordon, R.L. *Interviewing: Strategy technique and tactics*. Homewood, Illinois, Dorsey Press, 1975.

Hagedon, R.; Labovitz, S. *Introduction to social research*. New York, McGraw-Hill, 1972.

Hague, P. "Questionnaire design in postal surveys", in *Industrial Marketing Digest*, No. 4, 1979, pp. 137-144.

Harnett, D.L. *Statistical methods*. Reading, Massachusetts, Addison-Wesley, 3rd. edition, 1982. 730 pp.

Hardwyck, C.; Petrinovich, L.F. *Understanding research in the social sciences*. Sanders, 1975.

Herberlien, T.A.; Baumgartner, R. "Factors affecting response rates to mailed questionnaires: A quantitative analysis of the published literature", in *American Sociological Review*, 1978, Vol. 43, pp. 447-464.

Holsti, O.R. Content analysis for the social sciences and humanities, Reading, Massachusetts, Addison-Wesley, 1969.

Howard, K.; Sharp J.A. Management of a student project. Farnborough, Hampshire, United Kingdom, Gower Press, 1982.

Hughes, J.A. Sociological analysis: Methods of discovery. Nelson, 1976.

Jung, J.H. The experimenter's dilemma. New York, Harper and Row, 1971.

Keat, R.; Urry, J. Social theory as science. London, Routledge and Kegan Paul, 1975.

Krausz, E.; Miller, S.H. Social research design. London, Longman, 1974.

Lemon, N. Attitudes and their measurement. London, Batsford, 1973.

Linton, H.; Galls, P.S. The practical statistician: Simplified handbook of statistics. Monterey, California, Brooks/Cole, 1975.

McCall, G.J.; Simmons, J.L. Issues in participant observation. London, Addison-Wesley, 1969.

McFarlane-Smith, J. Interviewing in market and social research. London, Routledge and Kegan Paul, 1972.

Moser, C.A.; Kalton, G. Survey methods in social investigation. London, Heinemann, 1971.

Nachmias, D.; Nachmias, C. Research methods in the social sciences. London, Edward Arnold, 1976. Reckoned to be a good, clear, basic book.

Rescher, N. Methodological pragmatism: A systems theoretic approach to the theory of knowledge. Oxford, Blackwell, 1977.

Riley, G. Values, objectivity and the social sciences. Reading, Massachusetts, Addison-Wesley, 1974.

Ryan, A. _The philosophy of the social sciences_. London, Macmillan, 1970. Highly recommended on one book list for cover of epistemological and philosophical issues.

Siegel, M.H.; Zeiger, H.P. (eds.). _Psychological research: The inside story_. New York, Harper and Row, 1976.

Sudman, S. _Applied sampling_. Academic Press, 1976.

Tufte, E.R. (ed.). _The quantitative analysis of social problems_. Reading, Massachusetts, Addison-Wesley, 1970.

Warmington, A. "Action research: Its methods and its implications", in _Journal of Applied Systems Analysis_, No. 7. 1980, pp. 23-39.

Williamson, J.B.; Karp, D.A. _Research craft: Introduction to social science methods_. Little, 1977.

Wilson, M. (ed.). _Social and educational research in action_. London, Longman, 1978.

There is a lot of material to be found in the journals - far too much to be referred to here. The reader should search those journals relevant to the study area for appropriate articles. Collections of papers on research methods appear from time to time in special journal issues.

Some examples are:

_Administrative Science Quarterly_, Dec. 1979: special issue on qualitative methodology.

_Sociological Review_, Nov. 1979: special issue on handling qualitative data.

_American Behavioural Scientist_, July/Aug. 1980: special issue on methods in the social sciences.

_Academy of Management Review_, July 1982: several articles on research in management and organisations.